THE PRACTICAL SKEPTIC

CORE CONCEPTS IN SOCIOLOGY

Sixth Edition

Lisa J. McIntyre

Washington State University

Mc
Graw
Hill
Education

THE PRACTICAL SKEPTIC: CORE CONCEPTS IN SOCIOLOGY, SIXTH EDITION

Published by McGraw-Hill Education, 2 Penn Plaza, New York, NY 10121. Copyright © 2014 by McGraw-Hill Education. All rights reserved. Printed in the United States of America. Previous editions © 2011, 2008, and 2006. No part of this publication may be reproduced or distributed in any form or by any means, or stored in a database or retrieval system, without the prior written consent of McGraw-Hill Education, including, but not limited to, in any network or other electronic storage or transmission, or broadcast for distance learning.

Some ancillaries, including electronic and print components, may not be available to customers outside the United States.

This book is printed on acid-free paper.

9 10 LCR 21 20 19

ISBN   978-0-07-802687-4
MHID   0-07-802687-3

Senior Vice President, Products & Markets: *Kurt L. Strand*
Vice President, General Manager, Products & Markets: *Michael Ryan*
Vice President, Content Production & Technology Services: *Kimberly Meriwether David*
Managing Director: *Gina Boedeker*
Brand Manager: *Courtney Austermehle*
Director of Development: *Rhona Robbin*
Freelance Development Editor: *Nomi Sofer*
Marketing Manager: *Philip Weaver*
Marketing Coordinator: *Ryan Viviani*
Director, Content Production: *Terri Schiesl*
Content Project Manager: *Mary Jane Lampe*
Buyer: *Nichole Birkenholz*
Cover Designer: *Studio Montage, St. Louis, MO*
Cover Image: *Digital Vision / Getty Images*
Typeface: *10/12 Palatino*
Compositor: *Laserwords Private Limited*
Printer: *LSC Communications*

All credits appearing on page or at the end of the book are considered to be an extension of the copyright page.

Library of Congress Cataloging-in-Publication Data

McIntyre, Lisa J.
  The practical skeptic : core concepts in sociology / Lisa J. McIntyre, Washington State University. — Sixth edition.
     pages cm
  ISBN 978-0-07-802687-4 (alk. paper)
  1. Sociology. I. Title.
  HM586.M55 2014
  301—dc23

                                                                        2013008264

The Internet addresses listed in the text were accurate at the time of publication. The inclusion of a website does not indicate an endorsement by the authors or McGraw-Hill Education, and McGraw-Hill Education does not guarantee the accuracy of the information presented at these sites.

www.mhhe.com

CONTENTS

PREFACE

It wasn't until I was about halfway through my first decade of teaching that I finally had the opportunity to teach Introduction to Sociology. Did I *want* to teach Intro? You bet! I was ecstatic. I had been teaching various upper-division classes—research methods, social theory, criminology, law and society—but I wanted to be the one who introduced sociology to students. I wanted to share with students the enthusiasm that I felt for the entire sociological enterprise and to expose them to the power of sociological thought.

I tried to create an introductory course that would speak to the typical first-year student who isn't planning on majoring in sociology and, indeed, may not even know what sociology is. Even among sociology majors, very few plan on becoming sociologists. Each semester, I ask my beginning students, "Why are you here? What is it about sociology that interests you?" The very charitable say, "I don't know what sociology is, but I am sure that it will be interesting." Mostly, students are honest: "I'm here to fulfill my general education requirements." A few are more specific: "I have to take a social science class and my advisor said that sociology is easier than economics or political science."

I knew that once these students discovered sociology, they would find merit in it. Even if they didn't major in sociology, they would come away from the class with some important life knowledge. I quote Robert Bierstedt in my syllabus: "Sociology owns a proper place not only among the sciences, but also among the arts that liberate the human mind" (1960, 3). I paraphrase Peter Berger to suggest that students will find one of the most important lessons of sociology to be that "things are not what they seem" (1963, 23)—that sociological training encourages people to look beyond the surface and to be suspicious of what "everybody knows." I tell them that it hardly matters what sort of career they are working toward: learning how to be skeptical and how to think like a sociologist will help them understand and resolve complex and abstract problems on the job.

So, I knew how I wanted to structure the course—we would learn the basic concepts and then talk and read about how these worked in the real world. But I couldn't find a textbook whose author had anticipated my wishes. I wanted a book that would introduce students to sociology's foundational concepts—the scientific method, culture, social structure, socialization, deviance, inequality. I wanted a book that would not bury those concepts inside tons of empirical information but would present them in such a way that students could gain enough understanding to apply them to what they read elsewhere and what they encountered in life. It was the sociological perspective I wanted these students to come away with, not the details.

I was encouraged to pursue this vision by something I read in an article by Frederick Campbell, a sociologist from the University of Washington. In the book he co-edited with Hubert Blalock and Reece McGee, Campbell wrote that undergraduate courses in sociology ought to focus on *principles rather than facts:* "The mastery of sociology has a different meaning in the context of undergraduate education than in vocational training or a graduate program. A baccalaureate degree in sociology seldom prepares a student for a specific occupation or to pursue independent research. Emphasis on the subject matter, then, has little value if it means memorizing material that will soon go out of date for a job that does not exist. Mastery should move away from factual material and focus instead on the development of the mind" (1985, 13).

The longer I taught introductory sociology, however, the greater became my frustration with the available instructional material. So, one summer, I sat down to write some introductory and background materials for my students. My idea was that I would introduce them to the concepts that sociologists use, and we would then apply these to what we read in a variety of sociological articles and to what we encountered in real life (and in the media). My goal was to provide my students with the tools they needed to understand the social world through the eyes of sociologists. As everyone who has taught introductory courses probably knows, the foundational concepts of our discipline are not simple ones, and many students resist them. My goal was not to simplify the concepts but to make them accessible to students.

The set of essays I wrote that summer—on the history of sociology and the vocabulary of science, culture, social structure, socialization, deviance, and inequality—seemed to serve my students well. After students read them, we moved on with our shared vocabulary to other works by sociologists and to discussions of how these concepts applied to the real world. It worked. It was as Peter Berger had promised in his *Invitation to Sociology:* "It is not the excitement of coming upon the totally unfamiliar, but rather the excitement of finding the familiar becoming transformed in its meaning. The fascination of sociology lies in the fact that its perspective makes us see in a new light the very world in which we have lived all our lives" (1963, 21). Although I omitted much that is found in the typical sociology text (there are no chapters on family, religion, or politics), the concepts I did focus on (institutions, roles, values, and so on) allowed us to have relatively sophisticated discussions of those topics.

Be warned: I am not one of those sociologists who write in what Peter Berger called "a barbaric dialect." I've taken C. Wright Mills's caution to heart: "To get beyond sociological prose we must get beyond the sociologist's pose" (1959). Notwithstanding the fact that I once had a book rejected by a noted university press because it was "too much of a good read," I've persisted in my casual style and, whenever I couldn't help it, have indulged my odd sense of humor. Many sociological concepts are very complex, and I think I have done justice to that complexity, but I have tried to do it in ways that are accessible to students.

NEW TO THIS EDITION

This edition uses updated statistics from the most recent census and other agencies. In response to suggestions from my readers, I continue to augment the discussions of topics that many students find difficult. In this edition, you will find new sections on the relationship between correlation and causation, ethnography, the mutability of deviance and the relationship between gender and income.

The goal of the book remains the same: to introduce students to sociology in a way that makes the core concepts of our discipline accessible without losing the crucial complexity of these concepts in translation. Along the way, I hope that I have managed as well to convey my enthusiasm for sociology.

SUPPLEMENTS

Visit our Online Learning Center Web site at http://www.mhhe .com/mcintyre6e for student and instructor resources. This is a combined Web site for both *The Practical Skeptic: Core Concepts in Sociology,* and its companion reader, *The Practical Skeptic: Readings in Sociology.*

For Students
Student resources include comprehensive self-quizzes for both the text and reader.

For Instructors
The password-protected instructor portion of the Web site includes the instructor's manual (written by the author), containing discussion questions and activities, examples of lectures, tips specifically targeting new instructors, a comprehensive test bank, and all the tools available to students. Also included is a separate test bank for the reader with multiple choice, true/false, and essay questions for each reading.

THE COMPANION READER

Created to serve as a companion to the text, *The Practical Skeptic: Core Concepts in Sociology,* this reader, *The Practical Skeptic: Readings in Sociology,* includes classic sociological writings as well as recent writings on fascinating topics of interest to students. Corresponding to the conceptual organization of the text, each of the readings serves to illustrate key sociological concepts and ideas.

ACKNOWLEDGMENTS

My largest thanks go to the hundreds of students who have read *The Practical Skeptic* and shared their views of the text with me.

Many thanks to the following reviewers whose comments and suggestions shaped the sixth edition: Peter Adler, University of Denver; Mitch Berbrier, University of Alabama in Huntsville; Joslyn Brenton, North Carolina State University; Margaret Delehanty Kelly, University of Minnesota; Stacy Evans, Berkshire Community College; Susan Eichenberger, Seton Hill University; Catherine Leone, University of Wisconsin-Manitowoc; Pamela McMullin-Messier, Central Washington University; Janice L. Milner, Century College; Megan Peterson, William Rainey Harper College; Carly Sebastian, Mount Wachusett Community College.

Thank you to the following reviewers whose helpful comments and suggestions helped us in our preparation of the fifth edition: Elizabeth Larsen, California University of Pennsylvania; Lynda Dickson, University of Colorado at Colorado Springs; Kiren Ghei, Delta College; Thomas B. Gold, University of California at Berkeley; Patti Guiffre, Texas State University; Michael Collins,

UW Fox Valley in Menasha; Linda C. Evans, Drake University; Carolyn Kapinus, Ball State University; Carla Norris-Raynbird, Bemidji State University, C. Stephen Glennon, Iowa Western Community College; Doug Degher, North Arizona University; Kim Hennessee, Ball State University.

The fourth edition manuscript was reviewed by the following people, who responded with suggestions and pointed out necessary revisions, for which I am deeply grateful: Diane C. Bates, The College of New Jersey; Gretchen DeHart, Community College of Vermont; Esther Horrocks, Villa Julie College; Michael C. Maher, Spoon River College; Lida V. Nedilsky, North Park University; Deborah Thorne, Ohio University; and Craig Tollini, Western Illinois University.

I also appreciate the help of the third edition reviewers who offered many helpful comments and suggestions: Deborah A. Abowitz, Bucknell; Cheryl Albers, Buffalo State; Sue Cox, Bellevue Community College; Derek Greenfield, Highline Community College; Tiffany Hayes, Green River Community College; Barbara Karcher, Kennesaw; Susan Ross, Lycoming College; and Ann S. Stein, College of Charleston.

I thank the reviewers of the second edition for their thoughtful reading: Jerry Barrish, Bellevue Community College; Debra Cornelius, Shippensburg University; Jamie Dangler, SUNY Cortland; Laurel R. Davis, Springfield College; Gloria Y. Gadsden, Fairleigh Dickinson University; Alan G. Hill, Delta College; Susan E. Humphers-Ginther, Moorhead State University; Katherine Johnson, Niagara County Community College; Barbara Karcher, Kennesaw State University; Debra C. Lemke, Western Maryland College; Patricia A. Masters, George Mason University; Susan McWilliams, University of Southern Maine; Dan Pence, Southern Utah University; Marcella Thompson, University of Arkansas; Georgeanna M. Tryban, Indiana State University; and Brenda S. Zicha, Charles Stewart Mott Community College.

I would also like to thank the reviewers of the first edition: Peter Adler, University of Denver; Sheila M. Cordray, Oregon State University; Mary Patrice Erdmans, University of North Carolina–Greensboro; Valerie Jenness, University of California–Irvine; Frances V. Moulder, Three Rivers Community–Technical College; Karl T. Pfeiffer, University of Alaska; Martha L. Shockey, St. Ambrose University; Lisa Troyer, University of Iowa; and Georgeanna M. Tryban, Indiana State University.

Lisa J. McIntyre

INTRODUCTION

Have you ever caught yourself thinking about things that people do? Have you ever asked yourself, for example, questions about everyday things like these:

Why do some students always sit in the back of the classroom while others always sit in the front?

Why do African Americans on predominantly white college campuses frequently say "hi" to other African Americans, even if they don't know them?

Why do we dress baby girls in pink and baby boys in blue?

Why do people generally not look at one another in elevators—and always face front?

Why do young men, but not young women, spit?

Why do we go to such lengths to pretend we aren't embarrassed when we have to get naked in front of a doctor?

Why do people from small towns tend to act differently from people from big cities?

Why are most people less willing to seek professional help for mental or emotional problems than for physical problems?

Sociologists are trained to find answers to questions about people's behavior. We are especially interested in understanding the effects that people have on one another.

Sociologists are convinced that much of people's behavior is a result of what other people do. A sociologist reviewing the questions just listed would likely say that many of these behaviors result from how people are influenced by others.

1

This sociological conviction might offend you. Certainly, I like to think of myself as independent minded; you, too, may like to think that your behaviors are the results of choices you have made of your own free will. But allow me to persuade you that to understand people's behavior and the choices they make, it is important to take into account the influence of others in their environment.

Even when you think you are making your own choices, often you are picking only from the fairly limited range of options that others allow you. The simple fact is that, depending on your position in society—your age, gender, race, social class, and so on—people expect and allow you to act in various ways. Society places restrictions on your behavior with very little regard for your preferences.

Of course, you can choose not to live up to society's expectations, but if you decide to be contrary, you will pay a price. And, depending on the seriousness of your infraction, that price can range from endless nagging by your parents to a prison sentence and even to death!

Consider marriage. Surely, the decisions whether to get married, whom to marry, and when are very *personal* decisions. Actually, they are not. Examine this matter carefully and you will find that your marital choices are rather restricted. For example, in the United States, you can be married to only one person at a time. And (at least for the time being) you can marry only a person of the opposite sex—unless you live in one of the several states that allow same-sex marriage. Until the late 1960s, many states even had laws requiring people to marry within their own racial group—if you broke these laws, you could be sent to prison or exiled from the state.[1]

Chances are, your family places even more restrictions on your marriage choices. Have you noticed that there are, in effect, family "rules" about whom you can marry? These rules may be unspoken but clear: Your parents may wish you to wed someone of your own race and religion and from the same educational and social-class background. Of course, there is no *law* that says family rules must be followed, but we all know that families have ways of making us suffer.

Even your friends may restrict your marriage (and dating) choices. Consider how they would make you suffer if you started to date some seriously weird geek.

You really have to wonder, why does everyone care so much about whom we marry? Now *that* is a sociological question!

So, What Is Sociology?

Here is a technical definition of sociology: *Sociology is the scientific study of interactions and relations among human beings.*

---

[1]Some states have never rescinded these laws, but because such racial restrictions were ruled unconstitutional by the U.S. Supreme Court in 1967, even where they do exist, they do not have the force of law.

I hope the word *scientific* caught your attention. Including that word in the definition is a reminder that sociologists try to be very careful about how they find answers to their questions.

While the questions they ask are certainly influenced by their own interests and even their biases, they do not want their answers to be contaminated by bias or emotion or faulty logic—after all, they want their research to be persuasive to others. Therefore, as much as possible, they strive to be systematic in gathering data.

The Value of Sociology to Students

The goal of this book, and this course, is not so much to introduce you to new worlds as it is to inspire you to take a long hard look at familiar ones. And, I promise you, the reward for doing that will be much greater than the simple gratification of intellectual curiosity. There will be many practical rewards.

The practical value of taking a sociology course is that what you learn, by definition, *never will be irrelevant to your life*—present and future. Each of us lives in the social world; each of us is influenced by others and, to some extent, hopes to influence others. Studying sociology will strengthen your ability to understand how the social world operates and what your place is in it. Moreover, studying sociology will enhance your ability to act effectively in the social world.

Just to whet your appetite, let me share with you one of the most basic sociological truths as it was put into words in 1928 by the sociologist W. I. Thomas: "If people define situations as real, they are real in their consequences." The *Thomas theorem* articulated the sociological finding that had escaped many nonsociological observers. If one truly wants to understand why people do the things they do, one must take into account not only what is *really* going on in a particular situation but also what people *think* is going on. For example, if moviegoers believe the theater is on fire, they will react to the threat as if it were real, even if there is no fire. A consequence could be a panic in which people are trampled to death, even though the threat was never "real."

Thomas's insight helps us to understand how people live their everyday lives, too. Suppose the local newspaper runs a series of articles on how people are being victimized by crimes. The reporters pick the most interesting and most gruesome of criminal events on which to focus. Even if the reality is that these are uncommon events and that the actual rate of crime is going down, we would predict that people's fear of crime would increase, which would have important consequences. For example, more people might purchase handguns for protection just at the point when things really are becoming safer. The increase in handgun ownership might result in an increase in handgun deaths—kids playing with guns, panicked homeowners shooting neighbors stumbling around in the middle of the night, and so on.

Certainly, reality is important, because even when people do not define things as real, they can have real consequences. Thus, even if people do not know that the theater is on fire, they will die if they don't escape. But reality is only one factor that we must take into account to understand how people act and interact.

Sociology, then, is the discipline that studies the interactions and relationships among people—the realities and the perceived realities. Even given the seemingly countless variations in people's possible behaviors, sociologists are remarkably successful in shedding light on questions about why people do what they do and how they are influenced by one another.

My goal in this book has been to select the most important concepts that sociologists use and share them with you. My hope is that you, too, might apply these concepts as you work to move about in the social world more effectively and to understand it more thoroughly.

Tips for Studying Sociology— and an Invitation

To get the most out of your study of sociology, you will need to do more than simply read the book. Your goal should be to "own" the concepts—that is, not only to read, but to think about the concepts as well so that you can use them to understand social life. To help you achieve this goal, I have scattered Stop and Review questions throughout the book. I urge you to answer these questions. Many of my own students have told me that doing so makes it much easier to understand (and remember) sociological concepts. Several of my students tell me that they learn even more by making a list of the concepts for each chapter along with the definitions given in the book, and then writing their own definitions and examples.

Finally, I enjoy hearing from students (and their teachers, of course). If you have a question, comment, sociological example, or suggestion that you would like to share with me, please do so! I might use your example in the next edition of the book. (If I do that, I will be sure to give you credit—and I will make sure that you receive a copy of the book so that you can see your name in print.)

You can contact me via "snail mail" at Department of Sociology, Washington State University, Pullman, WA 99164-4020, or e-mail at ljmcint@wsu.edu. Please include your mail or e-mail address so that I can respond.

RESPONDING TO CHAOS

A Brief History of Sociology

"He who watches a thing grow has the best view of it."
—Heraclitus[1]

I have always suspected that what people choose to study is a result of something other than mere accident. It seems to me that people study what they feel they most need to understand, and frequently, these are things that frighten them.

To the first peoples of the world, nature was overwhelmingly powerful and fear inspiring; the physical environment dominated the lives of men and women. The time of year dictated daily tasks—planting, reaping, hunting. The available vegetation and game dictated what people ate. Even after plants and animals were domesticated, menus were limited by climate—if you lived in the Northern Hemisphere, probably you would die without ever having tasted a mango or a banana.

It is easy to understand, then, why the earliest people focused their intellectual efforts on gaining an understanding of the physical world. Theirs were pressing questions: Why did the sun rise each morning and set each evening? Would it continue to do so? What made it rain? Why did the wind blow?

Obviously, humankind has never "conquered" nature, yet by the beginning of the nineteenth century, humanity had succeeded in making the natural world seem more predictable. But then, just as Westerners seemed to be getting a handle on the natural, their *social* world became frighteningly chaotic. People were accustomed to wars with foreigners, but in the eighteenth century nearly every European nation faced internal war in the form of revolution. By the time the nineteenth century rolled around, the political, economic, and religious foundations of society appeared

---

[1]Heraclitus (hera-KLI-tus) was an ancient Greek philosopher (c. 540–480 B.C.E.).

to be on the verge of crumbling. Things were in chaos. People were frightened.

Inquiries into the Physical World

Although the most dramatic social upheavals occurred in the eighteenth century, rumblings had been heard as far back as the sixteenth century. It was during the sixteenth century that people started to question the validity of long-held beliefs about the fundamental nature of the world.

At first, these questions had to do with the physical world. In the second century of the common era,[2] Greek/Egyptian astronomer Claudius Ptolemy had determined that the earth was the center of the universe. (Actually this idea had been around at least since the fourth century B.C.E., but Ptolemy mathematically "proved" the theory using geometry.) More than a thousand years later, leaders of the Western Church still embraced Ptolemy's view because it meshed with other ideas they held: Of course, the earth is at the center of things—"man" was God's most important creation, and where else would God place man's world but at the center of the universe? Anyway, if things were otherwise—if the earth were not the center of things but revolved around the sun—wouldn't we feel the earth move?

In 1543, a Pole named Mikolaj Kopernik (better known now as Nicolaus Copernicus) in Frauenberg (a town in East Prussia)

---

[2]We are so accustomed to thinking that our ways of accounting for time are natural, that it comes as a shock to realize that these systems are very much human creations. For example, many people in Western societies distinguish between B.C. (Before Christ) and A.D. for *Anno Domini* (or "in the year of our Lord," and not "after death"). The B.C.–A.D. distinction did not appear spontaneously but was devised in 523 C.E. by the abbot of a Roman monastery, Dionysis Exiguus (also known as Peter the Little). Until then, the Church had followed the Roman tradition of dating events from the purported year of Rome's creation (*Anno urbia conditae*, or year of the establishment of the city). Dionysis Exiguus calculated that Jesus was born in 753 A.U.C. and designated that year as 1 A.D.

The monk's calculations have since been determined to be in error. Jesus of Nazareth was born during the reign of King Herod, and Herod died in 4 B.C. Thus, the birth of Jesus has traditionally been dated at least four years too late.

As an acknowledgment of the arbitrary beginnings of the Western calendar, many contemporary writers have substituted the terms B.C.E. ("before common era") and C.E. ("common era").

Of course, the Christian calendar has never been accepted everywhere in the world. The Islamic calendar, for example, dates the beginning of modern time from *Anno Hegirae* (A.H.), or the year of the Hegira—the year when Mohammed fled from Mecca to Medina (the Arabic word *hirira* means "flight"). The Prophet's flight took place in what the Western calendar calculates to be 622 C.E. (and more specifically on July 16); that means that the year 2000 C.E. on the Western calendar was 421 A.H. Moving back and forth between the Western/Christian and Islamic calendars is further complicated by the fact that their years are not the same length: The Western calendar is calculated according to solar movement, the Islamic calendar according to lunar movement.

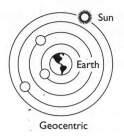

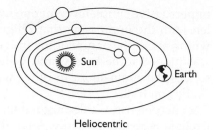

Geocentric   Heliocentric

Figure 1.1
*Competing Views
of the Cosmos.
Geocentric means
"earth-centered";
heliocentric means
"sun-centered" (Helios
was the sun god of
Greek mythology).*

published a book titled *On the Revolutions of Heavenly Bodies.* In this book Copernicus suggested that the *sun,* not the earth, was at the center of the universe and that the planets (including the earth) revolved around the sun. In other words, Copernicus properly described the cosmos as heliocentric, not geocentric (see figure 1.1).

The heliocentric perspective did not catch on right away. For one thing, Copernicus was such a timid fellow that he did not publish his theory until he was literally on his deathbed. And even after it was published, many people were reluctant to accept the Copernican view. Copernicus's ideas of the universe contradicted those espoused by the Church. Contradicting the Church meant facing possibly serious consequences (even death). Why risk it? At best, Copernicus's theory was a sophisticated guess. There was no way to test it.

Then, along came the Italian astronomer Galileo Galilei, who was born in Pisa in 1564. In 1609, Galileo was visiting Venice, where he learned of a new device invented by spectacle-maker Hans Lippershey: a telescope. Back home, in 1610, Galileo built his own telescope (one that was three times as powerful as Lippershey's original) and was the first to use the instrument to examine the heavens. Galileo found evidence to support the heliocentric theory. In 1632, Galileo presented this evidence in a book titled *Dialogoi ai due Massimi Sistemi,* or *Dialogue on the Two Great Systems of the World.*

Galileo understood the risk of publicly contradicting the teachings of the Church. In hopes of reducing his risk, Galileo wrote his book as if it were a dialogue between two scholars—one who argued for Ptolemy's (and the Church's) view, the other who propounded Copernicus's theory. At the end of the book, even though he had appeared to be winning the argument, the Copernican supporter suddenly gave up and admitted that the Ptolemaic view was the correct one. Because of this, asserted Galileo, his book *supported* the Church's teaching.

But Galileo had not been clever enough. The final surrender of the Copernican scholar did not make up for the fact that throughout the book the Ptolemaic supporter had been portrayed as an

*"The doctrine
that the earth is
neither the center
of the universe, nor
immovable, but
moves, even with
a daily rotation, is
absurd, and both
philosophically and
theologically false,
and at the least an
error of faith."*

—Rome's judgment
against Galileo

unpersuasive simpleton. Anyone who actually read the book was left with the impression that religious leaders had been proved wrong about the nature of the universe. Because of this, the book was judged to be heresy, and Galileo was summoned to Rome to face the Inquisition. In other words, the Church leaders put Galileo on trial.[3]

In his defense, Galileo argued that there was nothing unholy or irreligious about his theory. After all, as Galileo reminded Church officials, *it was God* who had made the planets revolve around the sun. Galileo even asked the judges to look through his telescope to see the truth for themselves. Some of the judges did look but, stuffed full of Church doctrine, failed or refused to see.

In fact, Galileo's crime (if we must call it that) was to question the authority of the Church. Cardinal Robert Bellarmine, a leading theologian of the Church, as much as told Galileo that it *didn't matter* what proof he had: "Physical reality is not to be explained by mathematics but by the Scriptures and Church fathers." Ultimately, faced with excommunication, Galileo was forced to recant—to take back his theory—and promise to be silent.[4]

Galileo died in 1642, having spent the final eight years of his life in enforced seclusion in Florence, Italy. Some twelve months later in England, Isaac Newton was born. Newton would salvage Galileo's reputation—and bring about the final undoing of the Church's authority over the workings of the natural world.

Newton was a brilliant mathematician—while still a student at Cambridge University, he discovered the binomial theorem—who became a professor at a very young age. His university career was put on hold in 1666, however, when the plague nearly turned London into a ghost town. Newton retreated to his family's farm in Lincolnshire. Farming was of little interest to Newton, so he built himself a laboratory wherein he might continue his research.

At least part of Newton's genius lay in his ability to look at data with a mind free of preconceived notions. He was not like the

$$v = \sqrt{2gh}$$

$$\sum_{i=1}^{n} \quad u = f(x, y)$$

Newton's most famous discovery, gravity, holds up planets. Newton also invented calculus, which often holds up students.

---

[3]The Inquisition was a tribunal or court of the Roman Catholic Church. It had been established in 1233 to deal with heresy, or crimes of unbelief. In 1542 (more than a century before it summoned Galileo), the Inquisition came to be called the Holy Office (though most still called it the Inquisition). In 1965 the Inquisition was replaced by the Roman Congregation for the Doctrine of Faith.

Don't confuse the Roman Inquisition with the much more notorious Spanish Inquisition. The latter had been established by King Ferdinand and Queen Isabella in 1478 to test the faith of converted Jews and, later, of converted Muslims. The Spanish Inquisition made frequent use of torture and capital punishment; the Roman Inquisition made only occasional use of such drastic measures.

[4]Galileo's reputation was eventually rehabilitated by the Catholic Church. In 1992, Pope John Paul II suggested that the condemnation of Galileo had been an error resulting from "tragic mutual incomprehension." The Church's acceptance of Galileo's contributions has not been total. In 2009, plans to place a statue of Galileo in the Vatican were quashed after church officials voiced concerns with the project.

Church officials, who looked but could not see. Newton studied the works of his predecessors, conducted his own experiments, and saw.

In a book titled *Philosophiae Naturalis Principia Mathematica* (1687), Newton posited his famous three laws of motion; from these Newton deduced the law of gravitation.[5]

First Law of Motion—The Law of Inertia

Nothing moves unless and until some force acts upon it.

Second Law of Motion—Law of Acceleration

Force is equal to mass times acceleration ($F = m \times a$).

Third Law of Motion—Law of Action and Reaction

To every action there is always an opposed and equal reaction.

Law of Gravitation

Every particle in the universe attracts every other particle with a force that is proportional to the product of the masses of the two particles, and inversely proportional to the square of the distance between their centers. This force is directed along a line between their centers.

Newton completely undid the traditional view of the cosmos by making it clear that the earth was not the center of the universe. But Newton did more: His simple laws explained the movement of everything visible in the universe. These laws explained not only how planets moved about in the cosmos, but also why buildings sometimes fell down and bridges sometimes collapsed. Because of Newton, astronomers could calculate the orbits of the planets, and engineers could build taller buildings and longer bridges.

> "Nature and Nature's laws lay hid in Night:
> God said, 'Let Newton be!'
> And all was light."
>
> —Alexander Pope

During the next century, religious leaders retreated from their position that their authority was the last word on the natural world. Newton's findings were so compelling that the Church *had* to retreat. But, the Church leaders maintained, it was still God, not gravity, that ordered the individual's place in the *social* world. As was frequently said, "The rich man in his castle, the poor man at his gate, God made them, high and lowly, and ordered their estate."[6] In short, each individual was born into a particular

---

[5]The story that Newton's discovery of the law of gravity was inspired when an apple fell on his head was first recounted by the French philosopher Voltaire (1694–1778), who claimed to have been told the tale by Newton's niece.

[6]This verse is from the hymn *All Things Bright and Beautiful*, by Irish poet Cecil Francis Alexander (1815–1895), published in 1848. Although this hymn is still sung in churches, this particular verse is omitted from modern hymnals.

"estate," or rigidly defined social group, and that was the condition in which he or she would die.

It is important to understand that a person's place in the social world was believed to be much more than an accident of birth: The estate or status into which the individual *was* born was the estate into which that person *ought* to have been born. According to religious leaders, God made kingly people kings, generally superior people rich, and generally inferior people poor. Moreover, men were superior to women, and (of course) Europeans were superior to everyone else. If you had been born a woman, or poor, or non-European, you had only gotten what you had deserved.

But people still wondered. Newton had stripped the universe of its great veil of mystery by showing that the planets were governed not by some unknowable cosmic force but by a few simple laws of physics. Surely the mysteries of the more immediate social world could be similarly resolved?

Technology, Urbanization, and Social Upheaval

And so it was that by the end of the eighteenth century, the traditional view of the social world came to be as suspect as the old views of the natural world. Skepticism ran deep. Were the rich really superior to the poor? Were men really superior to women? Were Europeans really superior to everyone else? Some people even had the audacity to propose that kings reigned not by divine right but simply to serve the needs of the people! If that was true, then if a king failed to serve his people, he should be replaced. This very revolutionary idea was reflected in the American Declaration of Independence in 1776 and the French Declaration of the Rights of Man and Citizen in 1789 and was behind the many revolutions that occurred in Europe in the late-eighteenth and early-to-mid-nineteenth centuries.

Still, this new world was a fragile one. It lacked political, economic, and social stability. Compounding the problem was the fact that technology kept bringing about even more changes. Richard Arkwright's invention of the water-powered spinning frame, for example, led to the building of giant textile mills. The prospects for employment in the huge mills and other new factories (or *manufactories*, as they were called) lured hordes of people from rural areas to cities. Throughout Europe, urban centers grew fast and furiously.

Consider: In 1800, 900,000 people lived in London, 600,000 people in Paris, and 170,000 people in Berlin. By 1900, the population of London was 4.7 million, of Paris 3.6 million, and of Berlin 2.7 million.

Among the new urbanites were millions of desperately poor people. Five-year-old children worked fifteen-hour days in factories, and countless numbers of unattached men and women could barely earn a living wage. Industry was dangerous, and if the factory didn't kill you, the open sewers and lack of clean water probably would. There was, of course, no health insurance. If you were injured and could not work, or if you lost your job for any reason, you would not eat. Here's how one medical historian has described the scene:

> In the big cities the death rate had reached such levels by the middle of the nineteenth century that there were serious doubts whether sufficient hands would be available for factories, and whether enough able-bodied recruits could be found for the . . . armies. . . . The big city slums represented reservoirs of infectious diseases and epidemics, menacing not only the poor, but the life and health of the upper classes as well. (Ackernecht 1982, 212)

In England, the life expectancy between 1540–1800 was around 37 years. This is not to say that no one lived until old age; the average life expectancy was affected by the fact that more than 50 percent of children died before the age of 15 years.

The new urbanites included many unfortunate souls—people working long hours for tiny wages, insufficient food, and inadequate shelter. These urban poor terrified the urban middle and upper classes—and it was easy to see why. There were obvious and strong links between poverty, riots, and revolutions. In France the urban poor were referred to as the dangerous classes.

The first European countries to experience widespread social upheaval were those countries that had first undergone industrialization: Britain, France, and Germany. It was thus no accident that the first sociologists emerged in those countries—these were the men (and a few women) who offered solutions to the pressing problems of modern industrial society.

One of the first to step forward was Auguste Comte. Born in France in 1798, Comte had witnessed firsthand the social chaos that had followed the French Revolution. Comte urged that some scholars should specialize in studying the problems of modern society and propose solutions. In 1832 Comte named this field of study *sociology*.[7]

Auguste Comte called himself the Great Priest of Humanity.

---

[7]Comte brought together the Greek word *socius*, or "companion," and the Latin word *logy*, or "study," to create the term *sociology*. In a similar fashion, it was Comte who coined the term *biology*.

As Comte came on the scene, people were saying that the main problem of modern society was that people no longer knew (or were satisfied with) their proper place in society. Instead of focusing on the good of the community and being content with their lot (or estate) in society, people had become selfish, greedy, and uppity. Generally, this sort of individualism was seen to be at the root of social chaos.

Comte's diagnosis was more specific. He argued that his contemporaries—people in this newly modern society—were suffering from "intellectual anarchy" because they no longer shared any beliefs about the way things ought to be.

Comte suggested that the history of people's understanding of things (including the social world) followed what he called the Law of Three Stages. In the first stage, which Comte called the theological stage, religious leaders were the major sources of knowledge and intellectual authority. In the second stage, which Comte called the metaphysical, people turned to philosophers for guidance. In the final stage, which Comte called the positive or scientific, knowledge would be based on scientific principles.

Comte believed that social chaos would be overcome when people accepted that it was time to move on to the third stage of knowledge. Then, through the science of sociology especially, social harmony would be restored. Scientific sociologists would be the experts on the earthly social world, just as astronomers were the experts on the heavens.

The word *scientist* was coined by the English mineralogist and philosopher William Whewell in 1840—about the same time that Comte coined the term *sociology*.

Sociologists would use scientific methods to gain knowledge of the social world. Then they would advise people about how life ought to be lived. Comte went so far as to argue that sociology should take the place of religion as a source of answers to life's important questions: What is right and wrong? What does justice require? Convinced that sociologists should serve as the high priests of the modern world, Comte even wrote to the Roman Catholic pope suggesting that he abdicate and let Comte take his place! Toward the end of his life, Comte began to sign his letters with the title The Founder of Universal Religion, Great Priest of Humanity (see Coser 1971).

Comte's grandiose plans gained him a number of disciples—even the English philosopher John Stuart Mill wrote admiringly of Comte in his *System of Logic*. Some of Comte's followers formed a cult known as Comtism. But eventually he went too far. Comte grew to be more than a tad odd; frankly, he became a quack. By the time Comte died in 1857, sociology was more or less a laughingstock in France.

It would be some time before anyone dared to raise the subject of sociology in France. Eventually, however, the mantle of the discipline was taken up by a scholar named Émile Durkheim.

The Origins of Modern Sociology in France: Émile Durkheim

Like many of his contemporaries, Émile Durkheim[8] was alarmed by the chaos he saw in society. It was important, Durkheim said, to study society and social dynamics to find out what was going on. Yet, whereas many of his contemporaries were repelled by the individualism that had emerged in the late-eighteenth and nineteenth centuries, Durkheim wasn't so sure individualism would be the undoing of society. In his first book, *The Division of Labor in Society*, published in 1893, Durkheim explored the sources of order and stability in the modern world. Based on his research, Durkheim argued that even a society filled with selfish individuals would hold together, because even selfish people *need* one another to survive.

Imagine, for example, a premodern society in which people's livelihoods depended on their herds of sheep and their crops of vegetables. In such a society, most people would spend their time raising sheep and tending crops. Thus, the interests of each individual in the community would coincide—a bad year for sheep or turnips would be a bad year for everyone, and a drought would bring catastrophe for the entire group. In such a society, Durkheim suggested, with a very simple division of labor, people's work would be alike, and so would the people.

This likeness was important, Durkheim claimed, because it was what held people in premodern societies together. Likeness allowed people to experience *solidarity*. Their similar circumstances led them to have shared ideas, values, and goals—or what Durkheim called a *collective conscience*. Durkheim called this sort of solidarity *mechanical* because people in the community functioned together as a simple machine.

Life in modern society is very different, Durkheim said. People's labor is more specialized, and their interests are thus different (and even conflicting). An especially hot summer might be bad for the vegetable farmers but great for the grape growers. A railroad strike might be a disaster for cattle ranchers but a bonanza for chicken farmers, who could easily ship via truck.

Because of this specialized division of labor, said Durkheim, modern society could not be held together by likeness. The collective conscience—people's shared ideas, values, and goals— existed but was a very small part of people's overall consciences. As the division of labor in society became more complex, people

One of his professors warned Émile Durkheim (1858–1917) to abandon his plans to become a sociologist because "sociology leads to madness."

---

[8]Émile is a man's name and is pronounced "A-meal," and not, as some mistakenly say, "Emily."

From *Suicide* (1897) and *The Rules of the Sociological Method* (1904)

ÉMILE DURKHEIM

What Is a Social Fact?

Sociological method as we practice it rests wholly on the basic principle that social facts must be studied as things, that is, as realities external to the individual.

The system of signs that I employ to express my thoughts, the monetary system I use to pay my debts, the credit instruments I utilize in my commercial relationships, the practices I follow in my profession, etc., all function independently of the use I make of them. Considering in turn each member of society, the foregoing remarks can be repeated for each single one of them. Thus there are ways of acting, thinking, and feeling which possess the remarkable property of existing outside the consciousness of the individual.

Not only are these types of behavior and thinking external to the individual, but they are endued with a compelling and coercive power by virtue of which, whether he wishes it or not, they impose themselves upon him. Undoubtedly when I conform to them of my own free will, this coercion is not felt or felt hardly at all, since it is unnecessary. . . . If I attempt to violate the rules of law they react against me so as to forestall my action, if there is still time. Alternatively, they annul it or make my action conform to the norm if it is already accomplished but capable of being reversed; or they cause me to pay the penalty for it if it is irreparable. . . . In other cases, although it may be indirect, constraint is no less effective. I am not forced to speak French with my compatriots, nor to use the legal currency, but it is impossible for me to do otherwise. . . .

Here, then, is a category of facts which present very special characteristics: *[social facts] consist of manners of acting, thinking and feeling external to the individual, which are invested with a coercive power by virtue of which they exercise control over him* [emphasis added].

[Social facts] have a reality *sui generis*.

---

became more different (and so, too, did their interests, values, beliefs, and the like).

This brought Durkheim to the point that was terrifying everyone else. If the collective conscience, or what people shared, was so limited, what would hold society together?

Durkheim reasoned that dissimilarity would not mean an end to group solidarity. Indeed, as people became more specialized and different, they grew more dependent on one another. For example, because they worked in specialized occupations, people needed each other as sources of trade. Durkheim called this sort of

Sui generis is a Latin phrase that means "of its (or her, his, their) own kind." It's pronounced "SOO-ee JEN-air-us" in English. Durkheim stressed that social facts could not be reduced to psychological or biological facts. By this he meant that social facts (e.g., suicide rates) could be explained only by other social facts (e.g., changes in industry or the economy), and not by individual facts.

solidarity *organic solidarity,* because society functioned as a complex entity that depended on the proper functioning of a variety of parts, or organs. In premodern society, people had been held together because of likeness; in modern society they were being held together because of their differences.

In *The Division of Labor in Society,* Durkheim thus articulated and resolved a paradox: However much they may want to be free and autonomous, people in modern society have no choice but to maintain social ties. The structure of society—especially the way labor is divided in modern society—*forces* people to interact and to maintain social relationships with one another.

In that first book, Durkheim not only made important discoveries about the relationship between the division of labor and social solidarity but also identified the key to understanding things sociologically. The way to understand society was to focus not on the psychological or biological attributes of individuals but on *the nature of society itself.* This led Durkheim to a fairly startling conclusion: Society and social phenomena actually do exist.

I call this a startling conclusion because prior to Durkheim, no one had really thought that social phenomena existed. Sure, the word *social* was used, but it meant little more than a group of individuals.

Throughout his life Durkheim continued to explore the social. He claimed that social phenomena have a reality *sui generis*—that is, a unique reality of their own—and that social facts must be distinguished from individual biological or psychological facts.

The discovery of the social provided Durkheim and his followers with a whole arsenal of tools with which to explain important and troubling phenomena. For example, Durkheim discovered that suicide was more than merely a personal thing—suicide *rates,* at least, were strongly influenced by social factors (the economy or political changes, for example).

Likewise, Durkheim would have held that if we want to understand why the rate of divorce increases or decreases, we should look for changes not in the psychological attributes of married people but in the wider society: divorce laws, the availability of child care, the economic pressures on family groups, and so on.

According to Durkheim, *sociology was to be the scientific study of social facts,* or of those things in society that transcend or are bigger than individuals. This is not to say, Durkheim observed, that individuals did not exist or play a role in the modern world. Yet, Durkheim insisted, individuals and individual facts were the domain of psychology and biology. Social facts were the domain of sociology.

STOP

&

REVIEW

Answers to Stop and Review questions are at the end of the chapter.

1.1 Carefully consider Durkheim's definition of a social fact: "manners of acting, thinking, and feeling external to the individual, which are invested with a coercive power by virtue of which they exercise control over him." One category of social facts that interested Durkheim was rules for behavior (what sociologists call norms). Are norms truly social facts? Test this for yourself. Does the rule or norm that one must wear clothing to class qualify as a social fact according to Durkheim's definition? Explain why or why not.

The Origins of Modern Sociology in Germany: Ferdinand Tönnies, Max Weber, and Karl Marx

As Durkheim was resolving the paradox of dependency in France, sociology was emerging in Germany under the leadership of Ferdinand Tönnies and Max Weber.[9] Like Durkheim, Tönnies compared premodern and modern societies to see how they differed. But Tönnies followed a different tack: He wished to understand how social relationships between people differed in the two types of societies.

His comparison of the premodern and modern social worlds led Tönnies to conclude that there are two basic categories of social relationships. The first category is made up of those social relationships that people enter into as *ends in and of themselves.* The second category includes social relationships that people enter into as *means to specific ends.*

People enter into relationships that are ends in and of themselves for emotional or affective reasons. An individual's relationship with his or her family is generally an example of this sort of relationship. Ideally, we value our families not for what they can buy for us but because of our affection for them. Tönnies called these emotion-based relationships *Gemeinschaft,* or communal, relationships.

Ferdinand Tönnies (1855–1936) was one of the first German sociologists.

---

[9]The umlaut (¨) over the *o* in Tönnies' name indicates that the *o* is pronounced differently than one might expect. The proper pronunciation of Tönnies is "TUH-nees."

It is also important to mention that Max Weber is pronounced "Max VAY-ber." (In German, *W*'s are typically pronounced as *V*'s.)

From *Gemeinschaft and Gesellschaft* (1887)

FERDINAND TÖNNIES

Gemeinschaft
(Guh-MINE-
shoft) intimate
association

Gesellschaft
(Guh-ZELL-
shoft)
impersonal
association

All intimate, private, and exclusive living together, so we discover, is understood as life in Gemeinschaft (community). Gesellschaft (society) is public life—it is the world itself. In Gemeinschaft with family, one lives from birth on, bound to it in weal and woe. One goes into Gesellschaft as one goes into a strange country.

A young man is warned against bad Gesellschaft, but the expression bad Gemeinschaft violates the meaning of the word. . . .

A bride or groom knows that he or she goes into marriage as a complete Gemeinschaft of life. A Gesellschaft of life would be a contradiction in and of itself. . . .

The Gesellschaft exists in the realm of business, travel, or sciences.

People enter into relationships that are a means to an end, not out of affection or natural affinity, but to achieve some specific goal (for example, financial gain). Tönnies called these goal-driven relationships *Gesellschaft,* or social, relationships.

In your own life, you no doubt experience both sorts of relationships. When you pick someone to be your friend because you enjoy his or her company (and hence think of the relationship itself as the end or benefit you seek), the nature of that friendship relationship is communal, or *Gemeinschaft.*

On the other hand, when you choose to associate with someone because it will help you achieve some goal, the relationship is *Gesellschaft.* For example, if you hire a tutor to help you with chemistry, your specific intention in creating the relationship is to achieve a better grade in chemistry. Of course, you may grow to like your tutor and continue to spend time with him or her even after you pass the final exam. In such a case, then, your relationship has changed from *Gesellschaft* to *Gemeinschaft.* Frequently, a particular relationship will have some elements of *Gemeinschaft* and some elements of *Gesellschaft*—for example, when you and your best friend decide to open a business together or when you join with a few other students to form a study group (which may involve as much socializing as studying).

Tönnies suggested that in modern society more relationships are means to an end, or *Gesellschaft,* than in premodern society, where most human relationships were *Gemeinschaft*, or communal. It is not so much that people themselves have changed. Rather, modern society itself forces people to work and live among others even when they lack emotional attachments. Think about your relationships with your professors. Chances are, these are *Gesellschaft*—means to ends and impersonal. In premodern times, students would have been more likely to experience one-on-one, personal relationships with their teachers.

In any particular society, one expects to find examples of both *Gemeinschaft* and *Gesellschaft* relationships, as well as relationships that change from one type to the other and relationships that are mixed. The difference between premodern and modern society, according to Tönnies, is that the proportions are different.

One of Tönnies' major contributions to the discipline of sociology was the suggestion that if we wish to understand social life, we have to understand that people enter into relationships for different reasons and that, depending on the type of relationship, we deal with people differently. *The type of the relationship determines the rules of the relationship.* If John believed that he was your best friend (a *Gemeinschaft* relationship), he would take it as a terrible betrayal if you sold him out to gain some benefit for yourself (that is, if you treated your relationship as *Gesellschaft*). On the other hand, the owner of the local supermarket should not be personally offended if you shop at a competitor's store to buy groceries at a cheaper price.

STOP & REVIEW

1.2 Which of the following types of relationships are most likely to be *Gemeinschaft?* Which are most likely to be *Gesellschaft?*

    a. friend–friend
    b. wife–husband
    c. doctor–patient
    d. retailer–customer
    e. minister–parishioner
    f. parent–child
    g. worker–boss

1.3 Generally, the banker–client relationship in modern society is *Gesellschaft.* Yet, from watching television advertisements for banks, one might conclude that the banker–client relationship is supposed to be *Gemeinschaft.* For example, many banks seem to make a big deal of claiming to be "friendly bankers" or "good neighbors."

Why would banks promote their services as *Gemeinschaft* rather than *Gesellschaft?*

What, if any, danger is there in thinking of your relationship with your banker as *Gemeinschaft* when it really is *Gesellschaft?*

Max Weber was intrigued with Tönnies' idea that people act with a variety of motives and that the type of motive makes a difference in what they do. In Weber's eyes, especially, the fact that people had begun to see one another more and more as means to ends was a part of a larger trend. Weber called this trend the growth of *rational behavior.*

In everyday life, we usually compare rational behavior and irrational behavior, as if to suggest that rational behavior is the only behavior that makes sense. But Weber used the term differently: For him, *rational* was synonymous with *calculating.* If you have a goal and you sit down to plot how to achieve that goal most efficiently, *that* is being rational.

The opposite of rational for Weber was not *irrational,* but *non*rational or noncalculating. To Weber, nonrational behavior was behavior that was not especially geared to achieving some goal but was simply to be experienced or appreciated for itself.

Max Weber (1864–1920) explored and expanded Tönnies' ideas about people's motivations for acting.

As he studied history, Weber discovered that people in premodern societies were more likely to engage in nonrational behavior. That is, they were less calculating and less concerned about achieving larger ends; they did things simply because such acts were pleasing. For example, when a premodern person had enough to eat and was living a comfortable life, he or she stopped working. Why not? What was the point of having more stuff than one needed? In premodern society, people farmed and produced crafts not merely to earn a living; farming and crafting were *ways of life,* not simply ways to live.

People live a different sort of existence in modern society, said Weber. In the modern world, individuals more frequently do things to achieve specific goals efficiently. Most of us work to live; we don't live to work. One way of behaving, for example, might be more fun or pleasing to us, but if there is a more efficient way to behave, we tend to choose efficiency over fun. In modern society, Weber observed, one is considered immature if one does things simply because one enjoys them!

This is not to say that everything that everyone does in modern society is rational (or done as a means to an end); nor is it to say that premodern people were never calculating. In any society, at any time, we can find examples of both kinds of behavior.

Consider art collectors. One sort of art collector, the nonrational, noncalculating kind, might acquire a painting because it evokes a feeling of beauty and awe. Another sort of art collector, the rational, calculating kind, might purchase the same painting but see it merely as a good investment.

Some golfers are nonrational. They play golf because they enjoy the challenge of chasing the little ball around the course so they can whack it. Then there are the rational players—they play golf because it is a good way to soften up customers or clients to make profitable deals.

In the university community, I have met both rational and non-rational students. The rational student sees college as a means to an end (for example, a high-paying job); the nonrational student enjoys college because of what he or she learns. (Of course, many students have a mixture of motives.)

Weber wanted to know what it was about modern life that tended to inspire people to choose rational over nonrational behavior. The fact that rationalism seemed to be increasing in the Western world suggested to Weber that something important was happening and that, if we were to understand society and our place in it, we needed to understand the underlying causes and consequences of this trend.[10]

S T O P
&
R E V I E W

1.4 Think about two things you do for what Weber would call rational reasons. In what respect are your motives rational?

1.5 Think about two things you do for what Weber would call nonrational reasons. In what respect are your motives nonrational?

Karl Marx

Karl Marx (1818–1883) is perhaps best known as the "father" of communism.

Although many sociologists rank Karl Marx among the most important founders of sociology (along with Durkheim and Weber), it is curious that they do so. As one of his biographers wrote, "To write about Marx as a sociologist is to be hedged in with perils." Marx did not think of himself as a sociologist, and indeed, he was contemptuous of the sociologists whom he knew. As far as Marx was concerned, their focus on the social was entirely misdirected; only economics counted.

Marx was born in Germany in 1818 and studied philosophy and law. His early political activities made it impossible for him to achieve an academic position and, ultimately, even to stay in Germany. When he fled to France and continued to criticize the German government, Germany prevailed upon France to expel Marx. After a short stint in Brussels, he found himself in England, where he would stay almost continuously until his death in 1883.

---

[10]Weber's most famous investigation focused on the relationship between religion and the growth of rationality. The result of this investigation, a book titled *The Protestant Ethic and the Spirit of Capitalism*, first published in 1904–1905, remains one of the most famous works in sociology.

With Friedrich Engels, he wrote and published *The Communist Manifesto* in 1848. This brief document helped shape the revolutions that re-created much of the world over the course of the next century.

Marx's conception of the world was a singular one. In his mind, the most crucial thing about a society was its primary mode of production and distribution of goods—that is, its economic system. Given this, Marx argued, the people of any society could be divided into two distinct classes: the bourgeoisie and the proletariat. The bourgeoisie consisted of the people who owned the means of production—specifically, the owners of the factories that produced the goods sold and distributed throughout society. The proletariat consisted of the workers—the people who survived by selling their labor to the bourgeoisie. As far as Marx was concerned, everything else—ideas, values, social conventions, art, literature, morals, law, and even religion—was "epiphenomenal," or secondary to and in the service of the economic realities of society.

Thus, for example, Marx argued that religion was the "opium of the people" and existed only to mask the inequalities and injuries of the economic system. Religion had no real importance in the overall scheme of things because once the people woke up and realized the real injustices of the economic system, there would be no need for religion, and it would disappear.

While Marx loathed sociology, he did have a great influence on the discipline. His influence was of two sorts. First, many "Marxist" sociologists have made important contributions to modern sociology. As you will read in chapter 3, a major school of sociologists is a proponent of what some call the *conflict tradition* or the *Marxist tradition*. As you will learn later in this text, many Marxist concepts (for example, ideology and alienation) have even been adopted by mainstream sociologists.

Second, Marx's work had a tremendous impact on sociology because of its influence on Max Weber. Weber was still in school when Marx died, but he came of age in an era when Marx's ideas were hotly debated in Germany. Indeed, it has been said that much of Weber's sociology was a *debate with the ghost of Karl Marx*. More specifically, much of what Weber wrote was a rejection of Marx's "monocausal" theory that the economic system was the driving force behind all things social. There are, Weber said, no *ultimate* causes—we must look not only at the influence of economic or material things but also at the influence of ideas and values.

The Origins of Modern Sociology in England: Herbert Spencer

The pioneering English sociologist Herbert Spencer believed that society was governed by laws in much the same way that the physical world was. His interest lay in understanding how societies evolve; his belief was that societies evolve just as animal species do.

Spencer's work on evolution was first published in 1852.[11] Seven years later, Charles Darwin published his theory of evolution in *On the Origin of Species by Means of Natural Selection, or the Preservation of Favored Races in the Struggle for Life.* After Darwin's work was published, Spencer's ideas came to be known as social Darwinism.[12]

Spencer's theories were very popular in some circles. Those who adhered to social Darwinism saw the world as a jungle in which only the superior ought to prosper. Especially popular was the principle that Spencer referred to as *survival of the fittest.* This principle summed up Spencer's basic thesis that if we simply leave people alone to compete, the best will survive and the inferior will perish. The overall result of natural social evolution, according to Spencer, is that society gets better over time. However, social improvement will continue only so long as people do not interfere with the natural course of things. Consequently, Spencer and his followers opposed any kind of state assistance to the poor; they even opposed public schools.

In the wrong hands this principle can be deadly. For example, it was used to justify the superior positions in society of whites over blacks and rich over poor. In this respect, Spencer's theory was hardly an improvement on ...e premodern theories of social status, which had held that God r ...ed people in the estates they deserved. Baldly stated, according ... Spencerian doctrine, if someone was rich, it was because he or ... was superior; if blacks had a difficult time thriving in white society, it was because they were inferior.

Herbert Spencer (1820–1903) promoted the theory of social Darwinism (sort of looked like Ebenezer Scrooge, didn't he?).

---

[11]"A Theory of Population, Deduced from the General Law of Animal Fertility," *Westminster Review* LVII (1852). It was in this work that Spencer introduced the phrase "survival of the fittest."

[12]Charles Darwin, the English naturalist, published *On the Origins of Species* in 1859. Given the timing, it is curious that Darwin's theory was not labeled "natural Spencerism" instead of Spencer's theory being labeled "social Darwinism."

Darwin's theory would have been published even later had it not been for what must have seemed (to Darwin, at least) the most appalling coincidence. Fourteen years after returning home from his famous trip on the HMS *Beagle,* Darwin was still gathering evidence for his theory (knowing it would be very controversial). Then, in 1857, another English scientist, Alfred Russel Wallace, fell ill in Borneo. According to the story, Wallace passed his three days in bed by working up a theory of evolution that was in many respects identical to Darwin's. Wallace sent his paper to Darwin for comments. Darwin was dumbfounded. Not wanting to become a historical also-ran, Darwin rushed his *On the Origin of Species* into print even though he believed it to be incomplete. For the rest of his life, Darwin referred to his work as a mere abstract.

In the United States and Germany, especially, there were many who found Spencer's ideas compelling. With social Darwinism they could justify the enslavement of Africans and the near genocide of Native Americans. Later, in Germany, principles of social Darwinism were invoked by the Nazis to justify their decision to exterminate the Jews.

Spencer viewed social competition as a kind of purifying process in which the weak were weeded out. Spencer cautioned his readers not to feel pity for the losers—the poor, weak, or otherwise disadvantaged. Social competition, Spencer claimed, is a "stern discipline, which is a little cruel that it may be very kind." He wrote about the pain and suffering (and deaths) of "inferior" people. These deaths only *seemed* to be tragic, said Spencer. They are not tragic, but beneficial to society!

Charles Loring Brace (1826–1890), who founded the Children's Aid Society in the United States, had this to say about Spencer's ideas:

"Would not mankind take chloroform if they had no future but Spencer's?"

> When regarded not separately but in connection with the interests of universal humanity, these harsh fatalities are seen to be full of beneficence—the same beneficence which brings to early graves the children of diseased parents and singles out [some but not others to be] victims of epidemics. (1852)

The bottom line, said Spencer, is that we must face facts: The competition to survive will be won by the best because those who survive and thrive, by definition, are the "best." Showing pity for social losers only leads to "spurious philanthropy" and is a waste of time, effort, and money. As one of Spencer's students warned,

> if we do not like survival of the fittest, we have only one possible alternative, and that is the survival of the unfittest. The former is the law of civilization; the latter is the law of anticivilization. We have our choice between the two, or we can go on, as in the past, vacillating between the two, but a third plan [offering help to the poor and helpless] for nourishing the unfittest and yet advancing civilization, no man will ever find. (Sumner 1934, II)

Sociology in the United States

Sociology came to prominence in the United States later than it had in Europe, possibly because the United States experienced the social chaos of the Industrial Revolution later than France, England, or Germany. Whereas the process of industrialization was virtually completed in the European nations by 1850, the United States did not experience full-fledged industrialization until after it fought its civil war in the 1860s.

The first sociology course was taught by William Graham Sumner, a professor at Yale University. The first sociology department in the United States was organized in 1892, at the University of Chicago. In 1905, sociologists organized the American

Sociological Society (soon changed to the American Sociological Association for reasons that might seem obvious). The goal of the ASA was and is to promote the scientific study of society.

Early U.S. sociologists differed from their European counterparts in that they did not focus all their efforts on building sweeping theories of society. In addition to theory building, the U.S. sociologists concentrated on solving the specific social problems—poverty, crime—that had arisen (or so it was thought) as a consequence of the large immigrant population. In other words, while European sociologists were attempting to build sociology into a *basic* science like physics or chemistry, many of the early U.S. sociologists treated sociology as an *applied* science, like engineering. Indeed, some of these sociologists called themselves social engineers.

Out of this initial enthusiasm for social engineering came the first sociologist to win the Nobel Prize: Jane Addams. In 1889, Addams and a colleague, Ellen Gates Starr, founded Hull House, a settlement house that served the needs of the poor in Chicago. Hull House was also the base from which Addams conducted her research into the causes and consequences of poverty. Other Chicago sociologists specialized in studying specific manifestations of modernity—hobos, dance hall girls, prostitution, gambling, and the like. In general, the focus of early sociology in the United States was as much on social reform as on theory building.

Jane Addams (1860–1935) was the first sociologist to win a Nobel Prize.

Born in Great Barrington, Massachusetts, William Edward Burghardt (W. E. B.) DuBois was the first person of African descent to receive a PhD from Harvard University. After a year-long stint as research assistant at the University of Pennsylvania, he took a job at Atlanta University in 1897. From 1933 to 1944, DuBois chaired the department of sociology at the university.

Like Marx, DuBois saw society as conflict-ridden; but DuBois argued that Marx had overlooked the importance of race and ethnicity in modern society. According to DuBois, it was not enough to focus on economic differences in society—racial differences were even more important. Convinced that once the injustice of the race system in the United States had been exposed, it would be remedied, DuBois published more than seventy books on race and race relations, including *The Philadelphia Negro* (1899), *The Souls of Black Folk* (1903), *Darkwater* (1920), and *Color and Democracy* (1945). Turning to direct political activism, in 1909 DuBois helped found the National Negro Committee, which soon came to be known as the National Association for the Advancement of Colored People (NAACP). DuBois was a vocal critic of other black leaders—like Booker T. Washington—whom he saw as too willing to compromise the position of blacks in American society. DuBois, it has been said, "took the lead in making the United States and the World recognize that racial prejudice was not a mere matter of Negroes being persecuted but was a cancer which poisoned the

W. E. B. DuBois (1868–1963) was highly critical of the race system in the United States.

One Small Step for Sociology

As a black man, DuBois had a difficult start in academics. He graduated with a bachelor's degree from Fisk College in Nashville, Tennessee, in 1888. DuBois applied to Harvard but was unable to begin graduate studies at that point because Harvard refused to accept the legitimacy of a degree from Fisk. DuBois repeated the final two years of his undergraduate work at Harvard, graduating cum laude in 1890. He went on to complete work for the Ph.D degree at Harvard, which he received in 1895. DuBois also studied in Germany with Max Weber at the University of Berlin. Below is a clip from the front page of the *New York Times* announcing his appointment as a research fellow at the University of Pennsylvania. Notice that the reporter took pains to assure readers that Dr. DuBois would have no interaction with students at the University.

FIRST COLORED "FELLOW" APPOINTED.

Philadelphia, Sept 20.—Dr. W. E. B. Dubois, colored, who was graduated from Harvard College several years ago, and who studied in the German universities, has been appointed to a Fellowship in Sociology at the University of Pennsylvania. He is the first one of his race to hold such a position in this university. He will be an assistant to Dr. Samuel Lindsay in sociology. Dr. Dubois will not be considered a member of the Faculty, and will not lecture at college. His work will be among the colored population of Philadelphia. He will make a house-to-house investigation of the colored settlements, giving to the university authorities the results of his observations. (*New York Times*, 30 Sept. 1896, p. 1)

In fact, W. E. B. DuBois, and not "university" authorities, compiled the results of his research into a book, *The Philadelphia Negro*, which was published by the University of Pennsylvania Press in 1899.

DuBois published widely throughout his career. But always, it seemed, he was distrusted. According to information gathered under the Freedom of Information Act, for example, we know that the United States Federal Bureau of Investigation opened a file on DuBois in 1942. Although he was widely quoted as saying he was not a communist, his politics came under close scrutiny for the last 50 years of his life. All told, the portions of the file made public included 927 pages. The final entries in that file (made in 1960, when DuBois was 92 years old) mentioned that "DuBois is alleged to be a 'champion' for equality among races and therefore . . ." (the rest of the paragraph was redacted by the FBI before the file was made public; alas, we will never know why being a champion for equality was perceived as threatening) (see http://www.foia.fbi.gov/foiaindex/dubois.htm).

whole civilization of the United States" (James 1967, 365). Many members of the NAACP found his ideas too radical—especially after he gave up on the idea of integration and began to promote the idea of segregation—and eventually he was dismissed from the NAACP. In 1961 DuBois renounced his U.S. citizenship and moved to Ghana, where he lived until his death.

The Place of Sociology in Modern Society

The founders of sociology in Europe—Durkheim, Tönnies, Weber, and Spencer, as well as Americans like Sumner, Addams, and DuBois who followed them—brought sociology from laughing-stock to prominence by the end of the nineteenth century. Although (fortunately) the more dangerous ideas of Spencer have been largely discredited, the works of the others are still held up as models of good sociological work. The articles and books by Durkheim and Weber, especially, continue to have a tremendous impact on sociologists. In spite of their many differences, each of these scholars insisted that the social world was worthy of study. Each believed that by bringing to bear the tools of science on the social world, he or she could help make sense of it. Like Copernicus, who was skeptical of the traditional view of the natural world, these sociologists were skeptical of traditional views of the social world. As we will explore in the following chapters, the tradition of skepticism continues.

Chapter Review

1. Below I have listed the major concepts discussed in this chapter and in the introduction to the book. Define each of the terms. (*Hint:* This exercise will be more helpful to you if, in addition to defining each concept, you create an example of it in your own words.)

   sociology (defined)
   W. I. Thomas
      Thomas theorem
   origins and development of natural sciences
   industrial revolution
   Auguste Comte
      Law of Three Stages
   Émile Durkheim
      mechanical and organic solidarity
      collective conscience
      social facts
      sui generis

Ferdinand Tönnies
   Gemeinschaft and *Gesellschaft*
Max Weber
   rational and nonrational behavior
   rationalization of society
Karl Marx
   all but economy is epiphenomenal
   proletariat
   bourgeoisie
   means of production
Herbert Spencer
   survival of the fittest
Jane Addams
W. E. B. DuBois

2. What sorts of social changes helped to lead people to question the nature of social reality (and thereby helped to spur the creation of sociology)?

3. List two of your relationships that are *Gemeinschaft* and two that are *Gesellschaft*. Explain why you have categorized each relationship as either *Gemeinschaft* or *Gesellschaft*. Then assume that you had to leave some of your relationships. Which would be easier to replace—those that are *Gemeinschaft* or those that are *Gesellschaft*? Why?

4. Weber distinguished between rational and nonrational behavior but said that many actual behaviors contain elements of both rationality and nonrationality. What is a behavior that you do that contains elements of both rationality and nonrationality? Explain what is rational and what is nonrational about this behavior.

Answers and Discussion

1.1 Durkheim said that social facts were "manners of acting, thinking and feeling external to the individual, which are vested with a coercive power by virtue of which they exercise control over him."

The norm that one must wear clothes is a social fact. It is external to the individual (it exists outside of him or her and would still exist even if the individual claimed it did not exist). Does this norm have coercive power? Yes. Imagine that you wanted to go to class in the nude. Wouldn't there be some coercion used against you either to prevent you from doing this or to punish you after the fact?

1.2 The types of relationships that are most likely to be *Gemeinschaft* (that is, personal and close) are friend–friend, wife–husband, minister–parishioner, and parent–child. The types of relationships most likely to be *Gesellschaft* are doctor–patient, retailer–customer, and worker–boss.

1.3 Why would banks advertise as if they had *Gemeinschaft* relations with their customers? Probably because they know that people would choose to interact with friends rather than cold and impersonal bankers. The thing is, however, a bank cannot be your friend. The law requires banks, for example, to treat people equally and to do such things as foreclose on mortgages when people don't pay on time. Those are certainly not behaviors one would expect from one's friends! The tension between *Gemeinschaft* and *Gesellschaft* relations also explains why many wise people advise against lending money to friends and family members.

1.4 and 1.5 These two questions could be answered in a number of ways. By way of example, here are my answers:

1.4 Two things I do for what Weber would call rational reasons:
   a. Pay my bills each month. Paying my bills is a clear example of doing something as a means to an end (keeping a decent credit rating).
   b. Show up for class on time. This is a means to a couple of practical ends: keeping my students calm (of course, they get upset if I'm late and they don't get to spend the entire class period with me) and keeping my chairperson happy.

1.5 Two things I do for what Weber would call nonrational reasons:
   a. Build furniture. Building things is a pleasurable activity. It is not a rational activity because it always costs me more to make something than it would to buy it. Moreover, although I have sold a few pieces of my furniture, I never have made more than I paid for the materials.
   b. Do graphics on my computer—it's fun.

My insight: As I was answering these questions, I stumbled onto an important insight: Question 1.5 was really hard to answer. I spent ten minutes not being able to think of a single thing that I do for nonrational reasons.

Did you have the same problem? Of course, I do nonrational things; it's just that I "rationalize" these activities. Consider one of my answers—building furniture. I was tempted to say that I build furniture as a means to an end—carpentry helps me reduce stress, and reducing stress is important if I am going to be a productive worker. But, really, carpentry is an end in and of itself; it's something I do because I enjoy it.

Similarly, I was tempted to claim that I do computer graphics because they help me teach. But it is simply not rational to spend forty-five minutes designing the perfect graphic to illustrate one sociological concept. Again, I do it because I enjoy it. It is a happy coincidence that I can use graphics in the classroom.

It is almost as if I am reluctant to admit to spending time in nonrational ways, as if nonrational behavior is wasteful. The fact that I rationalize my behavior this way suggests that Weber was on to something important when he observed that life was becoming more rational. I feel almost guilty when I do stuff for enjoyment and tend not to do fun stuff unless I can rationalize it—and thereby make it seem rational.

2

THE SOCIOLOGICAL EYE

Modern sociologists continue to be inspired by two important qualities stressed by early sociologists: (1) the focus on the social and (2) skepticism.

The Focus on the Social

It is the focus on the social that allows sociologists to see much that escapes the notice of other observers; it is what makes sociology unique. But, I should warn you, this focus on the social makes sociology difficult for newcomers to the discipline because most of them have been taught to view the world in ways that are distinctly nonsociological.

Let me explain: People in modern Western societies have been taught to embrace the principle of *individualism*. Individualism is the idea that in life people pursue their own ends, that people follow their own ideas. Why does Mary get better grades than Johnny? It must be that Mary is smarter, or works harder, than Johnny. Why does Chris get drunk every weekend? Well, frankly, Chris just doesn't make good choices.

You might be thinking—of course we focus on individuals! How else can it be? The fact is, in other cultures (and even in our own in earlier times) individuals are hardly noticeable, but are treated as extensions of their family, clan, or tribe. If one person does something heroic, the group receives the credit; likewise, if one person does something wrong, it is the group that is shamed. How unlike our own society. Imagine the day when you graduate from college: Your parents will be proud, but they will be proud

For American sociologist C. Wright Mills (1916–1962), the key to the sociological imagination was the ability to distinguish between personal troubles and social issues.

29

of *your* accomplishments. The diploma will have your name on it; all of the congratulations (and gifts) will be bestowed on you.

Sociologists have taught themselves not to be satisfied with explanations that focus on individuals, but to look at the social environment and the ways in which it affects people. What is it about the social context in which some people grow up and live that facilitates academic achievement? In what ways do particular social circumstances encourage some people to drink to excess?

More generally, sociologists understand that individuals make choices about how they will act, that they do have "free will," but sociologists know that it is the social environment that makes some choices easier and others harder.

Consider the case of the motorist who arrives at an intersection: Will she go right, left, or continue on? The naive observer might say that we cannot predict her next move, that it's *her choice.* Yet we can be confident that she will not shift into reverse and back up; neither will she choose to remain in the intersection for more than a few moments. Even if she doesn't want to go right, left, or ahead, the social circumstances (the rules of the road, not to mention the line of impatient drivers in the cars behind her) will push her to do so (McIntyre 2005, 19).

Why are sociologists unsatisfied with individualistic explanations for behavior? Allan G. Johnson, who has written a number of books for sociology students, explains it this way: *"The individualistic perspective that dominates current thinking about social life doesn't work"*:

> Nothing we do or experience takes place in a vacuum; everything is always related to a [social] context of some kind. When a wife and husband argue about who'll clean the bathroom, for example, or who'll take care of a sick child when they both work outside the home, the issue is never simply about the two of them even though it may seem that way at the time. We have to ask about the larger context in which this takes place. We might ask how this instance is related to living in a society organized in ways that privilege men over women, in part by not making men feel obliged to share equally in domestic work except when they choose to "help out." On an individual level, he may think she's being a nag; she may think he's being a jerk; but it's never as simple as that. What both may miss is that in a different kind of society, they might not be having this argument in the first place because both might feel obliged to take care of the home and children. In similar ways, when we see ourself as a unique result of the family we came from, we overlook how each family is connected to larger patterns. The emotional problems we struggle with as individuals aren't due simply to what kind of parents we had, for their participation in the social system—at work, in the community, in society as a whole—shaped them as people, including their roles as mothers and fathers.

> An individualistic model is misleading because it encourages us
> to explain human behavior and experience from a perspective that's
> so narrow it misses most of what's going on. (Johnson 1997, 20–21)

This is not to say that sociologists are uninterested in the behavior
of individuals. Many of us (myself included) are just as interested
in the goings-on of the people we encounter as you are; many of
us (myself included) watch and wonder about the antics of our
neighbors, colleagues (and, yes, our students) and seek explanations for what we see. The quality that makes sociologists
different from other people is the conviction that our ability to
understand and explain what we observe will be enhanced if we
look past the individuals involved to examine the impact of their
social and historical contexts.

The American sociologist C. Wright Mills sharpened the sociological perspective with his concept of the *sociological imagination*.
The defining quality of the sociological imagination, Mills said, is
the ability to look beyond what he called the *personal troubles* of
individuals to see the *public issues of social structure*—that is, the
social forces operating in the larger society.

> The first fruit of this imagination—and the lesson of the social
> science that embodies it—is the idea that the individual can
> understand his own experience and gauge his own fate only by
> locating himself within his period, that he can know his own
> chances in life only by becoming aware of those of all individuals
> in his circumstances. (1959, 5)

Mills observed that people in our society "often feel that their
private lives are a series of traps. They sense that within their
everyday worlds, they cannot overcome their troubles." In other
words, people feel unable to alter their circumstances. And, Mills
suggested, in this feeling of being trapped and impotent, people
"are often quite correct."

Mills suggests that people often misunderstand their own
circumstances because they have an individualistic bias. The individualistic bias leads people to think that their own situations are
wholly a result of their own behavior. They don't notice that there
are larger entities, forces outside of themselves, that shape their
behaviors.

Without guidance from the sociological imagination, our individualistic bias leads us to treat individuals as the source of problems. Of course, people frequently do make bad choices. But the
individualistic bias prevents us from discovering that some of our
worst problems are the result of *social forces*.

Consider John and Jill who, after nine years of marriage, have
just divorced. Jill is feeling like a failure. When she vowed "'til
death do us part," she meant it! Where did she go wrong? Her

own parents are still married after 32 years! John, too, is at a loss. Jill doesn't seem at all like the woman he fell in love with; she's changed. The passion is gone and they've grown apart.

John and Jill entered marriage with the understanding that it was up to them to make the union a success. As a result, as Mills would say, John and Jill regard the failure of their marriage as purely a *personal trouble*—a result of something they did or did not do.

Mills would understand John and Jill's point of view, but suggest it might be misguided. He pointed out that "inside a marriage a man and a woman may experience personal troubles," but when the divorce rate escalates, "this is an indication of a structural issue having to do with the institutions of marriage and the family and other institutions that bear upon them." John and Jill experience their divorce as a personal trouble, but current social arrangements (such as an economy that requires families to have two wage-earners and forces employees to work lots of overtime) has made marriage more difficult. Under such circumstances, Mills points out, "the problem of a satisfactory marriage remains incapable of purely private solution."

Here is the crucial sociological punch line: If people in society are concerned about the divorce rate and want to fix it, they must not focus on individuals; they must focus on the *social* structures and *social* arrangements that make marriage difficult.

Mills argued that most individuals feel trapped by the problems they encounter—and that their sense of entrapment comes from believing that their personal troubles are necessarily of their own making. Mills believed that the sociological imagination can help rescue people from such traps.

Without guidance from the sociological imagination, we are tempted to attack all problems by treating individuals. Again, this is because of our individualistic bias, which makes it hard for us to see beyond our own personal and immediate circumstances. With such a limited perspective, it's hard to see that some of our worst problems are a result of *social forces.*

The advantage of the sociological imagination or perspective, then, as Mills discovered, is that it opens up new resources for problem solving. Many of the most serious problems experienced by individuals, such as unemployment, have *social* causes, so it is futile to try to remedy or fix them at the individual level.

> When, in a city of 100,000, only one man is unemployed, that is his personal trouble, and for its relief we properly look to the character of the man, his skills, and his immediate opportunities. But when in a nation of 50 million employees, 15 million men are unemployed, that is a [social] issue, and we may not hope to find its solution within the range of opportunities open to any one individual. . . . Both the correct statement of the problem and the range of possible solutions

require us to consider the economic and political institutions of
society, and not merely the personal situation and character of a
scatter of individuals. (1959, 9)

As mentioned briefiy in chapter 1, the French sociologist Émile
Durkheim applied the sociological perspective to the problem of
suicide. To most of Durkheim's colleagues, the decision to kill
oneself seemed to be the most personal and individual of decisions. But, said Durkheim, *suicide is also a social issue.* From studying the differences in suicide statistics across different European
countries, Durkheim found that the rate of suicide tended to vary
with the degree of *social integration* in a particular society. In other
words, *the rate of suicide varies with the degree to which people have
strong ties to their social groups.*

More specifically, Durkheim found that people with weaker or
fewer ties to their social groups were more likely to commit suicide. This finding helped to explain the fact that single people had
higher rates of suicide than married people. Likewise, understanding the relationship between suicide and social integration helped
to explain why Protestants (who are encouraged by their religion
to be independent) had higher suicide rates than Catholics.

The sociological perspective of Durkheim, or what Mills later
called the sociological imagination, suggested that suicide is not
simply an individual problem, or personal trouble. Durkheim himself argued that the rate of suicide would decrease if more emphasis were placed on integrating people into society. To put it another
way, according to Durkheim, the rate of suicide would drop if
people were given more opportunities to bond with one another.

It is easy to find examples of situations in which the sociological
imagination or perspective adds to our understanding. Sociologists who study organizations, for example, have discovered
that working in a bureaucracy can have a tremendous impact
on people's behavior. Regardless of how warm and caring people are *off* the job, their "on-the-job personalities" can be rigid,
authoritarian, and uncaring—because that is how the structure of
the organization forces them to be. People who work in bureaucracies have to follow the rules and act without regard for differences among individual clients. (Just remember this the next time
you visit the registrar's office! If you want to make the system
work for you, you need to take into account the ways in which the
person across the counter is constrained by his or her position.)

Likewise, sociologists who study social inequality have examined the fact that people of different races are treated differently
in most societies. This inequity should come as no surprise to
you. But what may surprise you is that racial discrimination is
not merely a matter of individuals being nasty to one another.
Frequently, racism is a result of factors built into social systems.

Because of this *institutional racism*,[1] individuals may get locked into a larger pattern of racist behavior, perhaps without even being aware of it, let alone being able to resist it. The admissions officer at the exclusive private university who is told to give preference to the children of alumni is perpetuating racist admissions policies (because most of the alumni are white), even though he or she may personally abhor racism. The loan officer at the bank who is told not to approve loans for homes in certain parts of the city (populated mainly by African Americans) may not be racist, but her institution forces her to act as if she is. This does not, of course, excuse racist activities, but it does suggest that the fight against racism has to involve more than educating individuals. We have to treat this problem (or, as Mills would say, this *public issue*) at a higher level.

For most beginning sociology students raised in Western society, this idea of sociological imagination is a tough one. Because of their individualistic bias, Westerners tend to be unaware of the ways in which larger social forces affect people's beliefs and behaviors. If you find it difficult to understand this idea of

---

Agency and Structure

A caveat[2]

As you learned in the preceding material, the focus of this text is on the power of the social environment to influence individuals. Does that mean that sociologists do not believe that individuals have *agency*—that is, that individuals do not have the capacity to make decisions on their own and act to change their circumstances? While sociologists continue to argue how much agency individuals have, none doubt that people are capable of "critically evaluating and reconstructing the condition of their own lives" (Emirbayer and Mische 1998, 964)—that people have the capacity to act and influence their environment.

One goal of this text, however, is to persuade you that *social factors* influence the kinds of choices from which individuals choose. Typically, we do not even realize how much our choices are influenced by our social environment, and because of this, we may have trouble understanding why people act the way that they do.

---

[1] The term "institutionalized racism" was coined in the 1960s by Stokely Carmichael, a prominent black activist.

[2] A caveat is a warning or a caution.

a sociological imagination, take heart: The following chapters of this book will give you the tools you need to develop your own sociological imagination.

2.1 Describe the difference between crime as a personal trouble and crime as a public/social issue.

STOP
&
REVIEW

Skepticism

SOURCES OF SKEPTICISM

"Had it not been for the race problem early thrust upon me and enveloping me, I should have probably been an unquestioning worshipper at the shrine of the established social order into which I was born. But just that part of this social order which seemed to most of my fellows nearest perfection seemed to me most inequitable and wrong; and starting from that critique, I gradually, as the years went by, found other things to question in my environment."

—W. E. B. DuBois (1968)

Like their nineteenth-century predecessors, contemporary sociologists are skeptical of commonly accepted explanations of things. Indeed, skepticism is an important foundation of scientific curiosity. If one accepts everyday explanations for things, there is no reason to inquire further. For example, in years past, only those who were skeptical of the commonly accepted "fact" that humans could not fly attempted to build "aeroplanes." Similarly, in the early nineteenth century, engineers believed that buildings could not be constructed more than a few stories high. But the skeptics among them, working with technology and the laws of physics, designed the immense structures that dominate the skylines of modern cities.

Sociologists are especially skeptical about the impact of social things. As an outgrowth of his skepticism, American sociologist Robert K. Merton provided us with an important research technique. Merton said that really understanding social things involves identifying both their *manifest* (intended and obvious) and *latent* (unintended and frequently hidden) consequences. Merton called these consequences *functions*.

One of the most obvious examples of the importance of latent consequences involves the modern experience with prisons. The manifest function of the prison system is to protect society by locking up dangerous criminals. As many researchers have found, however, one of the latent functions of the prison system is the production of more knowledgeable criminals—that is, convicts learn from one another in prison about how to commit crimes!

Here are two more examples of manifest versus latent functions. The first has to do with medicine.

In the nineteenth century there were hundreds of medical schools throughout the United States. The quality of these schools was uneven: Some offered hands-on training while others stressed only theory. Some required three years of study after four years of college, while others required three years of medical study but no college degree. Some taught traditional (allopathic) medicine, while others pursued more novel approaches (such as homeopathy, osteopathy, chiropractic, and botanical medicine). Some had well-endowed laboratories and libraries, while others did not.

In the early twentieth century, some members of the American medical profession believed that society would be better off if its physicians were trained in a more scientific manner. In 1910 the American Medical Association (AMA) commissioned one of its members, Abraham Flexner, to conduct a study of medical schools throughout the country. As he would report to the AMA, Flexner was appalled at the variety of training methods he encountered. Citing the Flexner Report as evidence, the AMA lobbied government officials to clamp down on schools that did not offer a specific sort of training. As a result, hundreds of medical schools were forced to close their doors.

The manifest, or intended, consequence of tightening regulations for medical schools was to produce better-trained physicians. But this change in regulations had several latent consequences as well. One latent consequence was that practitioners who could not afford the more expensive training offered by traditional schools or who did not agree with traditional notions of medicine were forced out of the profession.[3] Tightened regulations also forced medical schools that trained women and African Americans to close their doors because they could not afford the expensive laboratory equipment and libraries that the AMA rules required. (Note that Flexner presented no evidence that the patients of physicians trained in alternative schools without laboratories and libraries were worse off than the patients of physicians who had trained at, say, Harvard.) And finally, doctors trained in the traditional manner no longer had to compete with the oftentimes more popular nontraditional practitioners.

---

[3] It is important to point out that even in the early twentieth century, regular (allopathic) medical practitioners could not successfully treat diseases like tuberculosis, syphilis, and polio. Nor were such things as the importance of wearing rubber gloves universally accepted among medical personnel (many hospitals did not provide gloves for surgeons, and most surgeons did not want the added expense of purchasing their own). Furthermore, regular medical treatments frequently did more harm than good. For example, during the nineteenth century, many people died from being "bled" by their physicians, who had hoped to drain out "bad humors" from the body. Some treatments even called for the letting of more blood than we now know exists in the entire body (George Washington was said to have met his death this way). In contrast, alternative medical approaches generally took a less invasive, more supportive approach. Thus, ironically, one was generally safer *not* being treated by regular medical personnel.

Nail Down That Distinction
Between Manifest and Latent Functions!

University Education

Manifest function: Educate young adults.

Latent function: Keep young adults out of the job market, thereby easing competition for older adults.

Mother's Day and Father's Day

Manifest function: Provide an opportunity to express gratitude to parents.

Latent function: Help greeting-card companies boost sales in the spring and summer months.

Carrying a Briefcase

Manifest function: Carry stuff.

Latent function: Indicate occupational status (for example, not manual laborer).

Here is an example of how unintended or latent functions may have an impact on one aspect of *your* life.

New college professors generally must endure a six-year probationary period. At the end of this time, the quality of the professor's teaching, research, and service work is evaluated by senior colleagues. If the accomplishments of the probationary professor are deemed acceptable, they will grant him or her *tenure.* But if he or she has not lived up to expectations, the professor is denied tenure and forced to leave the university.

In the past few decades, most universities and colleges have tightened up their tenure requirements. Fifty years ago, tenure was practically a given. Today, things are different; most junior professors[4] spend their first years working like crazy to fulfill tenure requirements. One of the most important requirements is to conduct research and publish the results. As a rule of thumb, if you don't publish a fair amount, you will be denied tenure (hence the so-called publish-or-perish rule).

The manifest function, or intended consequence, of emphasizing the importance of research for tenure is to produce more knowledge of the natural and social world. Universities do not want professors who simply sit around doing nothing. Professors should be out there, studying and making scholarly contributions. The latent

---

[4]Untenured professors typically are called assistant professors. Among the senior professors who have tenure, there are two ranks: associate professor and full professor.

function or consequence, however, is that some professors neglect their teaching responsibilities to do their research.[5]

This is not to say that all latent functions or consequences have a negative impact on society's usual functioning or are, as sociologists would put it, *dysfunctional*.[6] The unintended consequence of an action can be positive, or *functional*. For example, the manifest function of a neighborhood party is to have fun; a latent function can be to bring neighbors together or promote crime fighting. The manifest function of riding bicycles to work is to increase riders' fitness; a latent function can be fewer cars on the road or less air pollution.

Merton's distinction between manifest and latent functions is important. It reminds us to look beyond the obvious—frequently, the least obvious consequences are the most important ones.

2.2 For each of these common social events, list as many manifest and latent functions as you can:
- a. college athletics
- b. attending church
- c. attending sociology class

Chapter Review

1. Below I have listed the major concepts discussed in this chapter. Define each of the terms. (*Hint:* This exercise will be more helpful to you if, in addition to defining each concept, you create an example of it in your own words.)

individualism

C. W. Mills, sociological imagination

Émile Durkheim, suicide rates and integration

institutional racism

---

[5]Fortunately, as we begin the twenty-first century, university officials seem to be backtracking a bit and are once again beginning to emphasize the importance of teaching. At my own university, for example, candidates for tenure and promotion are required to show a measure of success in both teaching and research.

[6]Notice the spelling of *dysfunctional*. The *dys* prefix, which has its roots in the Greek language, suggests that something is defective, difficult, or painful. This prefix is frequently encountered in medicine—for example, *dysentery* (painful intestine), *dyspeptic* (painful digestion), or *dystrophy* (abnormal growth). On the other hand, the *dis* prefix, which is derived from Latin, tends to mean apart, asunder, or deprived of—for example, *dissemble*, *disable*, or *disrespect*. So, although the two prefixes are pronounced the same in English, they carry different meanings.

Robert K. Merton

   manifest and latent functions

   functions and dysfunctions

2. Sociologists often have a difficult time persuading lay-people that there is something to be gained by looking at divorce, racism, or poverty (or anything else, for that matter) as a social issue rather than just a personal trouble. In your considered judgment, why might this be so?

3. What is a possible benefit of looking for latent as well as manifest functions of things in the social world?

Answers and Discussion

2.1 According to Mills's perspective, crime as a personal trouble involves the circumstances and problems of the people who are directly touched by the crime. For example, Joe Student was arrested for breaking and entering. Why on earth did Joe do such a thing (seeking the cause of the crime in Joe's personal circumstances)?

Crime as a social issue involves looking at the larger aspects of crime and the ways these are affected by historical and social circumstances. For example, the rate of burglaries is on the increase. What is happening in the rest of society (perhaps in the economic arena) that might be influencing this?

2.2

   a. Manifest functions of college athletics include enhancing school spirit, helping students develop physical as well as mental skills, and increasing the fame of the college or university. Latent functions include helping students who otherwise would not be able to attend college (because of poverty, for example) to do so by winning athletic scholarships, acting as a training ground for future professional athletes, and exploiting the talents of athletes from underprivileged backgrounds without actually having to provide a real education for them. (That's pretty cynical, isn't it? That last one might be a dysfunction of college athletics.)

   b. Manifest functions of church attendance include worshiping and joining with others to celebrate important beliefs. Latent functions include having an opportunity to dress up and see what other people are wearing and how their children behave.

   c. Manifest functions of attending class regularly include learning the assigned material more thoroughly and having the opportunity to hear brilliant lectures by your professors. Latent functions include impressing your professors with the sincerity of your quest for knowledge and having more opportunities to make friends with other students, or even having a quiet time to write a letter.

3

SCIENCE AND FUZZY OBJECTS

Specialization in Sociology

"It is difficult to paint a clear picture of a fuzzy object."
—Ludwig Josef Wittgenstein (1959)

The first time I read Wittgenstein's statement,[1] I was struck by how profoundly it applied to sociology. As far as I was concerned, there was hardly anything more fuzzy than sociological phenomena. Many of my colleagues would probably not want to admit that what they do is study fuzzy stuff, but Wittgenstein's observation does help to explain why sociologists rarely make statements like "this causes that" or "if you do that, then this definitely will happen." Generally, sociologists do not like to commit themselves that far; they are more likely to say something to the effect that "if that happens, then it is likely that this will happen."

This really bugs some sociology students—the ones who like things cut and dried, who want their knowledge to be clear, definite, and certain. Unfortunately for these students, there is not much of that sort of knowledge in sociology.

I hasten to point out that the fact that many of sociologists' predictions about what will happen are probabilistic rather than certain is in no way the fault of sociology! That's where Wittgenstein's point that it is hard to paint a clear picture of a fuzzy object comes in. The stuff that sociologists study is some of the fuzziest in the universe.

Most sociologists long ago accepted that to understand a particular social event or interaction, they must take a multitude of factors into account. They also accepted that generally it is impossible to make predictions with absolute assurance. We can

---

[1]The philosopher Wittgenstein (VIT-gen-stine) was born in Vienna in 1889 but became a naturalized British subject in 1938. Before turning to philosophy, Wittgenstein had studied engineering.

40

frequently predict what *most* people will *likely* do under particular sets of circumstances, but we can offer no guarantees.

Of course, sociology is not the only science that studies fuzzy objects. But many of those working in other disciplines have demonstrated a tremendous ability to ignore the fuzzy qualities of the subjects that they study.

There have been important exceptions, however. In 1927, physicist Werner Heisenberg published his account of what he called the *uncertainty principle*. Heisenberg argued that there are important limits on science's ability to measure and predict the behavior of physical objects. To support his argument, Heisenberg demonstrated that *"it is impossible to measure, predict, or know both the position and momentum simultaneously of a particle, with unlimited precision in both quantities."* (For example, to measure a particle's position, one must interfere with its momentum.) Heisenberg's point stunned many physical scientists:

> [Many physicists believed] that if the positions and velocities of all the bits of matter in the universe were known at one time, and if all the various force laws were known, the positions and velocities of all these bits of matter could be calculated and predicted for any future time. All future effects would be the result of earlier causes. Even if the task of measuring all these positions and velocities were humanly impossible, and even if the discovery of all appropriate laws were impossible, nevertheless the positions and velocities did exist at a previous time and the laws do exist; therefore the future is predetermined.
>
> But Heisenberg's uncertainty principle says this is not so. It is, in principle, impossible to make the measurements with sufficient precision or even to calculate them from the future positions and velocities because we cannot know the future positions and velocities. (Speilberg and Anderson 1987, 218–219)

This was unsettling news to many physicists who wanted to believe that if they kept working at it, they would someday (at least theoretically) be able to measure and predict everything in the cosmos.

How have scientists learned to cope with the fuzziness or indeterminacy of the physical world? Some physical scientists seem simply to ignore it. And, in point of fact, a great deal of scientific progress can be made by treating phenomena as if they are predictable. Recently, however, some scientists have become more receptive to the unpredictable or chaotic nature of the world. And, once they open their eyes,

> chaos seems to be everywhere. A rising column of cigarette smoke breaks into wild swirls. A flag snaps back and forth in the wind. A dripping faucet goes from a steady pattern to a random one. Chaos

In 1926, Albert Einstein rejected Heisenberg's uncertainty principle on the grounds that "God does not play dice with the universe." One suspects, then, that Einstein—his hair not withstanding—was not comfortable with fuzzy objects.

Five decades later, physicist Stephen Hawking, referring to black holes in space, said this: "It appears that not only does God play dice, . . . he sometimes throws the dice where they cannot be seen."

appears in the behavior of the weather, the behavior of an airplane in flight, the behavior of cars clustering on an expressway, the behavior of oil flowing in underground pipes. . . . That realization has begun to change the way business executives make decisions about insurance, the way astronomers look at the solar system, the way political theorists talk about the stresses leading to armed conflict. (Gleick 1987, 5)

Chaos theorists work forward from the principle they call *sensitive dependence on initial conditions*—that is, the idea that a very small initial difference may lead to an enormous change to the outcome. In meteorological studies (studies of the weather), this principle is sometimes called the Butterfly Effect, based on the notion that a butterfly stirring the air today in Seattle can transform storm systems next month in Singapore.

You might be wondering why I have taken us so far afield from sociology. Why discuss physics? I do have a point: We must not dismiss scientific explanations and predictions merely because they do not pan out in all instances. The inability of physicists to predict both the position and momentum of particles with absolute accuracy does not undermine physics' claim to being a science. Likewise, the fact that sociologists cannot offer predictions with absolute certainty does not make their work less scientific. As many scientists in all disciplines are now learning, one must learn to accept the existence of fuzzy objects.

Dividing Up the Task

In addition to being fuzzy, the social world is big—so big that it is impossible to look at the whole of it at once. Therefore, most sociologists specialize by taking chunks of society and making these their particular concerns. Sociologists also tend to specialize in how they approach the study of their chunks. Understanding how sociologists divide things up will help you to understand how sociologists approach their work.

There are three sorts of divisions. The first has to do with what chunk of society a sociologist chooses to study; the second and third are a bit more complex and have to do with how particular sociologists approach their research.

What Sociologists Study
   1. Topic area or subject matter

How Sociologists Study
   2. Theoretical perspectives (paradigms)
   3. Levels of analysis

Table 3.1 Popular Topic Areas within Sociology

Age	Family and sex	Religion
Art	Formal organizations	Science and technology
Collective behavior	Gender	Small groups
Culture	Health care	Social change
Demography	Law	Social movements
Deviance	Mass media	Socialization
Economy	Military	Sports
Education	Political institutions	Stratification
Environment	Race and ethnicity	Work and occupations

Topic Area or Subject Matter

There are many topic areas within sociology—indeed, some sociologist, somewhere, probably is studying every social thing that exists. Table 3.1 lists some of the more popular subjects that are of interest to sociologists. Some sociologists focus their attention on only one area; others may divide their attention between two, three, or more areas. For example, my own major area of research is law, but I also study the family and work.

Theoretical Perspectives (Paradigms): Functionalist, Conflict, and Symbolic Interactionist

A more abstract way to divide up the discipline or field of sociology is in terms of theoretical perspectives, or paradigms (pronounced "PAIR-a-dimes"). A paradigm is akin to a framework or model of the world.

There are three major theoretical perspectives, or paradigms: functionalist, conflict, and symbolic interactionist. The differences between these perspectives mostly have to do with the sets of assumptions about the nature of the social world on which each paradigm is based.

THE FUNCTIONALIST PARADIGM

Sociologists who work from a functionalist paradigm tend to share three major assumptions about the nature of the social world:

1. Within a particular society, there is a great deal of consensus about what values and norms are important. In a particular

society, for example, there may be consensus that working hard is important, that murder is bad, that obtaining a lot of wealth is good, and so on. Regardless of the nature of the values and norms, functional perspectives assume that there is a general consensus about them in society.

2. Society is an entity or whole that is made up of many integrated parts. Because all the parts are integrated, or tied together, when one part of society changes, other parts will change in response. For example, if the economic system changes, then the education and family systems will change as well.

3. Society tends to seek stability and avoid conflict. Conflict is not normal, but is dysfunctional or pathological.

THE CONFLICT PARADIGM

Theories that emerge from the conflict paradigm tend to be based on assumptions that seem opposite to theories that grow out of the functionalist paradigm:

1. Within any particular society, there are subgroups of people who cherish different beliefs and have conflicting values and goals.

2. Society is made up of subgroups that are in ruthless competition for scarce resources.

3. Society is never harmonious; conflict is normal in a society.

THE SYMBOLIC INTERACTIONIST PARADIGM

Symbolic interactionists are sometimes called *social construction-ists* because of their interest in how people construct their own social worlds. The kinds of questions that symbolic interactionists ask have to do with such issues as how people use symbols to make sense of their environments. Most symbolic interactionists share four basic assumptions about the nature of the social world:

1. How people act depends on how they see and evaluate reality.

2. People learn from others how to see and evaluate reality.

3. People constantly work to interpret their own behavior and the behavior of others to determine what these behaviors "mean."

4. When people do not attach the same meanings to behaviors or perceive reality in the same way, there will be misunder-standing and conflict.

Which Paradigm Is Correct?

Many students are confused especially by the differences between the conflict and functionalist paradigms. They seem so opposite to one another—how can both be valid? That's a good question. A few sociologists would answer by stating that one of the two perspectives is wrong. But others (including me) would say that both are right—that there is both consensus and dissent in society, and that both consensus and conflict need to be studied. In my experience, the paradigm adopted depends on which of these aspects of society one judges to be the more interesting and important.

As you might guess, sociologists tend to ask different kinds of questions about their subject matter depending on the paradigm or perspective they hold. Those who have adopted the functionalist or consensus perspective tend to focus on what holds society together and on how changes in one part of society lead to changes in other parts. Those who have adopted the conflict perspective tend to focus on the kinds of things that create tension and conflict between people and groups and on the ways people from one group may exploit people from another group. Those who adopt the symbolic interactionist paradigm tend to look at how ideas emerge from social interaction and then affect that interaction.

Let me offer an example from two of my favorite subject areas: law and family. Here are some questions that sociologists working from the different paradigms might ask:

Functionalists

Law: As societies move from agricultural to industrial-based economies, how does this affect the functioning of their legal systems? How does the legal system function to help the economic

"But your honor—I'm so broke I don't even have a paradigm."

system run smoothly? How does law function to help build consensus and preserve order in society?

Family: What are the ways in which families contribute to the stability of society? How have changes in the law (e.g., divorce law) affected family?

Conflict Theorists

Law: How do people with power use the law to maintain their power? For example, how do rich people use property laws to keep poor people from making financial gains? How do powerful people use the law to force less powerful people to share the values of the rich (even when those values might have negative consequences for poor people)?

Family: How has the social organization of the family contributed to perpetuating sex discrimination in society?

Symbolic Interactionists

Law: How do the rules of evidence affect the way people can tell their stories in court? How do attorneys learn to plea bargain how much prison time a particular defendant should get? How are these bargains negotiated between defense attorneys and prosecutors?

Family: What behaviors are expected of different family members, and how are these negotiated between adults and children in the family? Given the changing roles of women and men in society, how do newlyweds negotiate their roles as wives and husbands?

Sociologists can become very attached—sometimes *too* attached—to one of these theoretical perspectives. Becoming too attached means forgetting that there is value in each of the three paradigms. Truth be told, understanding any complex phenomenon may require the sociologist to make use of the insights offered by all three paradigms. It is probably impossible, for example, to have a society in which there is no consensus or no dissent. Furthermore, in all societies, people have to work to communicate and negotiate the meaning of things. Therefore, because each paradigm offers a different window on the social world, each paradigm enhances our understanding.

3.1 In your own words, summarize the three major theoretical perspectives/paradigms used in sociology.

Levels of Analysis: Microsociology and Macrosociology

The third and most abstract way that sociologists divide up their discipline is to distinguish between different *levels* of analysis. Roughly speaking, depending on the level of analysis used, a sociologist might be doing *microsociology* or *macrosociology*. Micro-sociologists generally focus on the interactions of individuals and the context of those interactions. Macrosociologists, on the other hand, focus on broader social phenomena, such as whole social structures, systems, and institutions.

A sociologist who studies the family from a microsociological perspective might ask questions about the relationships between family members. For example, what kind of *division of labor* exists in the average American family? In other words, who does the dishes? Who makes the financial decisions? Who has primary responsibility for child care?

A sociologist who studies the family from a macrosociological perspective might look at the impact of economic change on divorce and birth rates in a particular society. Are advances in technology, for example, related to lower birth rates? Do changes in the occupational structure of a society have an impact on the divorce rate?

Although most sociologists tend to do either macrosociological or microsociological research (rather than combine the two), nearly everyone realizes that both kinds of work are important. If we want to gain an understanding of the family, or crime, or religion, or whatever, it is important to study the phenomenon from *both* perspectives.

3.2 In your own words, explain the difference between microsociology and macrosociology.

Chapter Review

1. Below I have listed the major concepts discussed in this chapter. Define each of the terms. *(Hint:* This exercise will be more helpful to you if, in addition to defining each concept, you create an example of it in your own words.)

Ludwig Wittgenstein on fuzzy objects
fuzzy objects in the physical sciences
   Werner Heisenberg, uncertainty principle
   Albert Einstein
   Stephen Hawking
   chaos theory
topic areas in sociology
paradigms in sociology
   functional
   conflict
   symbolic interaction
microsociology
macrosociology

2. Assume you were interested in gaining an understanding of the relationship between teachers and students in your college or university. What two or three questions would you ask if you were guided by a functionalist perspective? If you were guided by a conflict perspective? How about the symbolic interactionist perspective?

3. Look back over the questions you constructed in response to question 2. Do these tend to be the kinds of questions that a microsociologist would ask or a macrosociologist? Explain how you reached your conclusion.

STOP
&
REVIEW

Answers and Discussion

3.1

a. *Functionalist* (also known as the consensus perspective): Sociologists who operate from this perspective assume that there is a lot of consensus about values, goals, and so on in society. They focus on the kinds of things that help to maintain this consensus. For example, if a functionalist were interested in understanding the role of schools in society, he or she might examine the ways in which our schools help out the larger society (such as teaching the values and skills that adults believe children need in order to succeed). Functionalists see conflict as pathological; if it exists, then, something is wrong with the society.

b. *Conflict:* These sociologists assume that many groups with different values compete in society. Conflict is thus a normal part of social interaction. Conflict theorists focus on the nature of this conflict and the way it works. For example, how do men maintain their superior place in the labor market over women? In what ways do social institutions—like the criminal justice system—serve the needs of the powerful over the powerless?

c. *Symbolic interactionist:* These sociologists assume that people construct their own worlds and ask how this process takes place. How do people come to agree on what symbols mean? Symbolic interactionists assume that the process is one of negotiation. How does this work?

3.2 Microsociologists always include individuals somewhere in their focus; macrosociologists don't. For example, many sociologists study work. A microsociologist would be interested in how individuals select and learn their jobs, how they get along with their bosses, and how men and women relate in the workplace. A macrosociologist, on the other hand, would rather look at how, for example, changes in the political system affect the labor market or how technological changes affect the unemployment rate.

4

WHO'S AFRAID OF SOCIOLOGY?

Challenges to Skepticism

"All of us cherish our beliefs. They are, to a degree, self-defining. When someone comes along who challenges our belief system as insufficiently well-based—or who, like Socrates, merely asks embarrassing questions that we haven't thought of, or demonstrates that we've swept key underlying assumptions under the rug—it becomes much more than a search for knowledge. It feels like a personal assault."

—Carl Sagan (1996)

Once, on about the third day of the semester, a student in my introductory sociology class walked up to me and said, "Sociology is the work of the devil." Then he left.

I never saw that student again. But had he given me the chance, I would have told him that I disagreed with his assessment. In fact, I am sure that the devil hates sociology more than most things.

It is true that sociology emerged at a time in history when many individuals (including some sociologists) were questioning the authority of religious leaders. It is likewise true that a few of those early sociologists even thought that sociology might someday replace religion. But there is nothing inherently anti-religious about sociology. Of course, the skepticism and questioning attitude of sociologists do threaten some people in authority. (Whether that is a bad thing is for you to judge. In any case, as I will discuss shortly, whether something is good or bad is *not* a proper sociological question.)

As much as sociology may threaten religious leaders, it is not really a threat to the social institution of religion—and certainly it is no threat to God (just imagine!). Sociologists are concerned with issues of *observable facts*. In other words, sociologists (like other scientists) tend to be preoccupied with the *empirical* world.

The Empirical World and Inconvenient Facts

This concept of empirical is an important one in science. *Empirical* refers to things that can be observed through the use of one's physical senses—sight, hearing, touch, taste, and smell. If a thing cannot be seen, heard, touched, tasted, or smelled—or, more specifically, if it is not *observable*—it is of little interest to sociologists.

For example, a sociologist doing research might well ask, "Do people in a particular society believe in God?" or, "What impact do religious beliefs have on a person's behavior?" or, "What are the manifest and latent functions of religion in society?" But no working sociologist would ask, "Is there a God?" or, "Is God more fond of Buddhists, Christians, Jews, or Muslims?" or, "Is religion X more correct in its beliefs and practices than religion Y?" These are *not* sociological questions.

Admittedly, anyone who preaches unquestioned obedience to authority will be troubled by sociology. This is well evidenced by the fact that in the twentieth century, whenever a dictator came into power, one of his first acts was to reassign or fire all the sociologists—anything to keep them from making trouble by asking questions. Obviously, you cannot have a successful dictatorship as long as people are questioning authority and being skeptical about its claims. Sociology can flourish only in a free society.

I remember that *my* first sociology course was quite an awakening. Like my classmates, I frequently was appalled to learn some of the stuff that sociologists have uncovered about society. Still, that was in 1972, and in those days we were just learning not to be shocked when we found out that there is a dysfunctional underside to society.

As a sociology professor, I have observed that some students become uncomfortable when they encounter the results of sociological research. I guess that even now it can be shocking to discover that many of the things you always accepted as true are, in fact, false.

Max Weber had a term for those pieces of evidence that contradict what you have always believed and/or want to believe about the social world; he called them *inconvenient facts*. As far as Weber was concerned, it was the sociologist's duty to deal with inconvenient facts. Indeed, Weber argued that one of the best things a sociology teacher could do

> is to teach his students to recognize inconvenient facts—I mean facts that are inconvenient for their party [that is, political] opinions. And for every party opinion there are facts that are extremely inconvenient, for my own opinion no less than for others. I believe the teacher accomplishes more than a mere intellectual task if he compels his audience to accustom itself to the existence of such facts. (Weber 1918/1958, 147)

Here are some empirical facts that have upset some beginning sociology students; in the Weberian sense, these are examples of inconvenient facts. Keep in mind that each of these facts about life in the United States has been validated by a great deal of research.

> Even when they do the exact same jobs and have the exact same educational background, men tend to earn more money than women, and whites tend to earn more than African Americans. (See, for example, chapter 14 of this book.)
>
> The majority of adults who sexually abuse children are heterosexual. (See Greenberg 1988; Sullivan 1995.)
>
> Whether students get into college has more to do with their parents' socioeconomic standing than with their own intelligence or high school grades. (See chapters 12 and 13 of this book.)
>
> Friendships between people of different races are as stable as friendships between people of the same race. (See Hallinan and Williams 1987.)

When they hear such things in lectures or read them in articles or books assigned in sociology classes, some students react as if the professor (me) is trying to pull a fast one: How can it be true that there is still salary discrimination based on gender and race? How can it be true that most child molesters are heterosexual? How can it be that money and status will get you into college over brains and knowledge? How can such things happen in a society that promotes equality, or in which the supposed corrupting influence of homosexuals is so feared, or in which people are supposed to succeed on their own merit?

Our society, like all societies, aspires to many things. But, as with all societies, there can be discrepancies between the ideal world and the real world. It may be disturbing to learn of these discrepancies, but hiding from them will not make the world a better place.

It is important to remember that the goal of sociology is not to undermine society or people's beliefs. Still, I can assure you of one thing: Any belief that can't stand up to objective scrutiny is hardly worth having. Sociologists cultivate the skill of examining beliefs about the nature of the social world and seeing which ones stand up to the evidence.

4.1 What did Weber mean by the term *inconvenient fact*?

Ethnocentrism

The most difficult thing about doing sociology is examining people whose customs and traditions differ from our own. Each of us likes to believe that his or her own people's customs and traditions are best. And when we encounter people whose ways of life are different, our tendency is to make a value judgment. More specifically, we generally do not see difference as merely difference, but as an indication of inferiority.

The human tendency to judge others as inferior is very much evident in the written records of those who were the first to explore other countries and to encounter "foreigners." When Europeans first met Africans, for example, they found African customs so different from European ones that they doubted that the Africans were even human. It seems likely that the Africans' first responses to the Europeans were similar.

To the ancient Greeks, the language of foreigners sounded like nonsensical stammering, like "bar-bar-bar." Because of this, the ancient Greeks came to call all foreigners "barbarians." Similarly, the Aztec peoples called their own language *nahuatl*, meaning "pleasant sounding," but called other people's languages *nonotl*, meaning "stammering." Modern languages reflect a similarly near-universal disdain for foreign peoples:

> In Japanese, the word for foreigner means "stinking of foreign hair."[1] To the Czechs a Hungarian is "a pimple." Germans call cockroaches "Frenchmen," while the French call lice "Spaniards." We in the English-speaking world take French leave, but Italians and Norwegians talk about departing like an Englishman, and Germans talk of running like a Dutchman. Italians call syphilis "the French disease," while both French and Italians call con games "American swindle." Belgian taxi drivers call a poor tipper "un Anglais." (Bryson 1990, 17)

This process of judging other peoples and their customs and norms as inferior to one's own people, customs, and norms is

"[Ethnocentrism is the view] of things in which one's own group is the center of everything and all others are scaled and rated with references to it. . . . Each group nourishes its own pride and vanity, boasts itself superior, exalts its own divinities, and looks with contempt on outsiders."

—William G. Sumner (1906)

---

[1]A close reader of the first edition of this book told me that the Japanese word for foreigner is *gaikokujin*, or more frequently *gaijin*, "which translates to 'foreigner' or 'outsider.'" But, according to my reader, either word is "pejorative, and no one would use it in public except children who haven't been socialized not to repeat in public what their parents say in the home." I confess that my knowledge of Japanese is very limited; but I did quiz more than a dozen of my students who are from Japan. When I asked, "What word do the Japanese people use to refer to people from other countries?" each one told me *gaijin*. I am still investigating this matter!

Table 4.1 Ethnocentric Attitudes—toward One's Own Group and toward Outsiders

Toward Own Group	Toward Outsiders
See members as virtuous and superior	See outsiders as contemptible, immoral, and inferior
See own values as universal and intrinsically true	See outsiders' values as false (where they differ from own group's values)
See own customs as original and centrally human, as reflecting true "human nature"	See outsiders' customs as suspicious, ignorant, and lacking in humanity

For an excellent introduction to the issue of ethnocentrism, see Levine and Campbell 1972.

called *ethnocentrism*. Table 4.1 lists common ethnocentric attitudes toward one's own group and toward outsiders.

The positive side of ethnocentrism is that it brings together people and builds solidarity within a particular society. It is similar to believing that your team is the best team. Much as believing that one's team is the best helps to unite students and boost school spirit, believing that one's culture is the best helps to unite people in society. To use Durkheim's phrasing, ethnocentrism promotes social solidarity.

The negative (or dysfunctional) side of ethnocentrism is that it can lead to nasty consequences: prejudice, discrimination, even genocide or "ethnic cleansing."[2] For example, in 1619, a group of religious dissidents in England sought a place where they could have religious freedom. These Pilgrims chose North America. Why? Because no "people" lived there! Here's how one of their leaders, William Bradford, explained the Pilgrims' rationale:

> The place [the Pilgrims] had their thoughts on was some of those vast and unpeopled countries of America, which are fruitful and fit for habitation, being devoid of all civil inhabitants, where there are only savage and brutish men which range up and down, little otherwise than the wild beasts of the same. (Quoted in Holmes 1891, 36)

Because the native inhabitants of North America had different customs and lifestyles, they were seen by these English as less than human and more like "wild beasts." This sort of reasoning allowed many European settlers (and their descendants) to believe that they were as justified in killing Native Americans as they were in killing any dangerous animal.

---

[2]The term *genocide* was introduced by Raphael Lemkin. In 1944, in his study of the Axis (German–Italian) rule of occupied Europe during World War II, Lemkin proposed the term to denote the destruction of a nation or an ethnic group. He coined the word by joining the ancient Greek word *genos* ("race, tribe") with the Latin term *cide* ("killing").

In my own experience, many people who live in the United States are ethnocentric about being ethnocentric! What I mean is that people in our society seem to think that we are the only ones who are ethnocentric—implying, perhaps, that we are the only ones who have any right to feel superior.

It comes as a shock to many North Americans to find, for example, that we smell bad to many Asians (it's because of all the dairy products we consume). Likewise, when the Thonga people of Africa first saw visiting Europeans kissing, they reacted with horror and disgust: What sort of people would engage in "eating each other's saliva and dirt" (Hyde 1979, 18)?

On his Web site "EduPASS," Mark Kantrowitz cautions international students coming to the United States: "Don't believe all of the stereotypes you may have heard about Americans. Even the ones that are true in general may not be true about specific individuals or a large segment of the population." He says, "rid yourself of any preconceived notions of American behavior before you arrive."

Kantrowitz helpfully lists the "common stereotypes of American citizens"; these include, "boastful and arrogant, disrespectful of authority, drunkard, extravagant and wasteful, generous, insensitive, lazy, loud and obnoxious, promiscuous, racist, rich and wealthy, rude and immature, snobbish," and more.

What do you think are the origins of these stereotypes?

For sociologists, ethnocentrism is especially dangerous because it gets in the way of understanding. If we really want to understand why people in society X act the way they do, how their institutions work, and what their customs are, we have to see them in the context of *their* society. Ethnocentrism hinders such understanding because it means we are viewing society X in terms of our own society.

Avoiding Ethnocentrism Can Be Difficult

Even when we tell ourselves sternly that we must be objective, that we must examine the people of other cultures in terms of their cultures, it is difficult. Anthropologist Napoleon Chagnon gives a startling example of how difficult it can be to avoid being ethnocentric. Chagnon studied the Yanomamö Indians of South America by living among them for more than a year. Here's part of what he wrote about his first day in the field. Imagine yourself in his shoes: Could you have remained "objective"?

> My first day in the field illustrated to me what my teachers meant when they spoke of "culture shock.". . .

We arrived at the village, Biaasi-teri, about 2:00 P.M. and docked the boat along the muddy bank at the terminus of the path used by the Indians to fetch their drinking water. It was hot and muggy, and my clothing was soaked with perspiration. . . .

I looked up and gasped when I saw a dozen burly, naked, filthy, hideous men staring at us down the shafts of their drawn arrows! Immense wads of green tobacco were stuck between their lower teeth and lips making them look even more hideous, and strands of dark-green slime dripped or hung from their noses. We arrived at the village while the men were blowing a hallucinogenic drug up their noses. One of the side effects of the drug is a runny nose. The mucus is always saturated with green powder and the Indians usually let it run freely from their nostrils. My next discovery was that there were a dozen or so vicious, underfed dogs snapping at my legs, circling me as if I were going to be their next meal. I just stood there holding my notebook, helpless and pathetic. Then the stench of the decaying vegetation and filth struck me and I almost got sick. I was horrified. . . .

The whole situation was depressing, and I wondered why I ever decided to switch from civil engineering to anthropology in the first place. I had not eaten all day, I was soaking wet from perspiration, the gnats were biting me, and I was covered with red pigment, the result of a dozen or so complete examinations I had been given by as many burly Indians. These examinations capped an otherwise grim day. The Indians would blow their noses into their hands, flick as much of the mucus off that would separate in a snap of the wrist, wipe the residue into their hair, and then carefully examine my face, arms, legs, hair, and the contents of my pockets. I asked Mr. Barker [a local missionary and Chagnon's temporary guide] how to say "Your hands are dirty"; my comments were met by the Indians in the following way: They would "clean" their hands by spitting a quantity of slimy tobacco juice into them, rub them together, and then proceed with the examination. (Chagnon 1977, 4–7)

Our initial reaction to the Yanomamö likely would be one of horror and disgust—just as it was Chagnon's reaction. In time, however, if we tried to keep an open mind, we too could become accustomed to the Yanomamö ways—once we saw these in the context of their entire living situation.

Mr. Barker and I crossed the river and slung our hammocks. When he pulled his hammock out of a rubber bag, a heavy, disagreeable odor of mildewed cotton came with it. "Even the missionaries are filthy," I thought to myself. Within two weeks everything I owned smelled the same way, and I lived with the odor for the remainder of the field work. My own habits of personal cleanliness reached such levels that I didn't even mind being examined by the Indians, as I was not much cleaner than they were after I had adjusted to the circumstances. . . .

Encounters with different cultures challenge one's taken-for-granted assumptions about the way things are and ought to be. Social scientists refer to the resulting feeling of disorientation as culture shock.

"Culture shock refers to the whole set of feelings about being in an alien setting, and the resulting reactions. It is a chilly, creepy feeling of alienation, of being without some of the most ordinary, trivial—and therefore basic—cues of one's culture of origin."

—Conrad P. Kottak (1992)

I discovered that it was an enormously time-consuming task to maintain my own body in the manner to which it had grown accustomed in the relatively antiseptic environment of the northern United States. Either I could be relatively well fed and relatively comfortable in a fresh change of clothes and do very little fieldwork, or, I could do considerably more fieldwork and be less well fed and less comfortable. (Chagnon 1977, 4–7)

It could certainly be argued that Chagnon's experiences were extreme, that most social scientists do not venture into such exotic locales. But one does not have to go very far to experience the shock of cultural differences. Probably, even in your own city or town, there are groups of people who live their lives very differently than you do. Quite possibly, you experienced a bit of culture shock when you first arrived at college!

When encountering cultural strangers, a person's first reaction is likely to be the same as Chagnon's when he met the Yanomamö. Ethnocentrism is normal. However, because it gets in the way of understanding, social scientists work to overcome it.

4.2 What does it mean to be ethnocentric? What's an example of ethnocentrism?

4.3 What is culture shock? What's an example of culture shock?

Cultural Relativism

Ethnocentrism can lead to shocking cases of ignorance. During a debate over the merits of bilingual education, for example, one congressman quite seriously said to Dr. David Edwards (head of the Joint National Committee on Languages):

"If English was good enough for Jesus Christ, it's good enough for me."

—Quoted by Bill Bryson (1990)

Sociologists work to overcome their ethnocentrism by practicing something called *cultural relativism.* Cultural relativism is *the belief that other people and their ways of doing things can be understood only in terms of the cultural context of those people.* This is based on the assumption that if our goal is to truly understand people's behavior, we have to look for clues in *their* culture.

Some people have misunderstood this notion of cultural relativity. They suspect that it implies that any one way of doing things is as good as any other way. As far as sociologists are concerned, however, cultural relativity has nothing to do with assessing which ways of doing things are better or worse. Remember, "Which way is better or worse?" is *not* a legitimate sociological question.

For sociologists, cultural relativity means being objective enough to understand people's behaviors in terms of their culture and social situation. Sociology does not agree or disagree with, or approve or disapprove of, behavior; sociology seeks to understand and explain behavior. And understanding and explaining is difficult to do unless one is willing to look at things in their own context.

Chapter Review

1. Below I have listed the major concepts discussed in this chapter. Define each of the terms. (*Hint:* This exercise will be more helpful to you if, in addition to defining each concept, you create an example of it in your own words.)

   empirical
   Max Weber (inconvenient facts)
   ethnocentrism
   culture shock
   genocide
   Napoleon Chagnon, experiences with the Yanomamö
   cultural relativity

2. What is cultural relativism? Why is it considered crucial for sociologists?

Answers and Discussion

STOP
&
REVIEW

4.1 Weber used the term *inconvenient facts* to refer to facts or data that go against one's social and political beliefs. For example, suppose you are very much in favor of imposing the death penalty on convicted murderers. If that were the case, the following facts might be inconvenient for you:

    a. There is no evidence that the threat of the death penalty has any appreciable effect on a country's murder rate.

    b. In the United States, it costs more to put a person to death than to keep him or her in prison for life.

By the way, it is amazingly difficult to think of examples of inconvenient facts. That is not because they aren't there, but because it is easier to try to ignore them.

4.2 Your definition of ethnocentrism should include the ideas that it occurs in situations where we judge other people's customs and behaviors against the standards of our own culture. Asking a kilted Scotsman why he is dressed like a woman is ethnocentric.

4.3 Culture shock is that feeling of disorientation and even squeamishness that one feels when plunked down into a different culture. Chagnon felt this as he stood there and let the Yanomamö examine him.

5

THE VOCABULARY OF SCIENCE

"To speak of a science without concepts suggests all sorts of analogies— a carpenter without tools, a railroad without tracks, a mammal without bones, a love story without love."

—H. Blumer (1931)

During the past century, science has revolutionized the way we live and die. Yet scientists follow a relatively simple method. First, we specify some concepts of interest to us. Second, we posit, or suggest, some relationship between those concepts. Third, we test whether the posited relationship reflects what happens in the real world. If our testing shows that our posited relationship does reflect what goes on in the real world, we conclude that we have succeeded in understanding something about the nature of things in the world.

Simple, right? Well, you might well ask: If science is so simple, why is it that scientific reports seem so complex and that reading and untangling them is so daunting? The answer is that the simplicity of the scientific method becomes clear only when one has conquered the basic vocabulary used by scientists.

The good news is that science uses a language that crosses many academic disciplines. Therefore, learning this language not only is crucial for your sociology course work, but will help you in other sorts of classes as well.

Concepts and Constructs

Look outside your window—what do you see? There are things out there. But you do not perceive them as "things," you see cars,

Figure 5.1
*Elementary Exercises
In Conceptualization*

Circle the thing in
each box that does
not belong

apartment buildings, trees, street lamps, and so forth. The terms with which we organize these things are *concepts*. More technically, *a concept is a label that is applied to things with similar characteristics or attributes;* things that—in our minds—seem to belong to the same category.

Whether or not you have used the term *concept*, you've been taught to think conceptually beginning in primary school. You may, for example, recognize figure 5.1 from your first-grade language skills workbook. When your teacher asked you to mark the thing that does not belong, he or she was asking you to delineate a concept.

Some of the things we think about are not easily pictured because they are not material or tangible in substance: love, intelligence, speed, racism. These are all real in the sense that they exist and have tangible (empirical) effects on life (that is, they can make a difference in what happens to people), even though none of them can be directly observed. The words used to describe things that exist analytically but are not directly observable are called *constructs*—because to observe them we must rely on some constructed measure. To observe and measure racism, for example, we would need to construct a list of observable behaviors that would allow us to measure whether racism exists. Our list might include such behaviors as telling ethnic jokes, refusing to associate with people of different racial backgrounds, discriminating against certain categories of people, and so forth.

Variables

The first step in doing scientific research involves picking the concepts or constructs of interest to us. We call these concepts *variables*. When sociologists speak or write about their research, they tend to use the term *variable* a lot. To call a concept or a construct a variable means, in the first place, that it is a thing of interest in a particular piece of research.

Variables are special because they have two important characteristics. First, a variable is something that is thought to influence or be influenced by another thing. For example, suppose I were to assert that "income is thought to influence voting behavior." That assertion makes reference to two variables: income and voting behavior. The first, income, is a variable because it is thought to influence voting behavior. The second, voting behavior, is a variable because it is thought to be influenced by income.

Here are a few more examples. In each case I have italicized the variables.

Gender is thought to influence *occupation*.

Religious affiliation is thought to be influenced by *income*.

Educational attainment is thought to influence *income*.

Age is thought to influence *attitudes toward using computers*.

Income is thought to be influenced by *race*.

The second important characteristic of a variable has to do with the idea of variation or difference: A variable is a thing that has varying *attributes* (an attribute is a characteristic or a quality that describes a thing).

For example, the attributes of the variable gender vary from, or include, female and male. The attributes of religious affiliation vary from, or include, Catholic, Jewish, Protestant, other, and no religion. The attributes of the variable educational attainment vary from zero years of schooling to twelve or more years of schooling (with a number of steps in between those two extremes). The attributes of the variable income vary from zero dollars earned a year to $1 million or more earned a year, again with a number of steps in between.

Depending on the circumstances, the attributes of a particular variable will be defined in different ways. Table 5.1 illustrates two ways of listing the attributes of the variable religious affiliation.

How you define your list of attributes depends on the nature of the group you are studying. If the group is known or expected

Table 5.1 Attributes of Religious Affiliation

List 1		List 2
Baha'i	Protestant	Catholic
Buddhist	Roman Catholic	Jewish
Confucian	Rosicrucian	Protestant
Eastern Orthodox	Shinto	Other
Hindu	Tao	None
Islamic	Other	
Jewish	None	

to be very diverse, then something like list 1 is appropriate. If the group is known not to be very diverse (that is, if it is made up of people from only a few religions), then list 2 is more appropriate, as long as it includes the names of the religions to which most of the people you are studying are likely to be affiliated.

You will see right away that list 1 is quite a bit longer than list 2. But there is one crucial thing that is common to both lists: Each is totally inclusive—every person in the world has one of these attributes.

5.1

a. Identify the variables in each assertion.

Example
Marital status *is thought to influence a person's happiness.*

i. Number of beers consumed per week is thought to influence a student's GPA.
ii. Frequency of tooth brushing is thought to influence the number of cavities gotten each year.

b. Now go back and list the attributes of each variable.

Examples
Marital status: *never married, married, separated, divorced, widowed, other*
Happiness: *extremely happy, somewhat happy, somewhat unhappy, extremely unhappy*

c. "Thought question": One way sociologists define the term *variable* is as "a logical grouping of attributes." Explain what this definition means.

Hypotheses

Ultimately, scientists are interested in the relationships among different variables. So, after we identify the variables of interest to us, we posit a relationship between them. The result is called a *hypothesis.* Here are some simple hypotheses:

H_1: Gender affects occupation.
H_2: Age affects income.
H_3: Social class affects voting behavior.
H_4: Religious affiliation affects attitudes toward abortion.
H_5: Occupation affects income.

When we create a hypothesis, we are not asserting that it reflects something true. Hypotheses can be either true or false. We create them to test whether the posited relationships between the variables are true or false.

Each of the five hypotheses just given follows the same basic form: Variable X influences variable Y. This format is really a form of shorthand. The more precise way of stating the hypothesis is this: *Different attributes of variable X are related to different attributes of variable Y.*

Let's reexamine the first three of our five hypotheses for their more precise meaning.

Shorthand Version

H_1: Gender affects occupation.

Longhand Version

H_1: Differences in gender are related to differences in occupation. [That is, men and women tend to be employed in different occupations.]

Shorthand Version

H_2: Age affects income.

Longhand Version

H_2: Differences in age are related to differences in income. [That is, people in different age groups tend to receive different amounts of income.]

Shorthand Version

H_3: Social class affects voting behavior.

Longhand Version

H_3: Differences in social class are related to differences in voting behavior. [That is, people from higher social classes tend to vote differently than people from lower social classes.]

STOP
&
REVIEW

5.2 Now *you* translate the fourth and fifth hypotheses into their longer versions on a separate piece of paper.

Shorthand Version
H_4: *Religious affiliation affects attitudes toward abortion.*

Longhand Version
H_4: *Differences in _____ are related to _____.*
[That is, _____.]

Shorthand Version
H_5: *Occupation affects income.*

Longhand Version
H_5: *Differences in _____ are related to _____.*
[That is, _____.]

In the examples I have used thus far, it has been fairly easy to identify the variables. Sometimes, however, you might have to ponder a particular hypothesis for a while before you can identify the variables.

Here I have listed four sets of hypotheses. You should be able to confirm that the variables are the same for each hypothesis in a particular set. (Do not assume that the hypotheses in a particular set mean the same thing, however.)

Set A

H_{6A}: Gender influences occupation.
H_{6B}: Men and women tend to have different occupations.

Set B

H_{7A}: Age affects income.
H_{7B}: The very young and the very old tend to have less income than middle-aged workers.
H_{7C}: Younger workers are more likely to earn a minimum wage than older workers.

Set C

H_{8A}: Social class affects voting behavior.
H_{8B}: The higher one's social class standing, the more likely one is to vote Republican in national elections.
H_{8C}: The lower one's social class standing, the more likely one is to vote Democrat in national elections.

Set D

H_{9A}: Religion influences attitudes toward abortion.
H_{9B}: Catholics are more likely to oppose abortion than Protestants are.

5.3 Read the following hypotheses and identify the variables.

H_{10}: Poor people tend to commit street crimes, whereas rich people tend to commit white-collar crimes.
H_{11}: Catholics are more likely to oppose the death penalty than are Protestants and Jews.
H_{12}: Married people are more likely to own pets than single people are.
H_{13}: The hotter the weather, the more ice cream people will buy.
H_{14}: Students who earn good grades tend to study more than do students who earn poor grades.

Kinds of Variables: Independent Versus Dependent

Remember the first defining characteristic of a variable? (It's a thing that is thought to influence or be influenced by another thing.) The distinction between *influence* and *influenced by* is a clue that there are two kinds of variables: There are variables that influence other things and variables that are influenced by other things.

When a variable influences another thing, it is called a *cause*; when a variable is influenced by another thing, it is called an *effect*. So,

Variables that influence or affect other things = causes

Variables that are influenced or affected by other things = effects

With this new knowledge about variables as causes and as effects, let's look back at our original five hypotheses. Each hypothesis posits or suggests a cause-effect relationship.

H_1: Gender affects occupation.
H_2: Age affects income.
H_3: Social class affects voting behavior.
H_4: Religious affiliation affects attitudes toward abortion.
H_5: Occupation affects income.

Hypothesis 1, for example, posited that being a man or a woman causes individuals to choose different occupations. To make these cause-effect relationships more obvious, we could rephrase our hypotheses this way:

H_1: Gender differences (cause) occupational differences (effect).
H_2: Age differences (cause) income differences (effect).
H_3: Social class differences (cause) voting behavior differences (effect).
H_4: Differences in religious affiliation (cause) differences in attitudes toward abortion (effect).
H_5: Occupational differences (cause) income differences (effect).

As you might suspect, there are special names for these two types of variables. A variable that is believed to influence another variable (that is, to be a cause) is called an *independent variable.* A variable that is thought to be influenced by the independent variable (that is, to be an effect) is called a *dependent variable.* Therefore,

Independent variable/cause	affects	dependent variable/effect
H_1: gender	→	occupation
H_2: age	→	income
H_3: social class	→	voting behavior differences
H_5: occupation	→	income

This distinction between independent and dependent variables is really an important one. If you confuse them, you will make a big mess out of your analysis of the social world.

How can you remember that the independent variable is the cause and the dependent variable is the effect? One way is to recall that the effect depends on the cause just as *the dependent variable depends on the independent variable*. Another way to remember the difference is to think of the word *INCA: The INdependent variable is the CAuse*.

It might help to remember that the cause of something always happens before the effect. So, if one variable obviously comes before another variable, it will be the cause (INCA = independent variable). (Be careful, however; not all variables that come before another variable are causes of the variable. For example, one generally attends kindergarten before attending college, but we would not say that attending kindergarten is the cause of attending college!)

5.4 Identify the *independent variable* (the cause) in each of the following hypotheses:

H_{15}: Education affects income.

H_{16}: Income affects vacation choices.

H_{17}: Marital status affects vacation choices.

H_{18}: Mental health is affected by marital status.

H_{19}: Regularity of church attendance is influenced by marital status.

H_{20}: People with more education tend to have higher-paying jobs.

H_{21}: People with higher-paying jobs tend to own more computers.

H_{22}: People with light skin tones tend to sunburn more easily.

STOP & REVIEW

Kinds of Relationships: Directionality

Often you will discover that the relationships between two variables may be one of two types: positive or negative. The difference is fairly simple: *Variables that vary in the same direction have a positive relationship; variables that vary in the opposite direction have a negative relationship.*

How does this work? Consider the following hypothesis, which posits a *positive* relationship between eating and weight:

H_{23}: Increased eating causes increased weight.

The relationship between eating and weight is a positive one because these two variables vary in the same direction. That is, the *more* you eat, the *more* you weigh; and the *less* you eat, the *less* you weigh.

Now consider this hypothesis, which posits a *negative* relationship between exercise and weight:

H_{24}: Increased exercise causes decreased weight.

The relationship between exercise and weight is a negative one because these two variables vary in opposite directions. That is, the *more* you exercise, the *less* you weigh; and the *less* you exercise, the *more* you weigh.

In the abstract, *positive* relationships look like this:

$\uparrow$ independent variable $\rightarrow \uparrow$ dependent variable

or this:

$\downarrow$ independent variable $\rightarrow \downarrow$ dependent variable

That is, as the independent variable goes faster, or gets bigger, or becomes more important, the dependent variable goes faster, or gets bigger, or becomes more important. Or, as the independent variable goes slower, or gets smaller, or becomes less important, the dependent variable does, too.

On the other hand, *negative* relationships look like this:

$\uparrow$ independent variable $\rightarrow \downarrow$ dependent variable

or this:

$\downarrow$ independent variable $\rightarrow \uparrow$ dependent variable

STOP & REVIEW

5.5 Identify the variables in each hypothesis, and then indicate whether the posited relationship is positive or negative:

H_{25}: The longer you live, the more money you will earn.

H_{26}: The higher your social class, the more education you are likely to have.

H_{27}: The higher your social class, the less likely you are to be arrested for committing a crime.

H_{28}: Children are more likely than adults to take naps.

H_{29}: The more frequently an individual attends services at a church, temple, synagogue, or mosque, the more likely that person is to donate money to religious causes.

H_{30}: The more education one has, the less likely one is to be prejudiced against those of different races.

H_{31}: Older people tend to be less fearful of dying than younger people.

Operational Definitions

After we select the variables of interest and formulate hypotheses, we need to arrange things so that we can test our hypotheses. Recall our very first hypothesis: Gender affects occupation. When we set up that hypothesis, we posited a relationship between gender and occupation. To put it another way, we posited that men and women are likely to have different sorts of occupations. Testing this hypothesis will mean determining whether there is indeed a relationship between gender and occupation in the real world.

Before we can test our hypothesis, however, we must create something called an *operational definition* for each of our variables. Many people call this *operationalizing* the variables. Creating an operational definition essentially involves *transforming the variables into things that can be observed and measured.*

Generally, operationalizing a variable simply means listing its attributes so that you can count the presence or absence of those attributes in the real world. For example, in operationalizing gender, we can easily identify two attributes:

Gender

> woman
> man

Operationalizing occupation is a bit trickier, but we can still do it in a fairly straightforward manner. Here is one way we might operationalize occupation:

Occupation

> professional
> manager or owner of business
> skilled laborer
> unskilled laborer
> not employed
> other

Suppose I am interested in looking at the relationship between a student's major in college and how many hours per week that student studies. My hypothesis is that students who major in the sciences study more hours per week than do students who major in the humanities or social sciences. So, I have two basic variables: major field of study and hours per week spent studying. Here's how I might operationalize the variables of interest to me:

Primary Major

> social sciences
> humanities
> physical sciences
> other
> not yet declared

Hours Studied per Week

> none
> fewer than 5 hours per week
> 5–15 hours per week
> 16–25 hours per week
> more than 25 hours per week

There are two rules to keep in mind when operationalizing variables. First, the list of attributes must be *exhaustive;* that is, every thing or person being observed must fit into one category. Second, the list of attributes must be *mutually exclusive;* that is, no one person or thing should be able to fit into more than a single category.

Suppose we wanted to operationalize the variable type of car. Consider the following list of attributes:

two-door
four-door
station wagon

Is this a good way to operationalize type of car? No. The attributes on this list are not mutually exclusive, because a particular car could fit into two categories (for example, a two-door station wagon).

STOP & REVIEW

5.6 Operationalize the following variables.

Example
Year in college: *freshman, sophomore, junior, senior, other*

    or

Year in college: *first, second, third, fourth, other*

a. age
b. race
c. political party affiliation
d. amount of television watched per week
e. attitude toward capital punishment

Tables and Figures

The point of putting data (pieces of information) into a table or figure (such as a bar graph or pie chart) is to present those data clearly. Still, until you get some experience, tables and figures can be quite confusing. When you come across a table or figure in an article or a book, you might even be tempted to rely on the author's explanation of what that table or figure shows rather than take the time to study the data for yourself. But this can be dangerous because the author may not have interpreted the data correctly or may have written a misleading account of those data. Remember—be skeptical.

Usually, no matter how many pieces of information are packed into a figure or table, you can figure out what it means by following a few steps:

1. *Begin by reading the title of the table or figure carefully.* A proper title will, for example, tell you the name of each of the *variables* that is described in the table or depicted in the figure.

Table 5.2 Median Annual Total Earnings for Those 25 Years and Older by Gender, Educational Attainment, Race, and Hispanic Origins, 2007

Demographic Group	Educational Attainment			
	High School Graduate	Some College (no degree)	Associate's Degree	Bachelor's Degree
Men				
Asian	$31,545	$41,068	$40,716	$50,048
Black	29,474	32,425	37,398	50,079
Hispanic[a]	29,098	35,372	37,485	45,706
White	35,765	40,864	45,982	60,458
Women				
Asian	21,816	25,434	31,643	41,828
Black	21,641	27,853	30,152	40,197
Hispanic[a]	21,018	26,465	29,788	36,117
White	22,593	27,172	30,606	38,641

NOTE: These figures exclude workers with less than a high school degree as well as workers with a graduate degree.
[a]Hispanic may be of any race.
SOURCE: U.S. Census Bureau, *Current Population Survey, Annual Social and Economic Supplement, 2008.*

(When people misinterpret a table or figure, it is generally because they skipped this step. The title is so important!) The title of table 5.2 tells you that the table shows the variable median (or average) annual incomes of people in the United States. The title also reveals that the table shows the differences in the median income for people in different (variable) categories of gender, race, and educational background.

2. *Determine the source of the data.* Is it trustworthy? Data in table 5.2 are drawn from the U.S. Census (which is regarded as one of the most reliable sources). Would you be as likely to trust data from a call-in talk show? (I hope not!)

3. *Read any notes that accompany the table or figure.* Not all tables or figures have notes, but when they are included, notes give additional information about the data. The note in table 5.2, for example, explains that the table excludes information about workers with less than a high school degree as well as workers with more than a bachelor's degree.

4. *Examine any footnotes.* Footnote *a* in table 5.2 tells you that Hispanics may be of any race.

5. *Look for any trends in the data.* Be sure to look both *horizontally* and *vertically*. What does the table tell you about the relationship between the variables?
   a. *Horizontally.* For example, check the relationship between how much education workers have and how much money they make. This table shows that, generally, the more years of school an individual has, the more money he or she earns. In other words, *there is a positive relationship between income and years of education.* If you don't see this, keep looking!
   b. *Vertically.* For example, this table shows that, overall, men tend to earn more than women and that whites tend to earn more than Asians, blacks, and Hispanics.

Figure 5.2 shows some of the same data as table 5.2. To read figure 5.2, follow the same steps you did when reading table 5.2: Read the title, check the source and any notes, and look for trends.

The primary difference between tables and figures is that with figures, although the data are less precise, overall trends are easier to spot.

STOP & REVIEW

5.7 Use the data from table 5.2 to determine whether each of the following statements is true or false.
   a. Earnings tend to rise with increases in educational attainment, regardless of race or gender.

Figure 5.2 *Median Annual Total Earnings for High School and College (BA) Graduates, by Gender, Race, and Hispanic Origins, 2007*

SOURCE: U.S. Census Bureau, *Current Population Survey, Annual Social and Economic Supplement, 2008.*

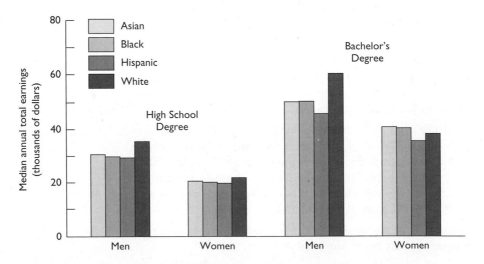

b. White male high school graduates have higher median earnings than white women with associate's degrees.

c. White women with bachelor's degrees have higher median earnings than white men with associate's degrees.

5.8 Given the data in table 5.2, what overall conclusion can you draw about the differences between men's and women's earnings?

5.9 Here's a more difficult question: Does race seem to make more of a difference in men's or women's earnings?

Table 5.3 Median Weekly Earnings of Selected Occupations, by Gender, 2008

	Males	Females
Low-Paying Jobs		
Bus Drivers	$605	$507
Cashiers	399	349
High-Paying Jobs		
Lawyers	1895	1509
Physicians/Surgeons	1911	1230

SOURCE: U.S. Department of Labor, Bureau of Labor Statistics, 2008.

5.10 Use the data from table 5.3 to determine whether each of the following statements is true or false.

a. It's true that males tend to earn more money than women in low-paying jobs, but there are only small differences between the earnings of men and women in high-paying jobs.

b. According to table 5.3, women are paid less than men because women are more likely than men to have low-paying jobs.

Table 5.4 Victims of Intimate Homicide, Rates per 100,000 Population by Victim Race, Gender, and Type of Intimate Relationship, 1993, 1998, 2003

	White Victims				Black Victims			
	Spouse or Ex-Spouse of Offender		Boyfriend or Girlfriend of Offender		Spouse or Ex-Spouse of Offender		Boyfriend or Girlfriend of Offender	
Year	Male	Female	Male	Female	Male	Female	Male	Female
1993	0.43	1.29	0.60	2.46	4.52	6.04	4.96	6.70
1998	0.28	1.21	0.46	1.96	1.84	1.96	3.08	4.73
2003	0.17	0.98	0.39	1.85	1.39	3.04	2.12	3.92

NOTE: Homicide and population data are for persons aged 20–44.

SOURCE: Bureau of Justice Statistics, FBI, *Supplemental Homicide Reports, 1976–2004.*

STOP
&
REVIEW

5.11 Use the data in table 5.4 to determine whether each of the following statements is true or false.

    a. The rates of fatal violence between intimates increased between 1993 and 2003.

    b. Overall, a female is more likely than a male to be killed by an intimate partner.

    c. For both men and women, there is less risk of being murdered by a spouse or ex-spouse than by a boyfriend/girlfriend.

    d. The rate of violence between intimates older than 44 years of age has decreased since 1998.

Table 5.5 Victim and Offender Relationships, Nonfatal Crimes of Violence, by Gender, in Percents

	Relationship of Offender to Victim					
Victim's Gender	Intimate	Other Relative	Friend or Acquaintance	Stranger	Don't Know	Total
Male	2.6	4.6	35.6	54.1	3.1	100%
Female	18.1	7.6	38.7	34.1	1.5	100%

NOTE: Data are for persons age 12 and over. Crimes of violence include rape, robbery, sexual assault, aggravated assault, simple assault.

SOURCE: Bureau of Justice, *Criminal Victimization in the United States, 2005.*

5.12 In 2005, there were about 5.2 million victims of (nonfatal) violent crime in the United States. Contrary to what you might suppose, fewer than half (46 percent) of the perpetrators of those offenses were strangers to their victims. In other words, people were more likely to be victimized by people known to them than by strangers. However, were men and women equally likely to be victimized by strangers? Find out by examining the data in table 5.5.

A NOTE ON COMMON STATISTICS

The data shown in figures 5.3 and 5.4 is from a recent survey of college students. Each figure shows the "average" credit card debt of U.S. college students. Figure 5.3 shows the "mean" credit card debt and figure 5.4 shows the "median" credit card debt. Why are these two averages, mean and median, so different? How does this work?

    Suppose you conduct research to determine how many times a day people in a work group send personal e-mails during the workday. Here are your results:

Jamal	1		Judy	4
Brian	1		Harold	4
Arthur	1		Mary	5
Traci	1		Hugh	160
David	3			

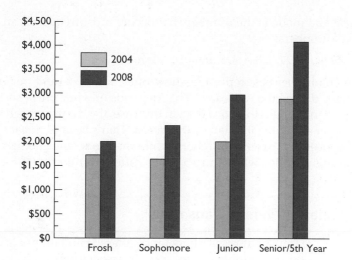

Figure 5.3 *Average/ Mean College Student Credit Card Debt, by Year in School, 2004 and 2008*

SOURCE: Sallie Mae, *How Undergraduate Students Use Credit Cards, National Study of Usage Rates and Trend 2009.*

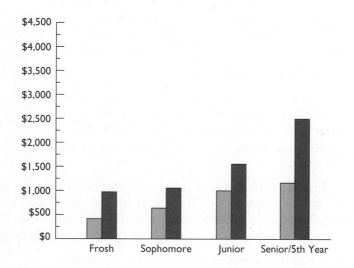

Figure 5.4 *Average/ Median College Student Credit Card Debt, by Year in School, 2004 and 2008*

SOURCE: Sallie Mae, *How Undergraduate Students Use Credit Cards, National Study of Usage Rates and Trend 2009.*

Mean As you no doubt know, to calculate a mean you simply add up all the values and divide the result by the number of cases. There are nine people in the group, so you have nine cases. Your calculation should look like this:

$$\text{Mean} = \frac{1 + 1 + 1 + 1 + 3 + 4 + 4 + 5 + 160}{9} = \frac{180}{9} = 20 \quad \text{So, the mean is 20}$$

Median The median is simply the number in the middle so that half the numbers in the set are above and half are below.

Median: 1, 1, 1, 1, 3, 4, 4, 5, 160   So, median is 3
                    ↑

Mode The mode is the number that occurs most frequently in the set of numbers.

Mode: *1, 1, 1, 1*, 3, 4, 4, 5, 160   So, the mode is 1

Which number best represents how often workers send personal e-mails during the workday? That depends on your purpose. The important thing is to notice that, in this case, the mean is much bigger than either the median or the mode. That's because means are influenced by extreme numbers while the mode and median are not. This explains why figure 5.3 is so different from figure 5.4.

Correlation Versus Causation[1]

One of the traps that researchers (and others!) can fall into is that of confusing correlation (a measure of association) with causation. Bottom line: Just because two things are associated does not mean that one of them causes the other. Before we conclude that there is a causal relationship between variables, we should ask these questions:

1. Is there an association between the variables?
2. Does the variable we suspect is a "cause" occur before the variable we suspect is an "effect"? (In the Western world, we believe that causes must occur before effects.)
3. Is there something else that might be influencing both variables?

For example, suppose research shows that there is a strong association between ice-cream sales and deaths by drowning: As ice-cream sales go up, so too does the rate of death by drowning. Does it make sense to conclude that eating ice cream causes drowning?

1. There is an association between sales of ice cream and drowning rates.
2. The sales of ice cream seem to go up before drowning rates do.
3. Another factor explains both: Increase in outside temperatures.

In other words, when it gets hot, more people might cool off by eating ice cream and by swimming; as the number of people swimming increases the so, too, does the likelihood of more drownings.

Recently, Bob Kingsbury, a state legislator from New Hampshire announced that his research showed that going to kindergarten made children more likely to grow up and commit crimes:

---

[1]http://healthland.time.com/2012/07/06/does-kindergarten-lead-to-crime-fact-checking-n-h-legislators-research/

The sources I have is [*sic*] I went to the [state] Department of Education and got a list of kindergartens and I went to the safety department and got the crime report. . . . In general, the towns with a
kindergarten have 400 percent more crime than other towns in the
same county. In every county the towns and cities with kindergarten
had more crime. (Szalavitz 2012)

Based on his research, Kingsbury concluded that going to kindergarten greatly increased the likelihood that children would turn
to a life of crime. Why? Kingsbury concluded it was because "We
are taking children away from their mothers too soon" (Claffey
2012).

   Be skeptical: What other factors might account for the association between kindergarten and crime rates? (If the question stumps you, check out this article: http://healthland.time
.com/2012/07/06/does-kindergarten-lead-to-crime-fact-
checking-n-h-legislators-research/#ixzz27896dgmq)

Chapter Review

1. Below I have listed the major concepts discussed in this chapter. Define each of the terms. (*Hint:* This exercise will be more
   helpful to you if, in addition to defining each concept, you
   create an example of it in your own words.)

   variables
   attributes
   hypothesis
   dependent variables
   independent variables
   positive relations
   negative relations
   operational definitions
   tables and figures (how to read them)
   averages: means, medians, modes
   correlation vs. causation

2. Go to chapter 14 and examine table 14.3.
   a. What is/are the dependent variable(s) in this table?
   b. What is/are the independent variable(s)?
   c. What do the data suggest? (In other words, what are the
      relationships between the independent and dependent
      variables?)

3. Convert the data in table 14.3 into a figure (see figure 5.1
   for an example). Which makes the relationships between the
   independent and dependent variables more clear—the table
   or the figure?

4. Research shows there is a very strong association/correlation between sleeping with shoes on and waking up with a headache. Ought we to conclude that sleeping with shoes on *causes* headaches?

STOP & REVIEW

Answers and Discussion

5.1

a.
  i.   *Number of beers consumed per week is thought to influence a student's GPA.*
  ii. *Frequency of tooth brushing is thought to influence the number of cavities gotten each year.*

b.   *Number of beers per week:*
     This variable could be operationalized by creating categories or by the exact number:
     none
     1–2
     3–4
     5–8
     9–12
     more than 12 or 0, 1, 2, 3, 4, 5, 6, 7, 8, 9, 10, 11, 12, 13 . . .
     Student's GPA
     0.0–2.0
     2.1–2.5
     2.6–3.0
     3.1–3.5
     3.6–4.0 or 0.0, 0.1, 0.2, 0.3, 0.4, 0.5, 0.6 . . .
     Frequency of tooth brushing
     never
     less than once a day
     1 or 2 times a day
     3 times a day or more
     Number of cavities gotten each year
     0
     1
     2–3
     4 or more or 0, 1, 2, 3, 4, 5, 6, 7 . . .

Hint: When you use categories, make sure that they are relevant ones. If every one of your respondents gets more than five cavities a year, they will all check the same category. This won't help you. It may be that those who brush more frequently do get fewer cavities, but 10 as opposed to 20 cavities. How do you tell what categories are important? Ask around! Find out what the range is.

c.   Attributes are characteristics of a variable. The variable sex, for example, has two attributes: male and female. If we knew only the attributes and applied some logic, we could name the variable. For example, consider these three attributes: felony, gross misdemeanor, misdemeanor. What's the variable? (Levels of seriousness in crime.) Likewise, consider these attributes: private, corporal, sergeant, lieutenant, captain, major, colonel, general. What's the variable? If you apply logic, you can figure it out (military rank).

5.2

H_4: Differences in religious affiliation are related to differences in attitudes toward abortion. That is, people who belong to different religions tend to have different attitudes toward the issue of abortion.

H_5: Differences in occupation are related to differences in income. That is, people in certain occupations tend to earn less than people in other occupations.

5.3

H_{10}: level of wealth or poverty, type of crime committed
H_{11}: religious affiliation, attitude toward the death penalty
H_{12}: marital status, pet ownership
H_{13}: temperature, sales of ice cream
H_{14}: amount of time spent studying, grades

5.4 *Hint:* When faced with a choice between variables, logically the cause has to come before the effect.

H_{15}: *Education* affects income.
H_{16}: *Income* affects vacation choices.
H_{17}: *Marital status* affects vacation choices.
H_{18}: Mental health is affected by *marital status*.
H_{19}: Regularity of church attendance is influenced by *marital status*.
H_{20}: People with more *education* tend to have higher-paying jobs.
H_{21}: People with *higher-paying jobs* tend to own more computers.
H_{22}: People with *light skin tones* tend to sunburn more easily.

5.5

H_{25}:
    variables: age, income
    direction: positive (that is, as your age increases, your income increases)

H_{26}:
    variables: social class, education
    direction: positive (the higher the social class, the higher the education)

H_{27}:
    variables: social class, likelihood of being arrested
    direction: negative (the higher the social class, the less likely you are to be arrested)

STOP
&
REVIEW

H_{28}:
  variables: age, likelihood of taking naps
  direction: negative (the older a person is, the less likely he or she is
  to nap)

H_{29}:
  variables: frequency of attendance at religious services, amount
  donated to religious causes
  direction: positive (the more one attends, the more one gives)

H_{30}:
  variables: education, prejudice
  direction: negative (the more the education, the less the prejudice)

H_{31}:
  variables: age, fear of dying
  direction: negative (as age increases, fear decreases)

5.6 (Remember, *operationalizing* simply means turning a variable into
something that can be observed and measured, which generally involves
coming up with a list of the variable's attributes. Each list of attributes
must be exhaustive, and the attributes must be mutually exclusive.)
  a. Age (either in categories or as straight numbers)
        less than 5 years old
        5–8 years old
        9–15 years old
        16–21 years old
        more than 21 years old or 0, 1, 2, 3, 4, 5, 6, 7, 8, 9, 10, . . .
  b. Race
        black
        white
        Asian
        Hispanic
        other
  c. Political party affiliation
        Democrat   (You could add to your list the name of
        Independent   any political party you know of. But always
        Republican   remember to add the "other" and "none"
        other   categories. That's really the only way to
        none   be sure your list is exhaustive—or inclusive of
                         every possible person.)
  d. Amount of television watched per week
        none
        no more than 2 hours
        2–5 hours
        6–10 hours
        more than 10 hours or 0, 1, 2, 3, 4, 5, . . .

e. Attitude toward capital punishment
   strongly oppose   or: On a scale of 1 to 10, with 1 being
   somewhat oppose   strongly opposed and 10 being strongly
   somewhat in favor   in favor, rate your attitude toward capital
   strongly in favor   punishment.

5.7

a. For the most part, this is true. The only exception is that Asian men with associate's degrees earned less than Asian men with only "some college."

b. This is true. White males with a high school diploma have average annual earnings of $35,765; white females with associate's degrees have average annual earnings of $30,606.

c. This is false. White women with bachelor's degrees have average yearly earnings of $38,641; white men with associate's degrees have average yearly earnings of $60,458.

5.8 At every level of education, men tend to earn more than women. This is true for each racial/ethnic group mentioned in the table.

5.9 This is a more complicated question. In the following table 5.2a, I've reworked the data to show the earnings of Asians, blacks, and Hispanics as

Table 5.2a Median Annual Total Earnings for those 25 Years and Older by Gender, Educational Attainment, Race, and Hispanic Origins, as Percent of Whites' Earnings, 2007

Demographic Group	Educational Attainment			
	High School Graduate	Some College (no degree)	Associate's Degree	Bachelor's Degree
Men				
Asian	88.2%	100%	88.6%	82.7%
Black	82.4%	79.4%	81.3%	82.8%
Hispanic[a]	56.2%	86.6%	81.5%	75.6%
White	100.0%	100.0%	100.0%	100.0%
Women				
Asian	96.6%	93.6%	100.0%	100.8%
Black	95.8%	100.0%	98.5%	100.4%
Hispanic[a]	93.0%	97.4%	97.3%	93.5%
White	100.0%	100.0%	100.0%	100.0%

NOTE: These figures exclude workers with less than a high school degree as well as workers with a graduate degree.
[a]Hispanic may be of any race.
SOURCE: U.S. Census Bureau, *Current Population Survey, Annual Social and Economic Supplement, 2008.*

STOP

&

REVIEW

percentages of the earnings of whites. Table 5.2a shows, for example, that male high school graduates of Asian descent earn an average 82 percent of what white men with high school diplomas earn. Study the table and you will see that there are greater differences in earnings among men than among women.

5.10

    a. This is false. The gap between men's and women's salaries for higher-paying jobs is about as large, if not larger, for lawyers and physicians/surgeons as for bus drivers and cashiers.

    b. This is false. Table 5.3 compares the average weekly earnings of men and women in the *same* jobs.

5.11

    a. False. The 2003 rates are lower in every category than they were in 1993. (There was an increase in 2003 in the murders of black women compared to 1998, although the 2003 rate is still lower than it was in 1993.)

    b. This is true. If you study table 5.4, you will see that the rate of intimate-partner killings (whether done by spouses, ex-spouses, or boyfriends/girlfriends) is in all cases higher for women than for men.

    c. This is true. For example, in 2003, white men died at the hands of their wives or ex-wives at a rate of .17 per 100,000 compared to .39 per 100,000 at the hands of their boyfriends/girlfriends. Black women died at the hands of their husbands or ex-husbands at a rate of 3.04 but at the hands of their boyfriends/girlfriends at the rate of 3.92.

    d. Okay, this was kind of a trick question. If you read the note at the bottom of the table, you would know that table 5.4 includes no information about victims older than 44 years of age.

5.12 Table 5.5 shows that, among male victims of nonfatal violent crimes, more than half of the perpetrators (54.1 percent) were strangers. Among female victims, only 34.1 percent of the perpetrators were strangers. On the other hand, notice that female victims of nonfatal violence were nearly 7 times more likely than men to have been victims of violent crimes perpetrated by intimates. (Only 2.6 percent of men who were victims of nonfatal violent crimes were victimized by intimates, compared to 18.1 percent of women.)

6

DOING SOCIAL RESEARCH

A ny sociologist worth her (or his) salt has a broad repertoire of techniques or methods for finding answers to questions. This must be so because finding good answers to different kinds of questions requires different kinds of techniques. So, it will be the nature of the questions to which you want to find answers that determines your choice of method.

Two Traditions: Quantitative and Qualitative Research

There are two major approaches to or traditions of sociological inquiry. One tradition can be traced back to the work of the French sociologist Émile Durkheim. As you will recall from chapter 1, Durkheim saw sociology as the study of social facts. Sociologists, he said, should study social facts in much the same way that chemists study chemical facts and biologists study biological facts. Durkheim was proposing, in other words, that sociology follow the research model established by natural scientists. As scientists, sociologists should observe and measure the actions of social facts. For Durkheim, the goal of sociology was to discover the laws that govern social behavior—just as Newton had discovered the laws that govern planetary behavior. Because research done according to the natural sciences model gathers data that are easily expressed in numbers, this research tradition is often referred to as *quantitative research*.

The second sociological research tradition can be traced back to the work of the German sociologist Max Weber. Weber, too, saw sociology as a science, but he argued that because the subject matter of sociology differs from that of the natural sciences, its research techniques should also differ. According to Weber, following the natural sciences model would leave sociological work incomplete. Human beings have important qualities that set them apart from the objects of natural sciences investigation—that is, human beings think and feel, and they frequently do things for reasons. Thus, said Weber, sociology must go beyond the natural sciences model and be an *interpretative science*—it must take into account the social meanings/reasons attached to behaviors. Weber proposed that sociologists adopt two goals: predicting and understanding social behavior. This sort of research is frequently called *qualitative research* because it focuses not only on the objective nature of behavior but on its meaning (or quality) as well. Although qualitative researchers often use numbers to quantify certain kinds of data, they are more focused on obtaining data that are difficult to quantify. Qualitative research reports generally devote more space to people's descriptive accounts of their own experiences than to numbers that quantify these experiences.

In this chapter, I will describe a variety of methods used by sociologists. Whether they practice in the quantitative or qualitative research tradition, sociologists typically follow one of four basic methods for obtaining data: surveys, observation, and unobtrusive methods. As you read through the description of each method, be aware that each method has its own strengths and weaknesses and is best suited for answering particular types of research questions.

First Things First: The Lit Review

No matter which research method sociologists ultimately choose, the first stage is always the same: a review of existing literature on the topic. Many call this phase of research the *lit review*. Now, when you are eager to actually do some research, spending time in the library doing a lit review may seem a wearisome prospect. But it is never a waste of time!

In the first place, someone may have already found an answer to your question—possibly even a good answer. If that's the case, wouldn't you want to know before wasting your time and energy? Of course, you may indeed find a better answer, but your task will be much easier if you start by determining what is already known.

American sociologist Pitirim Sorokin once compared the researcher seeking sociological knowledge to the explorer seeking out new lands. How tragic for the researcher, Sorokin suggested, to arrive at his or her destination only to hear, "Been there, done that."

Not knowing that a certain theory has been developed long ago, or that a certain problem has been carefully studied by many predecessors, a sociologist may easily devote his time and energy to the discovery of a new sociological America after it was discovered long ago. Instead of a comfortable crossing of the scientific Atlantic in the short period of time necessary for the study of what has been done before, such a sociologist has to undergo all the hardships of Columbus to find, only after his time and energy are wasted, that his discovery has been made long ago, and that his hardships have been useless. Such a finding is a tragedy for the scholar, and a waste of valuable ability for sociology and society. (1928, xviii–xix)

Personally, I think Sorokin missed the most important point: How embarrassing to arrive back from sailing the theoretical Atlantic and announce, "The world is flat!" In other words, even worse than reinventing the wheel is inventing *a wheel that will not roll!*

Even if your search of the literature reveals no answer to your particular question, inevitably you will find important clues. Studying what other people have already done, for example, may suggest ways of phrasing your questions or focusing your research in more interesting ways.

The importance of the literature review first really struck me as I was doing research for my PhD dissertation. My topic was public defense attorneys—those attorneys who are paid by the state to defend people who cannot afford a lawyer of their own. When I began my research, my question was fairly simple: How could these attorneys defend clients whom they knew to be guilty of horrible crimes?

So, I did what every good researcher does—I went to the library and started looking for what other social scientists had already found out. The time I spent in the library was enlightening, but in an unexpected way: I found *no* answers to my research question because, according to my predecessors, public defense attorneys *really do not defend their clients!* What? The sociological point of view was that because public defenders are paid by the same agency that pays the prosecutors (the state), they are really just fake lawyers. Even many of the public defenders' clients said that! I particularly recall reading an interview of Eldridge Cleaver in *Playboy* magazine in which he stated that PD stands not for public defender but for "penitentiary dispatcher."[1]

What I personally observed during the first few days in the courtrooms watching these attorneys work made me very skeptical of the conventional wisdom about public defenders. Indeed, I would discover a great deal of evidence that public defenders did about as well for their clients as private attorneys do for theirs.

---

[1]It's interesting what one gets to read in the course of doing research, isn't it? A friend of mine did her dissertation on romantic love in American society. Parts of her data were gleaned from so-called romance magazines (such as *True Romance*) and tabloids (like the *National Enquirer*)—all in the name of science.

To put it baldly, the information I obtained seriously undermined the work of my predecessors. They, not me, were the flat-earthers who had fallen for the conventional wisdom.

Does this mean that I regard my time in the library reading the existing literature as a waste of my time? No way! What I learned from my lit review forced me to phrase my questions about public defenders in much more interesting ways. The issue was not simply how public defenders defend their clients, but also why no one thinks they do!

Moreover, what would have happened had I published my findings without taking the time to discuss previous studies and to explain why their conclusions were wrong and mine were right? My readers likely would have thought that I was terribly naive (at best) or an idiot (at worst).

So, the time spent reviewing the work of others is time well spent. The more you know about your predecessors' work, the better you will be prepared to make your own contribution.

The Survey

The idea of the survey is pretty straightforward: If you want to get answers to your questions, simply ask! More specifically, if your research question requires knowing who people are and/or what they think about something, the survey is a good method.

More technically, a *survey* is a series of questions asked of a number of people. Sometimes we ask these questions orally, either face-to-face or over the phone. Other times, we give people the list of questions on paper and ask them to write their own answers. The first method is generally referred to as an *interview*; the second method is generally called a *self-administered questionnaire*.

The survey method is popular in sociology because surveys are particularly suited to obtaining information from large numbers of people. Indeed, this capability to obtain data from large numbers of people is the main strength of the survey method. Frequently, survey researchers can obtain information from hundreds, or even thousands, of people in their research.

Surveys are especially appropriate for discovering basic "demographic information" (such as age, gender, income, education, and religious affiliation).[2]

---

[2]The term *demography* is derived from the Greek *demos* ("people") and *graphein* ("to draw or describe"). It was first used, as near as we can tell, by Achille Guillard in his 1855 book *The Elements of Human Statistics*. Demographers study such things as the size of populations and the factors that affect population growth and composition—for example, the rates of marriage, birth, death, and immigration.

Another strength of the survey method is that it allows research-ers to obtain information about things that cannot be observed directly, such as attitudes. Using survey techniques allows researchers to tap into people's attitudes on a large variety of issues (for example, "Do you think the president is doing a good job?" or "Do you approve or disapprove of same-sex marriage?").

The weakness of the survey method is that, although it can get at people's attitudes, it is not a good way to measure people's actual behavior. If you want to know about what people *do*, a sur-vey might provide you with misleading information.

Information about people's behavior that is obtained from sur-veys can be misleading for a number of reasons. For one thing, people might not want to admit (even to themselves) certain behaviors. But more important, many people cannot give an accu-rate account of their behaviors even when they want to. People may remember, for example, which candidate they voted for in the last election, but they will probably not be able to remember how much campaign literature they read and whether it influ-enced their decision to vote.

TYPES OF SURVEY QUESTIONS

When you ask questions in a survey, it is important to phrase them in ways that make it possible for respondents to answer. Survey researchers ask two types of questions: *closed-ended* and *open-ended.*

Using the closed-ended format requires that you not only ask the question but also provide answer categories. The respondent answers the question by picking a particular category. Here are some examples of closed-ended questions:

1. Are you: _____ male _____ female?

2. What is your present marital status?

   _____ never married
   _____ married
   _____ separated
   _____ divorced
   _____ widowed

Closed-ended questions can be quite complex:

1. Do any children under the age of 18 live with you full time?

   _____ no _____ yes

   If yes, how many?
   _____ 1–2
   _____ 3–4
   _____ 5 or more

2. Are you presently employed?

_____ no _____ yes

If yes, is your work:
_____ full time

_____ part time

_____ other

A particular kind of closed-ended question is frequently used to ask people about their attitudes on sets of issues. This sort of question is sometimes called a *matrix* question because the answer categories look like a matrix, or array of numbers:

Here are some statements that have been made by students from your college. Please indicate the degree to which you agree or disagree with each by circling the appropriate number to the right of the statement.

	Agree Strongly	Agree Somewhat	Disagree Somewhat	Disagree Strongly
1. No student should be allowed to consume alcohol on campus.	1	2	3	4
2. Students should be required to study a minimum of 6 hours each school night.	1	2	3	4
3. Students who miss a class more than once a term should be suspended.	1	2	3	4
4. Faculty should be subject to a dress code.	1	2	3	4

To ask a closed-ended question, you have to know what the appropriate answer categories might be. Sometimes you might not be able to determine these categories in advance. Or you might want to hear or read respondents' answers in their own words. In such cases, open-ended questions should be used:

1. What is the most important thing you have learned so far in this sociology class? Why does that seem important to you? (Please explain.)

2. What is the thing that you like *most* about your sociology class? Why?

3. What is the thing that you like *least* about your sociology class? Why?

Six Guidelines for Crafting Survey Questions

1. *Adapt the phrasing of questions to the educational level of respondents, but do not be insulting.* "What is your GPA—that is, your grade point average?" sounds patronizing, because it seems to presume that people do not know what GPA stands for. Yet, we do have to deal with the fact that some people may not know what a GPA is. To explain the meaning of your question without sounding patronizing, try rephrasing: "What is your grade point average, that is, your GPA?"

2. *Avoid double negatives in a question.* Here's an example: "Do you oppose denying students access to their files or not?" What!?

3. *Avoid "marathon" questions.* Consider this example: "What do you think we should do about cheating on campus— should we abolish take-home exams, even if this means that students only get tested on writing that they have rushed through, as in in-class exams, or should we allow take-home exams even if this means a number of students will cheat?" Whew!

4. *Don't ask "double-barreled" questions.* That is, ask only one question at a time. Here's a double-barreled question: "Do you favor or oppose giving medical care to small babies and bums?" Well, gee, how can I answer that?

5. *Don't ask "leading" or "loaded" questions.* That is, avoid wording questions in ways that will lead respondents to answer one way over another in spite of their true opinions. Here's a loaded or leading question: "Do you agree with the Democrats that we ought to keep religion and the state separate?" As soon as your respondent sees the word *Democrat*, it will influence his or her answer. ("What, me agree with Democrats? No way; I don't care what the subject is!")

6. *Don't ask questions that your respondents cannot answer.* Unanswerable questions range from ones that ask for inaccessible information ("How many ice cubes did you use last year?" or "Do you believe that the chaos theory poses a serious threat to quantum physics?") to illogical ones ("Have you stopped beating your wife?" or "Quick, is Mickey Mouse a cat or a dog?").

THE ART OF ASKING QUESTIONS

In his book *The Art of Asking Questions*, Stanley L. Payne pointed out that it is pretty cheeky to expect people to answer survey questions:

> People are being exceedingly gracious when they consent to be interviewed. We may ask them to give us anywhere from a few minutes to many hours of their time in a single interview. We may ask them to expose their ignorance with no promise of enlightenment. We may try to probe their innermost thinking on untold subjects. We may sometimes request their cooperation before telling them who the sponsor is and before indicating the nature of our questions—for fear of prejudicing their answers. (1951, 114)

Payne argued that researchers must work hard to not annoy their respondents but rather to treat respondents graciously.

S T O P
&
R E V I E W

6.1 Here are five poorly constructed survey questions. Indicate what is wrong with each of them.
   a. Do you agree that pulchritude possesses exclusively cutaneous profundity?
   b. Do you agree that colleges ought to do away with homework and drinking alcoholic beverages on campus?
   c. How old were you when you learned to spell *president*?
   d. At what point will you stop lying to me about your answers to these questions?
   e. Do you approve of the practice of bogarting?

Observation

Of course, all forms of research—even lit reviews—involve some sort of observation. But when sociologists talk about *observational research,* they generally mean a particular research technique in which the researcher directly observes the behavior of individuals in their usual social environments, not in a laboratory. Some sociologists refer to observational research as *field research,* because the normal social world is the field in which sociologists conduct their research.

Different strategies are used in observational or field research. In one strategy, the researcher acts as a *complete participant.* The complete participant essentially goes "undercover" and does not tell the people being observed that he or she is doing research. At the other extreme is the *complete observer,* who views things from a distance (or from behind a one-way mirror) or somehow blends into the social scenery. The complete observer is generally unknown to the people being observed. Finally, midway between these two extremes, is the *participant observer*, who admits to being a researcher so that people know they are being studied.

The particular strength of observing people in the field is that this technique enables researchers not only to observe behavior (that can be done in a laboratory!) but to observe behavior *in its natural context*. When we observe behavior in its natural context, we glean important clues about the impact of context on behavior. Moreover, observational research enables the researcher to get information about individuals, such as small children who are not able to fill out questionnaires or respond to oral survey questions.

The weakness of observational methods includes the fact that only relatively small groups can be observed at once. Moreover, observational research is probably the most labor-intensive kind of research. Finally, the very fact of researcher participation in field research can influence subjects, and therefore findings, in what is known as the *Hawthorne effect*. Here is how the Hawthorne effect is typically described:

> Back in the 1920s, a group of social scientists wanted to investigate the sorts of things that could influence worker productivity. They chose to study this issue in a factory that made electrical parts: the Western Electric Hawthorne Works in Chicago.
>
> A number of workers agreed to go along with the study—even though they were not told the exact nature and goals of the research. These workers were divided into control and experimental subjects and were placed in special rooms in the factory where they could be easily observed and where the working conditions could be controlled by the scientists.
>
> The researchers believed that worker productivity could be improved by introducing better working conditions (for example, more light, rest breaks, earlier quitting times, meals). So, they provided the workers in the experimental group with these benefits. As expected, worker productivity increased.
>
> What was not expected was the increase in productivity that workers in the control group demonstrated. What was going on here? Even though these workers received none of the benefits enjoyed by the workers in the experimental group, their productivity increased.
>
> As it turned out, what was going on was that the real independent variable was the increased attention that the workers were receiving from the researchers! The increase in productivity in both cases was caused simply by participation in an experiment!
>
> The Hawthorne effect (as it is now called) is an example of what social researchers call the *reactive* effects of research. We know now that reactive effects are not limited to experiments but can take place when there is contact between researcher and subject or when subjects know they are the objects of research.

The problem with this description is that it's essentially misleading. A series of experiments was done at Western Electric's Hawthorne plant but, in retrospect, the research plan was problematic. For example, the lights were changed always on Sunday; when workers' output increased the following day, their productivity could just as well be explained by the fact that workers generally produce more at the beginning of the week than at the end.

Because of the study's flaws, some social scientists refer to the Hawthorne effect as nothing more than "a glorified anecdote." (*The New York Times*, 6 December 1998). But social scientists tend to accept the point of the Hawthorne effect: Care must be taken to avoid reactive effects that cause the research process to influence the outcome.

Unobtrusive (Nonreactive) Research

Most research methods have an impact of some sort on the people being studied. People may respond to surveys in ways they think the interviewer wants them to respond or in ways they think make them seem to be better people. As the idea of the Hawthorne effect suggests, simply knowing that one is being studied can have an impact on one's behavior. Unobtrusive methods are strategies for studying people's behavior in ways that do not have an impact on the subjects.

ARTIFACTS

Archeologists use unobtrusive measures. They dig up the sites of ancient settlements and look for the artifacts that inhabitants left behind. From these artifacts, they can tell a great deal about a people's culture. This sort of unobtrusive research uses what sociologists call *accretion measures.* Similar techniques can be used to build an understanding of contemporary social processes.

On a particular college campus, the dean of students receives phone calls from parents who are concerned that students might be drinking too much alcohol. The dean decides to do some research to determine just how much drinking is taking place on campus. Her first thought might be, "If I want to know something, why not simply ask?" So, she designs a questionnaire that asks about drinking behaviors and sends a copy to each student on campus. The dean tabulates the responses with a sigh of relief: 99.99 percent of the students say that they rarely drink more than one beer a week.

The assistant dean (who majored in sociology) warns his boss that the data from the questionnaire might be biased. It's possible, he says, that the students did not wish to reveal the true amount of drinking because they were afraid of the consequences. It is also possible that some of the students were so drunk when they filled out the questionnaire that they had no idea of how much they had been drinking.

The assistant dean (who got an A in his introductory sociology class) suggests an alternative: What about taking an unobtrusive approach to the question? He sketches out a research design and carries it out. What he finds is that there probably is a drinking problem on campus and that something ought to be done about it.

So, what was the research design? The assistant dean used a kind of trace measure to determine the amount of drinking. More specifically, he got up early one Saturday morning, visited each residence hall, and counted the beer bottles and cans that had been left in the recycling bins and garbage cans. There are 600 students in the school, yet he found 7200 empty beer cans and bottles! Because he knows that the garbage cans and recycling bins are emptied each Friday morning, he is fairly confident that the average student in the college drank 12 cans or bottles of beer sometime between Friday morning and Saturday morning.

As you might guess, a great deal of information can be obtained from what people throw away! Next time you think of it, check your own garbage—I'm betting that you will find clues to your social class origins, your student status, and possibly even your grade point average.

USE OF EXISTING STATISTICS

The U.S. government gathers and publishes incredible amounts of data on everything from how many bedrooms people have in their houses to how many people are arrested for robbery. These data are readily available in libraries and through computer searches and are great starting places for researchers. If you are interested in the differences between men's and women's salaries, for example, the data have already been collected. If you are interested in prisons—their size, their rate of growth, their population—the data are in the library and online. Businesses and other organizations gather and publish data, too.

CONTENT ANALYSIS

Content analysis involves subjecting some text to careful scrutiny to see what it reveals about its author, the times in which it was written, and so on. The texts that may be studied with content analysis include personal diaries, literature, television shows, radio commercials, magazines and newspapers, and even rock and roll music.

Children's books have frequently been subjected to content analysis, and the results are quite revealing:

> Throughout the 1970s, parents and educators conducted studies to document objectively how men and women were portrayed in the curriculum. . . . It was easy to investigate, there was no need to use time-lapse photography to stop the action. The messages were already frozen on the textbook pages.
>
> [One group of researchers] studied 134 elementary school readers from 16 different publishers and found the following ratios:

Boy-centered stories to girl-centered stories	5:2
Adult male characters to adult female characters	3:1
Male biographies to female biographies	6:1
Male fairy tale stories to female fairy tale stories	4:1

In a study of award-winning children's books, the results were similar:

> When girls and women were included, they were typecast. They looked in mirrors, watched boys, cried, needed help, served others, gave up, betrayed secrets, acted selfishly, and waited to be rescued. While men were involved in 150 different jobs, women were housewives. When they took off their aprons and discarded their dishtowels, they worked outside the home only as teachers and nurses.
>
> Children's literature and school texts routinely included derogatory comments about being female. For example,
>
> "Women's advice is never worth two pennies. Yours isn't worth even a penny."
> "Look at her, Mothers, just look at her. She is just like a girl. She gives up."
> "We are willing to share our great thoughts with mankind. However, you happen to be a girl." (Sadker and Sadker 1994, 69–70)

The strength of unobtrusive methods is that they do not require the cooperation of the people being studied. Moreover, the research process itself does not in any way affect the behavior being studied. Unobtrusive researchers study social things after they have occurred. The weakness is that unobtrusive research can study only things that leave traces. Moreover, these traces must be solid enough to last until they can be observed.

The Importance of Triangulation

Triangulation is a term that social researchers borrowed from geodetic surveying—a discipline that has developed techniques for determining the size and shape of the earth and the location of specific landmarks. In geodetics, one uses knowledge of

Ethnography

Many of those who engage in qualitative field research specialize in ethnography.[3] In the tradition of the best qualitative work, the goal of ethnography is to make sense of the social world in terms of the meaning it has for people who inhabit it. This requires a special mindset because doing good ethnography requires "entering the field without totally predefining the domain of interest and without presuming that you already know what is universal, because most of the time those presumptive universals are generated out of one's own perspective-dependent, context-dependent, and hence local world" (Shweder 1997, 154).

Successful ethnographers must arm themselves with a variety of methods—historical, unobtrusive, interviewing, observation—in order to study people where they live, work and play. Frequently, ethnographers will be dealing with number (quantitative data) as well.

Ethnography is hard and never fast work: Gaining an understanding of the world from someone else's point of view requires, to an extent, becoming an insider in their neighborhood, families, and work groups.

As you can imagine, this process can involve negotiating such delicate issues as gaining access to the groups and building trust with people (often, with people who have reason to distrust outsiders).

Ethnography is labor intensive, but the rewards are impressive. Unlike nonqualitative research methods, the goal is not proving a theory or testing a hypothesis; the goal is surprise.

Anthropologist Richard Shweder explained it this way: "Ethnography is about discovery. Skillful ethnography is about making some room for the creative imagination and some disciplined intuition.

Consider, for example, the events that led up to the tragedy that befell the astronauts on the U.S. Space Shuttle Challenger in January 1986: Seventy-three seconds into the flight, the shuttle began to disintegrate; a fuel tank exploded and all seven astronauts were killed. Those astronauts included Christa McAuliffe, a teacher from New Hampshire who had been selected as the first teacher in space.

Six days after the accident, President Reagan created a presidential commission to investigate. The commission, which came

—continued

---

[3]From the Greek terms *ethnos* (people) and *grapho* (to write).

to be known as the Rogers Commission (after its chair, William P. Rogers), issued its five-volume report five months later and concluded that the cause of the disaster was found to be the failure of an O-ring; an O-ring that was known by NASA engineers to be flawed.[4] The Rogers Commission report faulted both NASA and its contractor for failing to correct the O-ring design (1986, 40, 120).

Nine months after the Challenger disaster, in October 1986, the U.S. House of Representatives Committee on Science and Technology published its report. "As a rule," the Committee agreed "with the findings reached by the Rogers Commission". However, the House Report located primary blame on the poor judgment of the people in charge.

Ten years after the disaster, sociologist Diane Vaughan published her research on the space shuttle accident—it took her a long time to do her research:

> When I started, it was from the point of view that it was misconduct. I kept looking for "rule violations," but I didn't find any. . . . After about a year I had to throw everything out and start over. . . . I relied on thousands of documents in the US National Archives that were placed there by the government investigation. Many of these were engineering documents and memos. Doing the research involved learning engineering and NASA language. In the Challenger case there is this notion of "levels" of "acceptable risk," for example. These were called "Criticality Levels." Each part on the shuttle had to be classified at a Criticality level, meaning the probability of failure. . . . NASA's risk assessment procedures were very complicated. The reality was that every attempt they made to quantify and clarify risk gave them no help because there were thousands of technical components on the shuttle. Instead of clarifying, it was just overwhelming. (Vaughan, 2008)

Based on what she discovered from those thousands of documents, as well as from extensive interviews with NASA personnel, Vaughan concluded that the "real" cause of the disaster was something built into NASA's organizational structure—a "normalization of deviance." As Vaughan explained the concept:

> Social normalization of deviance means that people within the organization become so much accustomed to a deviant behavior that they don't consider it as deviant, despite the fact that they far exceed their own rules for the elementary safety. But it is a complex process with some kind of organizational acceptance. The people outside see the situation as deviant

—continued

---

[4]An O-ring is a flat rubber or plastic gasket. It's used to create a tight seal between joints.

whereas the people inside get accustomed to it and do not.
The more they do it, the more they get accustomed. For
instance in the Challenger case there were design flaws in the
famous "O-rings," although they considered that by design
the O-rings would not be damaged. In fact it happened
that they suffered some recurrent damage. The first time the
O-rings were damaged the engineers found a solution and
decided the space transportation system to be flying with
"acceptable risk." The second time damage occurred, they
thought the trouble came from something else. Because in
their mind they believed they fixed the newest trouble, they
again defined it as an acceptable risk and just kept monitor-
ing the problem. And as they recurrently observed the problem with no consequence they got to the point that flying
with the flaw was normal and acceptable. Of course, after the
accident, they were shocked and horrified as they saw what
they had done. (Vaughan 2008)

trigonometry to locate a third point by taking bearings from two
fixed points that are a known distance apart.

In sociology, we use the term *triangulation* to refer to a research
strategy that helps us zero in on social phenomena. Because each
research method has both weaknesses and strengths (in other words,
because there are advantages and disadvantages to every method),
whenever possible, researchers use more than one method to obtain
data. More specifically, researchers try to use methods whose
strengths and weaknesses balance out. When methods are combined so that the strengths of one method overcome the weaknesses
of another method, we speak of triangulating research methods.

For example, my interviews with public defenders (of all ranks)
suggested that they were paid less than prosecutors. Even the
prosecutors agreed. But I was suspicious about the validity of this
notion because how much people earn tends to be a closely held
secret. I triangulated by checking the official budgets for the public
defenders' and prosecutors' offices. What I found was that there
was no appreciable difference between how much public defenders and prosecutors were paid. However, I did find some important
clues to why the lawyers might feel differently rewarded for their
work. The budget for the prosecutors' office included a lot more
money for amenities (phones, photocopying, law journals, inves-
tigators, secretaries, and the like). No doubt, the sense that public
defenders were being paid less was tied to their perception that
they received fewer perks and resources for actually doing the job.

Here my triangulation (even though it was really only "bian-
gulation") was successful. The advantage of using existing statistics (for example, budgets) is that they lay out the facts in a fairly

reliable manner, whereas data from interviews may not be so reliable. However, the facts of the budget did not speak for themselves; it was only through my interviews that I discovered the sense of deprivation that one set of lawyers had when compared to the others. They were right about being relatively deprived, just not right about the source of this feeling.

Sampling

After you have selected your method (or, whenever possible, your methods), you have some decisions to make about whom you will interview, observe, or experiment on. In other words, you have to make some decisions about your sample. The *sample* is that portion of the larger population that you will study to make inferences about the larger population.

Why not simply study the entire population? Generally, the cost of studying an entire population is beyond the financial resources of researchers. Anyway, if one's sample is selected properly, the results can be as valid as results obtained from the entire population.

Drawing a sample is both a science and an art. In fact, some social researchers make their living simply by helping others draw good representative samples. I will not go into much detail here, but I will share the basics of this process with you.

How big your sample should be depends on one thing especially: how diverse the population is. If the population is very diverse (*heterogeneous*), then you will have to draw a large sample to get representativeness. Imagine two jars filled with gum balls. The first one contains 50 gum balls—10 each of 5 different flavors. The second one contains 50 gum balls of the same flavor. If I drew only one gum ball from the second jar, my sample would be absolutely representative. But if I drew only one gum ball from the first jar, I would miss four of the flavors. I would need at least five different gum balls to accurately reflect the contents of the first jar. So, as a general rule, we can say that *the more diverse a population is, the larger the sample needs to be.*

When you hear about surveys done before elections, for example, you will frequently hear about two sorts: scientific and nonscientific. The difference usually has to do with the sampling technique used. Scientific surveys use samples that are drawn according to the rules of random sampling; unscientific surveys use nonrandom sampling techniques.

Don't be confused about this. In science, the word *random* has a specific technical meaning—*every element in the population has the same probability of being in the sample.* To be able to say that one has obtained a true random sample of, say, students at Home Town U requires that every college student who attends HTU have the same probability of being picked to be in the sample. Thus, for example, if I wanted to pick a random sample of students, I would not use the dean's list, because students with low GPAs would not have the same probability of being included. I would also not draw my sample only from students who lived in residence halls, because students who lived off-campus would have no chance of being in the sample.

To get a random sample of students at HTU, I would have to obtain a list of every student taking college courses and pick from that.

Standing on the street corner with a clipboard and asking questions of people passing by is not using random sampling! (This sort of sample is called a *convenience sample*.)

6.2 For each of the following research questions, indicate which would be your first choice of research methods and why.

    a. How will people vote in the upcoming municipal elections?

    b. How do preschool boys and girls interact with each other compared to how sixth-grade boys and girls interact?

    c. How does a particular secret organization socialize its new members?

    d. What are the effects of increasing wages on employee productivity?

STOP
&
REVIEW

Ethics and Social Research

When researchers make decisions about how to do their research, they are guided by two important concerns. One concern is, Which method is best, given the nature of my research problem? But the second, and more important, concern is, What is the risk that my research might harm someone—one of the research participants or even other people in the community?

This is not to say that research that involves risk cannot be done. But today's researcher is required to reduce the risk as much as possible. And, where risk is necessary and the benefits of the research are great, the researcher is required to obtain *informed consent* from any person who participates in the research. What is informed consent? It is consent that is obtained after the potential research participant has been told what he or she will be asked to do, what the benefits will be, and what the possible harms are.

To help researchers make ethical decisions (and to help ensure that they do), most universities and colleges have established Institutional Review Boards (IRBs). These review boards are made up of members of the faculty as well as members of the community. Their job is to examine each research plan to ensure that the researchers who designed it have given the appropriate amount of thought to the possible risks and benefits of the research.

e. Are women or men more likely to have their personal space invaded when waiting in line (for example, at the grocery store or bank machine)?

f. To what degree do people who live in the United States believe that people from other countries are honest?

g. Has the number of children in the average family increased or decreased since the 1950s?

h. The Ajax company has instituted a program for recycling paper. Are employees actually recycling paper?

i. Do patients recover from surgery faster when taken care of by physicians specially trained to have a sympathetic bedside manner?

j. Are professors in the humanities more or less likely to publish articles and books than professors in the social sciences?

Chapter Review

1. Below I have listed the major concepts discussed in this chapter. Define each of the terms. *(Hint:* This exercise will be more helpful to you if, in addition to defining each concept, you create an example of it in your own words.)

quantitative research
qualitative research
literature review
survey
self-administered questionnaire
open-ended versus closed-ended questions
matrix questions
demographics
field research
observational research
participant observation
Hawthorne effect
reactive effects
accretion measures
content analysis
unobtrusive methods
artifacts
ethnography
triangulation
sampling
heterogeneity
convenience sample
random sample
ethics
IRB

2. Describe the essential difference between unobtrusive and obtrusive research strategies.

3. Why is triangulation important in social research?

4. Suppose you wanted to test the following hypothesis (in your location): College men drink more beer than college women.

   a. Which research strategy would be your first choice to test this hypothesis? Why?

   b. Explain how you would triangulate your research and why.

Answers and Discussion

STOP
&
REVIEW

6.1

   a. The high-falutin' phrasing of the question makes it unclear. Simplify the phrasing: "Do you agree that beauty is only skin deep?"

   b. This is a double-barreled question; it asks two questions. It is very likely that most people would have different opinions on the two things being asked about, and so they would have trouble answering this question. If you really want to know people's views on these matters, ask two separate questions.

   c. This is a good example of a question that asks for information that will probably not be accessible to the subject. So, you would probably receive a lot of "I don't knows" in response—or people would make some wild guesses.

   d. This is not a question that all people could answer. A person who has been lying to the interviewer could answer this question, but a person who has not been lying would have trouble answering, because it's illogical.

   e. This question may be unclear to many respondents because it uses a slang term ("bogarting" was a term used years ago to refer to anyone who hogged a marijuana cigarette for too long before passing it along to the next person in the group).

6.2

   a. The best way would be to ask people how they intend to vote. There really is no other way (that I can think of).

   b. A survey probably would not work because the children are so young that they wouldn't be able to articulate their interaction patterns. Observation of boys and girls interacting would be best.

   c. This could be tricky. On the one hand, you could ask members of secret organizations how they socialize their new members. It is likely, however, that members of such organizations would be reluctant to tell an interviewer their secrets. It is possible, though not likely, that you could find some documentation on this, perhaps a booklet titled *How to Socialize New Members of Our Secret Organization.* Ordinarily, such documents published by organizations are great sources of information, but secret organizations probably don't publish much stuff. Of course, many secret organizations might publish their secrets to help out their members, and you might steal such a document. However, the ethics of this are questionable (at best). The most obvious method would be covert observation, also ethically questionable.

d. Observation.

e. Probably a survey (either self-administered or interview format). The survey is a good way of getting at people's attitudes.

f. The use of existing statistics, such as census data, would be the most straightforward and reliable method. Why pay to do a survey when the government has already collected the data?

g. You could ask the employees whether they are following through, but the best way would be to look in the garbage: Are there recyclable materials there?

h. Again, you could survey a number of professors. However, many likely would be "mistaken" about how much they have published or might exaggerate to look better. It would be better to look at lists of publications and count for yourself. Or you could ask professors for copies of their résumés (called curriculum vitae in academia). Generally, professors are pretty diligent about recording their publications on their vitae.

7

CULTURE

As I sit down to write about culture, I feel like an ant trying to describe an elephant. The first thing that must be said about culture is that it's *big*. But my task is more difficult than the ant's—an ant can turn away from the elephant and not see it. I cannot escape from culture; it surrounds me, it's inside of me, and I take it wherever I go. In short, culture is ubiquitous.[1]

Not only is it always and everywhere, but culture makes a difference in how I live my life. My culture influences what I eat, how I speak, what I believe, how I behave, and what I value. Clearly an understanding of culture is essential for anyone who wants to understand people's behaviors and interactions with others.

Two eminent anthropologists defined culture this way:

> Culture consists of patterns, explicit and implicit, of and for behavior acquired and transmitted by symbols, constituting the distinctive achievements of human groups, including their embodiments in artifacts; the essential core of culture consists of traditional (i.e., historically derived and selected) ideas [beliefs] and especially their attached values; culture systems may, on the one hand, be considered as products of action, on the other, as conditioning elements of further action. (Kroeber and Kluckhohn 1952, 181)

That's a pretty tough introduction to culture, so in this chapter I am going to make understanding culture easier by separating out its various parts.

"No matter how eloquently a dog may bark, he cannot tell you that his parents were poor but honest."

—Bertrand Russell

---

[1]If you don't know this word, look it up—it's everywhere!

Humans Are to Culture as Fish Are to Water

"The last thing which a dweller in the deep sea would be likely to discover would be water. He would become conscious of its existence only if some accident brought him to the surface and introduced him to air. Man, throughout most of his history, has been only vaguely conscious of the existence of culture and has owed even this consciousness to contrast between the customs of his own society and those of some other with which he happened to be brought into contact."

—Ralph Linton (1945)

Material and Nonmaterial Culture

Culture has both material and nonmaterial attributes. *Material culture* includes all those things that humans make or adapt from the raw stuff of nature: computers, houses, forks, bulldozers, jewelry, telephones, socks, bologna sandwiches, oil paintings, and so on.

As this list suggests, material culture includes some very sophisticated and complex objects. But to create a piece of material culture, one does not have to bring a thing very far from its natural state. Suppose I pick up a stick in the forest and use it to help me keep my balance. This walking stick becomes as much a part of material culture as my personal computer.

There is a difference, however, between my walking stick and the sticks that I ignored: The sticks that remain on the floor of the forest are merely sticks. They have no other meaning and are not, therefore, pieces of material culture.

To put it more technically, I can say that *material culture is made up of artifacts*. Artifacts are by-products of human behavior.[2]

NONMATERIAL CULTURE

Nonmaterial culture is different first of all because it is made up of intangible things—and these intangible things also vary from simple to complex. Our ideas about truth and beauty, about happiness and boredom, about what is funny and what is not, about right and wrong—all these are part of nonmaterial culture. So, too, are the words with which we express these ideas. We can divide up nonmaterial culture into five basic categories: symbols, language, norms, values, and beliefs.

SYMBOLS

A symbol is anything that represents something else to more than one person. The symbols on my computer keyboard include $ (dollar), % (percent), & (and), £ (English pound), § (section), ¶ (paragraph), © (copyright), and ™ (trademark). Each of these marks is a symbol because it stands for something other than itself—a ¶ is not a paragraph, but merely symbolizes a paragraph.

Some objects are symbols in that they mean something other than themselves. In the English language of flowers, giving someone a red rose means something different from giving someone a lily.

By definition, symbols are social things—if an object has meaning only to one individual, it is not a symbol. So, let's say

---

[2]The linguistic root of *artifact* is similar to the Latin root for *artificial,* which means "made by humans."

"John and Mary sitting in a tree,
K-I-S-S-I-N-G.
First comes love, then comes marriage,
then comes Mary with a baby carriage.
How many babies did she have?
1, 2, 3, 4 . . ."

"I'm a little Dutch girl, dressed in blue.
Here are the things that I like to do:
Salute to the captain, curtsy to the queen,
and hit them both with a rotten tangerine."

"Johnny on the ocean, Johnny on the sea,
Johnny broke a bottle, and he blamed it on me.
I told Ma, Ma told Pa,
and Johnny got a lickin', ha-ha-ha.
How many lickin's did he get?"

"Cinderella dressed in yella,
went upstairs to meet her fella.
On the way her girdle busted.
How many people were disgusted?
1, 2, 3, 4 . . ."

Different parts of a culture system tend to reinforce one another. Notice how these children's jumping rhymes tend to reinforce traditional gender-role expectations.

that a symbol is anything that at least two people agree represents something other than itself.

Ugh. That sounds so dry. I want to convey the fact that symbols are worthy of study by sociologists because in the interaction between human beings, symbols are powerful things. *They are powerful because we react to them as if they were the real thing.* For example, if someone gives me a rose, I am apt to feel pleasure; if someone paints a swastika (the symbol of Nazi Germany) on my synagogue, I will get very angry. Symbols do not simply convey information—they are powerful enough to invoke emotions!

LANGUAGE

Language is an organized set of symbols, but language is such an essential part of nonmaterial culture that I think it deserves its own section. Many sociologists argue, in fact, that without language, there can be no culture at all. After all, to have symbols, we need some means of learning what these objects stand for— and the best way of conveying such meanings between people is through the use of language. It would be difficult to sustain non-material culture without language. Certainly any activity that requires cooperation between individuals (from hunting game to building rockets) is facilitated by language.

Language is made up of certain kinds of symbols (spoken or written words and gestures) and rules (such as grammar and syntax[3]) for using these. Language-use rules are important because words in and of themselves cannot convey complex meanings very clearly. Although sometimes it might seem as if having to follow the rules of grammar gets in the way of being able to express ourselves, without such rules we would be hard-pressed to understand

---

[3]Rules of syntax have to do with proper word ordering.

one another. Examine the following pairs of statements; they demonstrate how syntax can make all the difference:

"Man shot in head accidentally dies"

versus

"Man accidentally shot in head dies"

"Congressman sat informally on the carpet and discussed food prices and the cost of living with several women"

versus

"Congressman sat informally on the carpet with several women and discussed food prices and the cost of living"

Or how about this headline: "Missouri Pacific to drop passengers from three trains" (Lederer 1987, 83).

Gestures are part of language as well. Nodding your head up and down, for example, communicates a different message than shaking your head back and forth does.

NORMS

In sociology we call rules about behavior *norms*. Norms also are part of nonmaterial culture. Some norms, of course, are more important than others. Consider these three norms about how women should dress when they attend a church or temple in the United States:

Women must not wear jeans.

Women must not wear clothing that exposes their navels.

Women must not wear clothing that exposes their breasts.

Compared to the others, the first norm seems pretty trivial. Someone who violated it would probably only be punished by a quick glance of disapproval. Depending on the church, someone who violated the second norm might get anything from a long nasty stare to a request to leave. The same can be said for the second norm—but many would see a violation of the "no navel" norm as possibly more offensive than a violation of the "no jeans" norm. However, the woman who arrives at church with bare breasts will not be able to ignore her punishment. She will not only receive disapproving looks from other members of the church but might even be arrested.

This brings us to an important point: The way to judge the importance of a norm (and even whether it exists) is to observe how people respond to behavior. Based on the church members' responses, we can not only identify the norms but also get a sense of how important they are.

TYPES OF NORMS

Having observed lots of norm violations and responses to norm violators in many societies, social scientists realized that there were different categories of norms.

In his book *Folkways* (1906), sociologist William Graham Sumner divided norms into two categories:

1. *Folkways.* These represent casual norms; violations are not taken very seriously. For example, when riding in an elevator, face the door; do not look at strangers' faces, do not enter into strangers' conversations. At worst, the punishment for violating a folkway might be a dirty look, rolled eyes, or disapproving comment.

2. *Mores.* These are anything but casual. Mores reflect important rules, such as the norms against unjustified assaults on other persons.[4]

Later, sociologists added a third category:

3. *Taboos.* There are norms that are so deeply held that even the *thought* of violating them upsets people. For example, in the United States, there is a taboo against eating human flesh.

Sociologist Ian Robertson illustrated the difference between folkways and mores this way:

"A man who walks down a street wearing nothing on the upper half of his body is violating a folkway; a man who walks down the street wearing nothing on the lower half of his body is violating one of our most important mores, the requirement that people cover their genitals and buttocks in public." (1987, 62)

7.1 Think of at least one example of each of the following norms: folkway, mos, and taboo. Explain why your example fits the definition of each norm.

SANCTIONS

If you violate a norm, you can expect a certain type of response from others—what sociologists call a *negative sanction*. The seriousness of this negative sanction depends on the importance of the norm. Violations of folkways might be sanctioned by a comment or a nasty look. Violations of taboos, on the other hand, might be sanctioned by expulsion from the social group, imprisonment, or even death.

The form of the negative sanction can vary as well. Sociologists distinguish between formal and informal negative sanctions.

Formal sanctions are official responses from specific organizations within society, such as the government, universities, or churches. Formal negative sanctions meted out by the government include prison sentences and fines. Formal negative sanctions

---

[4]*Mores* (pronounced "MORE-rays") is the plural of *mos*. Technically one would write that "the rule against murder is an important mos, and one of the most important mores." For some reason, hardly anyone ever refers to a particular mos; generally, the issue is discussed in terms of the plural—*mores*.

> ## The Power of Informal Sanctions
>
> As I suggest in the text, there is no necessary correspondence between the type of a negative sanction (formal or informal) and its effect or consequences. Nonetheless, many of my students seem to presume that being at the receiving end of a formal sanction must be worse than being the victim of an informal sanction. William James, an early psychologist, knew that informal sanctions can be much more powerful:
>
> > If no one turned round when we entered, answered when we spoke, or minded what we did, but if every person "cut us dead," and acted as if we were nonexisting things, a kind of rage and impotent despair would ere long well up in us, from which the cruellest bodily tortures would be a relief; for these [tortures] would make us feel that, however bad might be our plight, we had not sunk to such a depth as to be unworthy of attention at all. (1890)

doled out by a university range from library fines to expulsion. Formal negative sanctions given by a church range from penance to being excommunicated.

Informal sanctions come from the individuals in social groups. Informal negative sanctions can range from being laughed at and made to feel humiliated to being given the cold shoulder by everyone in the group.

There is no cut-and-dried correspondence between the form of a negative sanction and its effect or consequences. The formal negative sanction of a parking ticket is less painful to many than the informal sanction of being laughed at or ignored by one's friends or family.

Note, too, that someone who violates a norm can (and frequently does) receive both a formal and an informal sanction. Students caught cheating in a sociology course, for example, may receive the formal negative sanction of a failing grade and the informal negative sanction of expressions of disgust from friends and family.

Of course, it is not simply norm *violating* that evokes responses from others. If your behavior is in keeping with a norm or, especially, if it goes beyond what is expected, you may be rewarded with a *positive sanction*. Positive sanctions also range from small to large and can be either formal or informal. Formal positive sanctions are those given out officially by some organization and can range from receiving an A in a sociology course to winning the Nobel Peace Prize. Informal positive sanctions range from a smile to a standing ovation.

7.2 Using the diagram below as a model, write appropriate examples of each type of sanction.

Types of Sanctions

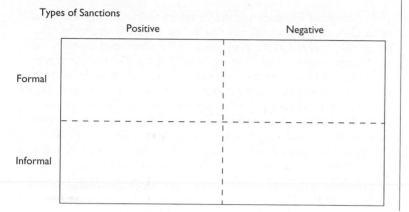

VALUES

In important respects, norms are one way that people in society have of expressing their values. So, after you have identified a group's norms, you can begin to see its values. For example, when you observe a negative sanction being given to someone who cheated, you might suspect that honesty is a value. (Or perhaps not getting caught is the thing that is valued.)

Values are general or abstract ideas about what is good and desirable, as opposed to what is bad and undesirable, in a society. For example, in a particular society, honesty might be valued over dishonesty, loyalty over disloyalty, liberty over restraint, and order over disorder.

The abstractness of values sometimes creates problems of conflict. The values themselves might not necessarily conflict, but the real-world implications might. A group of people might accept

What Do Americans Value?
(Williams 1970)

Achievement and success
Hard work
Efficiency and practicality
Science and rationality
Progress
Material comfort
Equality
Freedom
Democracy
The superiority of their own group

Ideology

The concept of ideology generally refers to knowledge that has been distorted by social, economic, or political interests. The term was invented at the beginning of the nineteenth century by the French philosopher Antoine Louis Claude Destutt de Tracy, who used it to distinguish his new science of ideas from both the old study of philosophy and the study of empirical facts. But the concept of ideology gained currency only when it was taken up by Karl Marx and Friedrich Engels in their book *The German Ideology*. Marx and Engels used ideology to refer specifically to the set of ideas found in law, religion, literature, and art that the upper classes use to maintain their economic superiority:

> The ideas of the ruling class are in every epoch the ruling ideas: i.e., the class, which is the ruling material [economic] force of society, is at the same time its ruling intellectual force. The class which has the means of material production at its disposal, has control at the same time over the means of mental production, so that thereby, generally speaking, the ideas of those who lack the means of mental production are subject to it. The ruling ideas are nothing more than the ideal expression of the dominant material relationships . . . ; hence, of the relationships which make the one class the ruling one, therefore the ideas of its dominance. (1845–46/1963, 39)

In 1929 Karl Mannheim (a Hungarian sociologist who established the sociology of knowledge as an important field of study) published a work titled *Ideology and Utopia*. In that book Mannheim expanded on Marx and Engel's use of the concept. As Mannheim pointed out, it is not only the ruling or upper class that has a particular worldview (or, to use the German term, *Weltanschauung*). The *Weltanschauung*—or the beliefs, worldviews, and ideas of people in all sorts of groups (ethnic and racial as well as economic)—can likewise be distorted by their social, political, and economic interests.

the same values in principle but find that they cannot agree on how to put these values into practice. For example, if your best friend asks to copy your test answers, does your loyalty to your friend win out over your commitment to honesty?[5]

Similarly, in our society we value freedom, but we also value safety and security. For example, should we pass laws that take away from people's liberty to preserve order in society? Since its founding, the U.S. legal system has struggled to balance laws that protect freedom with laws that protect people's safety.

---

[5]Allow me to interject a personal observation by suggesting that this is no real dilemma—what *friend* would ask you to cheat and thereby place you in jeopardy of failing the course?

> ### Ponder
>
> Think of some instances of values in conflict. For example, in what ways might the values of *achievement* and *success* conflict with the value of *equality?* How about *democracy* and *freedom?*

> ### Statements of Belief
>
> Men are stronger than women.
>
> God exists.
>
> Hard work leads to personal success.
>
> The earth is round.
>
> Women are smarter than men.
>
> The heart is the seat of emotion.
>
> Germs cause disease.
>
> Two plus two equals four.

IDEAS AND BELIEFS

Social scientists use the term *belief* to refer to *people's ideas about what is real and what is not real.* Beliefs, then, have to do with what people accept as factual. For example, as I mentioned in chapter 1, people once believed that the earth was the center of the universe.

Beliefs and values are frequently related. Church leaders were reluctant to let go of their beliefs about the geocentric nature of the cosmos because it was in keeping with their values. But beliefs and values are different, too. Most people in society regard the preservation of human life as an important value, but many disagree with respect to their beliefs about who qualifies as a human being.

How It Adds Up

Having separated out the different elements of culture, it is time to reexamine that definition of culture. Read it through again—this time, it should make more sense.

> Culture consists of patterns [norms], explicit and implicit, of and for behavior acquired and transmitted by symbols, constituting the distinctive achievements of human groups, including their embodiments in artifacts; the essential core of culture consists of traditional (i.e., historically derived and selected) ideas [beliefs] and especially their attached values;

As you may recall, there was a final part of the definition:

> *culture systems may, on the one hand, be considered as products of action, on the other, as conditioning elements of further action.*
> [emphasis added]

Let's explore this final part of the definition by distinguishing between culture as a product of action and as a conditioning element of further action.

Culture as a Product of Action

In Great Britain and in other countries, these gestures have distinctly different meanings.

"Up yours!"   *"Victory!"*

This part is fairly simple: Culture systems (the total package of material and nonmaterial cultural things) are created by humans and in this sense are products of action. Because culture is a product of human action and interaction, we would expect different groups of humans to have different cultures. And thus it is that the content of culture systems varies widely across societies.

That being the case, any examination of a culture system can reveal a great deal about the people who share in that culture. Think of how much archeologists have learned merely by examining the remains of material culture, such as a clay bowl or hammered piece of metal, left behind by peoples long dead. These artifacts can tell us a great deal about the level of technology in a society, as well as its members' norms, values, and beliefs.

The *content* of language itself reveals a great deal about a culture. What can you deduce from the fact that the Masai of Africa have seventeen terms for *cattle?* That the Ifugeos of the Philippines have twenty terms for *rice?* That the residents of the Trobriand islands of Papua, New Guinea, have a hundred words for *yams?* That the people of the Solomon Islands have nine words for *coconut?* For that matter, what can you deduce from the fact that college students may have upward of two dozen words for *vomit?*

In the United States, thumbs-up means "good job" or "A-OK." In Australia, Nigeria, and other places, this is a very rude gesture.

Even parts of our language that we assume mimic natural sounds are cultural. A dog may say "bow-wow" in English, but Spanish dogs say "gua-gua," Russian dogs say "af-af," and Japanese dogs say "wan-wan."

It is not just the spoken word that varies across societies. Gestures have different meanings to different peoples as well. Nodding your head up and down means you agree—right? (Nod your head.) But if you were visiting Bulgaria, parts of Greece, the former Yugoslavia, Turkey, Iran, or Bengal and you nodded your head up and down, it would be read as disagreement (Axtell 1991, 60).

So much of what we take for granted as "natural," as instinctual or genetic, is really a product of culture. For example, linguist Ray L. Birdwhistell observed that "we have found no gesture or body motion which has the same social meaning in all societies" (1970, 35). In his book *Word Play*, Peter Farb adds that "human beings every-where rotate their heads upon their necks, blink and open wide their eyes, move their arms and hands—but the significance of these nonverbal signals varies from society to society" (1993, 204).

Norms, values, and beliefs vary from culture to culture, just as language does. These differences can often result in travelers feeling a sense of "culture shock."[6]

Culture as a Conditioning Element of Further Action

The easiest way to explain how culture conditions our actions or behaviors is to say that culture puts us all in the same rut. For the most part, it is a reasonably comfortable rut, but it is a rut nonetheless.

Every society has problems that must be solved, such as providing shelter, food, and clothing. Once a particular problem has been solved in a satisfactory way, people tend to stick with that solution. And their children repeat these solutions, as do their children. Along the way, of course, the solutions are likely to become more elaborate, but they do tend to follow the established path. In other words, once a track through the problems of life is established, people tend to stay on that track.

This rut, or the influence of culture, is so comfortable to most of us (after all, most of us have never experienced anything else) that it is difficult to see until you really look. But it can be seen! Consider the following examples.

As you drive through town, you will notice (if you look) that most people have solved the problem of shelter in the same basic ways. The houses and apartment buildings themselves look remarkably alike. They all have doors and windows. And in spite of the fact that there are many colors from which to choose, most people paint their houses white, gray, light blue, or some "earth tone."

The next time you go out to dinner, watch the people around you to see how they have solved the problem of *how* to eat. In the United States people tend not to eat Jell-O with their fingers; they use a spoon. Most people will lick an ice cream cone but not a bowl of ice cream (even when the bowl is made of edible material). Tomatoes are served in a green (vegetable) salad but not in a fruit salad—even though a tomato is really a fruit. And most people eat the main course before the dessert.

---

[6]Recall Chagnon's response to the Yanomamö (described in chapter 4). That was a great illustration of culture shock.

Problems Identified and Resolved in All Known Cultures
(Murdock 1945)

Beliefs about death	Numerals
Bodily adornment	Personal names
Calendar	Population policy
Cleanliness training	Property rights
Cooking	Puberty customs
Cosmology	Religious rituals
Courtship	Sexual restrictions
Dance	Soul concepts
Decorative art	Sports
Divination	Superstition
Dream interpretation	Surgery
Education	Toolmaking
Ethics	Trade
Etiquette	Weaning
Faith healing	Weather control

Varieties of Cultural Wisdom

Proverbs are one repository of cultural wisdom. You've heard them: "You can't tell a book by its cover," "A bird in the hand is worth two in the bush." Every culture has them—for example, Haitians caution, "Do not insult the mother alligator until after you have crossed the river"; and the Greeks warn that "white hair is not a sign of wisdom, only age." The Irish suggest that "it is better to be a coward for a minute than dead for the rest of your life," and according to the Japanese, "The nail that sticks up gets hammered down." Finally, a Turkish proverb suggests that "he became an infidel hesitating between two mosques."

Notwithstanding their heritage, some of these sayings seem to provide lessons that are universal; others are harder to understand unless we know more about the culture which gave rise to them. Consider the following Yiddish proverbs. Which of them make sense to you?

"When a poor man gets to eat a chicken, one of them is sick."

"When a father gives to his son, both laugh; when a son gives to his father, both cry."

"If God were living on earth, people would break his windows."

"One fool can ask more questions than ten sages can answer."

"What good is a cow that gives plenty of milk and then kicks over the pail?"

The next time you go to class, look around at your classmates and see how they have solved the problem of clothing themselves. How many of the women are wearing fancy dresses? You know that a woman is likely to have at least one such dress in her closet, but even if it is her favorite dress, she won't wear it to class. How many of the men are wearing lipstick? Why are several people wearing baseball caps, but not a single one is wearing a football helmet?

The similarities in our solutions to the everyday problems of shelter, food, and clothing are more than coincidental. The ways in which we construct our dwellings, eat our food (and even what we consider to be food), and cover our bodies are not the only possible solutions to the problems of shelter, food, and clothing. But they are the solutions chosen by those who have gone before us, and though we have elaborated on them, these traditions or customs influence how we live our lives.

Social Institutions

Some solutions to problems are given special status—these solutions are called *institutions*. In everyday speech, people may refer to a specific organization as an institution ("This university is an institution of higher learning"). But to a sociologist, the term has a different meaning: *an institution is a set of ideas about the way a specific important social need ought to be addressed.* Institutional responses to problems tend to be justified by important social values and beliefs, and they tend to be slow to change. An institution, then, is part of nonmaterial culture.

Another way to put this is to say that after a particular pattern of responding to important social needs has become established, it becomes *institutionalized*. As parts of nonmaterial culture, institutions vary across societies, but (as you will see in chapter 9) all societies must address the same core of crucial problems.

Within a particular society, there is some latitude for difference in responding to basic social needs, but not too much. Take religion, for example. Even in our society, where people pride themselves on having freedom of religion, one's religious practices cannot stray too far from the accepted institutional pattern. If your religion requires you to participate in the sacrifice of the Eucharist or holy communion, that is okay. Sacrificing goats or chickens is getting a bit too far from the institutionalized line and may earn you an informal negative sanction. But sacrificing virgins is quite another thing—freedom of religion does not extend that far even in the United States.

Social Change: Cultural Diffusion and Leveling

Not every solution to a society's problems has been inherited from its ancestors. Depending on the extent of communication and contact between people of different cultures, people can adopt some of the solutions to life's problems from other cultures. Sociologists call the process by which cultural things are adopted *cultural diffusion*. For example, Americans have adopted sushi bars from the Japanese culture, and the Japanese have adopted baseball from American culture.

Elements of nonmaterial culture may diffuse, or spread, from one society to another as well. But the diffusion of nonmaterial culture is frequently more problematic. It is one thing to adopt American hamburgers, but quite another to adopt American ideas about women's role in society! Adopting a piece of material culture is easier because it is often easier to separate tangible things from their intangible meanings, which may not mesh or be congruent with a culture's values.

As cultural diffusion increases, the differences between cultures decrease. When you walk down a street in London, New York, Moscow, or Singapore and see someone eating a Big Mac or a Whopper while talking on a cell phone or listening to Nine Inch Nails on an iPod or Zune, you experience this sense of cultural *leveling*.

Subcultures and Countercultures

Culture is a powerful force not only in shaping people's behavior, but their thoughts and emotions as well. But it is a mistake to speak of culture as if it were shared equally by every person in a particular society—especially in modern societies. There are groups of people within society whose *shared values, norms, beliefs, or use of material culture sets them apart from other people in that society; these groups become subcultures.*

Subcultures can emerge for a variety of reasons. Some are occupational: As a result of their work, for example, police officers tend to see the world in ways that set them apart from civilians, and many police officers come to feel uncomfortable hanging out with anyone who is not a member of their ranks.

Deeply felt shared religious beliefs can also bring subcultures into being. Members of some religious groups have practices and beliefs that set them apart from the rest of society.

Regional differences also give rise to subcultures. For example, people who live in the southern United States tend to have in common special folkways, food, and even accents that make them distinct from other Americans.

Subcultures may be based on shared ethnic or racial heritage; others may be based on age, social class, sexual orientation, political beliefs, and even hobbies.

Some subcultures are long-lived. The Amish have managed to remain within and apart from the larger American culture since they began their migration from Switzerland to North America in 1720. Many subcultures are less enduring (the "flower children" or hippies of the 1960s come to mind).

What happens to subcultures? Frequently, subcultures disappear because aspects of their adherents' beliefs, values, or use of material culture are adopted by members of the larger culture, thereby leveling the difference between what was once a subculture and its *parent* culture. To the degree that middle-class youth begin to adopt the clothing, mannerisms, and argot[7] of hip hop, for example, hip hop loses much of what sets it apart from the larger culture. In other cases, members of a subculture may take steps to level the differences between themselves and those of the larger culture. For example, when the leaders of the Church of Jesus Christ of Latter-Day Saints (commonly known as the Mormon Church) outlawed plural marriage, they took a significant step toward bringing the culture of their church into line with mainstream American culture.

A *counterculture* is a special form of subculture (Yinger 1960, 1977). When members of a subculture hold values, share norms, or utilize material culture in ways that not only set them apart from the larger culture, but are perceived to threaten the parent culture, they have what's called a counterculture. The Ku Klux Klan is a famous example: it proclaims a racism that most Americans find repugnant. The Klan has birthed more modern countercultures—including much of the contemporary militia movement: "Many members of the militia movement are hard-core racists and neo-Nazis; weekend warriors who wear camouflage fatigues, revel in paramilitary activities, threaten and commit violence and who are determined to defy the federal government. . . . One could call [them] the Khaki Klan" (Wade 1987, viii).

I must admit that the concept of subculture is a fuzzy one. At what point does the culture of a particular group (i.e., its values, norms, beliefs, and use of material culture) become distinct enough to qualify it as a subculture? For sure, the Amish are a subculture, but are members of a college sorority? How about Freemasons or Rotarians?

---

[7]Argot is a sociological term of art (i.e., a piece of jargon); the term refers to the specialized language of a particular group.

The distinction between subculture and countercultures is likewise fuzzy: Who determines when the values of a subculture are not only distinct from but also in opposition to those of the parent culture? It is obvious (to most people) that the Ku Klux Klan is not only a subculture but a counterculture as well, but what about Goths? Ravers? Vegans?

Yet the fuzzy quality of these concepts does not render them useless; arguably, the fuzzy nature of these concepts merely reflects the fuzzy nature of social reality.

Finally, it must be observed that although members of any subculture hold values (and so forth) that set them apart from the larger culture, their members do not totally escape the power of the parent culture. Even the Hells Angels,[8] that motorcycle "club" whose members' values and beliefs would seem to be in complete opposition to the larger American culture has not been entirely able to escape its influence:

> They call themselves the one-percenters, "the one percent that don't fit and don't care." They refer to members of the "straight" world as "citizens," which implies that they themselves are not. They have opted out of the structural system. Nevertheless . . . they constitute a formal organization complete with complex initiation ceremonies and grades of membership emblematized by badges. They have a set of by-laws, an executive committee, consisting of president, vice-president, secretary, treasurer, and sergeant-at-arms, and formal weekly meetings. (Turner 1969, 194)

Moreover, Hells Angels appears to have adopted American capitalism: Even "civilians" can go online and purchase their stuff—pins, t-shirts, and beanies (at chapter Web sites or on eBay). In 2006, the Hells Angels announced they were going to sue the Disney Company for infringing on its trademark—for developing a film called *Wild Hogs*. (The Death head logo is also a registered trademark of the Hells Angels.)

Idiocultures

Although whether or not a group is a subculture (let alone a counterculture) is sometimes difficult to tell, I can say with certainty that not all groups constitute subcultures. Indeed, culturally

---

[8]In previous editions of this book, I mistakenly wrote "Hell's Angels." The next year I received an e-mail from a member of the Hells Angels who informed me that my use of the possessive apostrophe was wrong. I wrote him to thank him for his correction and to inquire how it came to be that a member of the Hells Angels was reading a sociology textbook. He never responded. Perhaps I offended him by implicitly stereotyping Hells Angels as nonsociologists.

speaking, most groups are simply microcosms of the larger society. In other words, the culture of most groups mirrors that of the larger culture. That doesn't mean, for example, that there is nothing worth noting about the culture of groups that don't qualify as subcultures.

Noted sociologist Gary Alan Fine reminded us that "every group has to some extent a culture of its own." He called these groups *idiocultures:*

> Idioculture consists of a system of knowledge, beliefs, behaviors, and customs shared by members of an interacting group to which members can refer and employ as the basis of further interaction. Members recognize that they share experiences in common and these experiences can be referred to with the expectation that they will be understood by other members, and further can be employed to construct a social reality. (Fine 1979, 734)

Over time, as people interact on a regular basis, they develop shared knowledge, beliefs, and customs, and these become important to their future interactions. To illustrate the concept, Fine shared the results of his own research—three years of participant observation of five Little League baseball teams. He found that each team developed its own norms (e.g., gum chewing allowed or not) and customs (e.g., appropriate joking topics and nicknames). By the end of the season, each group had developed its own distinct group culture—that is, its own idioculture.

It might be difficult for you to conceive of a group to which you belong having a culture (like the fish that doesn't notice the water), but what about your family? Different families have different customs about how to celebrate holidays, for example. My dad grew up in the Depression and (for some reason) had fond memories of eating such things as rutabagas and turnips. The kids in my family referred to those as "Depression vegetables," and refused to eat more than a token amount (or, in my case, none). Yet, on rare occasions when we get together to share a holiday meal, the rutabagas and turnips appear on the table.[9] Everyone in the family knows the meaning of those vegetables, and they are a running (through the generations) joke.[10]

---

[9]Rutabagas apparently lost favor with most Americans after they had consumed so many during food shortages during WWI. In modern Europe, these vegetables are grown extensively as animal feed.

[10]One semester, the students in one of the sections of my sociology class seemed to have a fairly well-developed idioculture: They started a *facebook* group to honor their graduate student discussion leader; the group's officers have such names as "The Sociological Imagination," "The Taboo," and "Role Strain."

7.3 Distinguish between subculture and counterculture. Give at least two examples of each.

7.4

    a. Margaret Visser states, "The extent to which we take every-day objects for granted is the precise extent to which they govern and inform our lives." What did she mean by that?

    b. Think of at least five ways in which culture has influenced your behavior today.

Chapter Review

1. Below I have listed the major concepts discussed in this chapter. Define each of the terms. *(Hint:* This exercise will be more helpful to you if, in addition to defining each concept, you create an example of it in your own words.)

    culture (defined)
    material culture (artifacts)
    nonmaterial culture
    symbols, language/gestures
    norms
    William Graham Sumner
    folkways
    mores/mos
    taboos
    sanctions (formal and informal)
    values
    beliefs and ideology
    social institutions
    cultural leveling and diffusion
    subculture
    counterculture
    idioculture
    culture as a product of action
    culture as a conditioning element of action

2. Explain how culture can be both a product of action and a producer of action.

3. Was the author of the following sentence exhibiting ethno-centrism or cultural relativity? What do you interpret the quotation to mean?

    "Natives who beat drums to drive off evil spirits are objects of scorn to smart Americans who blow horns to break up traffic jams."

4. New norms must be created in response to changes in society. Describe the norms that have evolved governing the use of cell phones or e-mail. As far as you have observed, how widespread are these norms? What sanctions come to people who violate these norms?

5. In your judgment, which of the following are subcultures? Justify your answer.

Goths
Nudists
Ravers
Skaters
Starbucks customers
Vegans
Yoga practitioners

Answers and Discussion

7.1 Check your examples. Is your example of a folkway a "gentle rule" about how things are usually done (blowing your nose in your handkerchief, not on your sleeve; eating with a fork, not a knife)? How about your example of a mos—is it a rule about something that is important? Is your example of a taboo something that is so disgusting you can't even imagine violating it (having sex with your brother)?

Remember, folkways, mores, and taboos are all types of norms. So, *norm* is the generic term for social rules of behavior.

7.2 There are many ways to answer this question. Here is how I filled in the boxes:

Types of Sanctions

	Positive	Negative
Formal	Good conduct medal Promotion on job	Getting fired Being fined
Informal	Cheers Being toasted	People not talking to you Being glared at Being hissed

Here are some things to remember about sanctions: They can be positive or negative, formal or informal. Formal positive sanctions are not necessarily better than informal positive sanctions; formal negative sanctions are not necessarily worse than informal negative sanctions. The point of sanctioning people—positively or negatively—is to encourage/force them to comply with social norms.

7.3 A subculture is a group of people whose values, language, dress, and so on set them apart from the larger society. A counterculture is a subculture whose values, language, dress, and so on are not only *different from* but are *in opposition to* those of the dominant culture. Most occupational subcultures (police, academics, and so on) are not countercultures. "Outlaw" groups (the Hells Angels, the KKK) are subcultures that are also countercultures.

Because the defining characteristic of a counterculture is that it is in opposition to the dominant culture, you have to know something about the dominant culture to determine whether a subculture is also a counterculture. For example, in a communist or socialist country, a group of Young Republicans would be seen as a counterculture but not so in U.S. society.

7.4

a. The power of everyday objects has to do precisely with the fact that *we feel as if* we can't live without them. I don't feel quite comfortable sitting on a chair that's lower than knee high. No matter how hungry I am, before I start on that baked potato, I have to find a fork. A spoon might work as well, but it wouldn't feel right. (Although I will use chopsticks when I am eating in a Chinese restaurant, I never feel as comfortable with them because I can't eat without thinking about what I'm doing.) Even though I keep my office door open and am not generally bothered by traffic in and out, I know I would be constantly annoyed if my colleague, whose office is next door, had to pass through my office to reach his—no matter how quietly he did so. Visser goes on to say that having these things now prevents us from being different.

b. If you had trouble with this one, look back to the quote from Ralph Linton. His point is that culture is everywhere, so it's hard to see (just as a fish likely would never have cause to notice it was swimming in water). Culture influences almost everything you do—so, what have you done today?

> I got up in the morning (instead of sleeping through the day). My culture demands that I participate during daylight hours!

> I ate breakfast. I wasn't particularly hungry, but "it's the most important meal of the day."

> I didn't take a nap. Naps are not prescribed for adults in my culture.

> I ate with a fork. I didn't have fried cat for lunch or dinner.

> I came to school and went to class. I spoke English all day.

8

SOCIAL STRUCTURE

When sociologists look at societies, or smaller groups such as colleges, or even families or Cub Scout troops, they see more than just assemblies of people; they see social structures. A social structure is a set of relatively stable *roles*, that is, patterned relationships among *statuses*. The definition is complicated, but in this chapter you will find the keys that will unlock that complexity.

Statuses

A social *status* is simply a position that a person occupies in a social structure. In modern Western societies, there is a wide variety of social statuses. These include *family* statuses (mother, father, child, grandparent), *occupational* statuses (president of the United States, lawyer, physician, firefighter, computer programmer), *social class* statuses (upper class, middle class, lower class). Other statuses are based on *age, race, sex, ethnicity,* and the like.

How do individuals come to occupy certain statuses? As you might guess from the examples given in the preceding paragraph, it varies. Some statuses are *achieved* by individuals. Achieved statuses in modern Western society might include being a spouse, a sociology major, a college graduate, a chamber of commerce member, a lawyer, or a convicted mass murderer. These are all positions in the social structure that individuals achieve for themselves (though, as in the case of the convicted mass murderer, not always on purpose). Other statuses are *ascribed.* That is,

ascribed

individuals are placed, generally at birth, in a status—sex, race, ethnicity, age, and so on—that they cannot escape.

Understanding where people fit within a social structure is crucial to everyday life. For this reason, when we meet new people, our first inclination is to find out something about their social statuses. Knowledge of the social positions or statuses that people occupy helps us to know how to interact with them.

Imagine you're at a party where strangers are forced to mingle. What sorts of questions do people ask of one another under those circumstances? "What do you do for a living?" "Are you married?" "Do you have children?"

These are all questions about social status or position in the social structure: "What do you do for a living?" translates into "What is your occupational status?" Similarly, "Are you married?" translates into "What is your marital status?" And "Do you have children?" becomes "What is your parental status?"

The nature of your response to others is likely to depend on what you know (or assume) about their social statuses. Probably you will respond differently to someone who is married than to someone who is single. If someone tells you that she is the governor, you are likely to respond to her differently than if she says she is a carpenter.

Even if we do not have an opportunity to ask others about their social statuses, we can detect many clues simply by watching and listening. These clues are _status symbols._ The police officer's uniform is a symbol of his occupational status; his wedding ring is a symbol of his marital status. The microphone the professor wears while lecturing is a clue to her status. A book bag might be a symbol of the status of student, though it is not as clear a symbol as a wedding ring.

After we know something about people's statuses, we generally feel more comfortable interacting with them. The reason for this is that each status is accompanied by certain expectations about how the _incumbent_ (that is, the individual occupying the status) is supposed to behave and how others are to behave toward the incumbent. In other words, when we know an individual's status, we have some good ideas about how he or she may act and expect to be treated.

Usually we find out about people's statuses and respond appropriately without even being conscious of what we are doing. Things get interesting, however, when we arrive at the wrong conclusion about someone else's social status—because they withheld crucial status information or provided misleading data or simply because we misread the clues. The results can be embarrassing and make clear that it is really a myth that we treat people equally in this society.

I can recall a number of occasions on which people have misguessed my status and I have found it can be embarrassing not only for me but for them! When I started driving, I was always losing the car keys. Finally my mother gave me a key ring that would attach to the belt loop on my jeans. I've had that same key ring for more than 25 years now—and I still frequently wear it attached to the belt loop on my jeans. Of course, now that I am fully adult, I have a lot more keys (one of the status clues to adulthood?). And, when I attach these to my belt loop, they make a lot of noise. Because of this, and because of my casual attire, I have on several occasions been mistaken for one of the janitors or maintenance engineers on campus by people looking for someone to fix a light fixture or unplug a toilet! (A couple of times, I have helped to change a light bulb, but I've stopped short of helping to fix toilets.)

8.1

    a. List two of your ascribed statuses.

    b. List two of your achieved statuses.

Roles

Sociologists define a *role* as *the sum total of expectations about the behavior attached to a particular social status.*

Consider my sociology class. In that social structure, my *status* is professor. My *role* is to teach—I'm expected to stand up in the front of the classroom and say things that will provoke students into thinking profound thoughts about the nature of society.[1] I am also expected to give assignments that I will evaluate and grade. These are some of the expectations that are attached to my professorial status; these are some parts of my role.

You occupy the status of student, and the behavior expectations attached to your status are different. That is, your role is different. Your role is to come to class, be properly appreciative of your teacher's sociological insights, think profound thoughts about the nature of society, and prepare and turn in assignments.

Here is an important fact about statuses and roles: They exist independently of their incumbents or occupants. Regardless of who the professor is, he or she must meet certain minimal role expectations. If you were to look for the common denominator among all professors—putting their idiosyncrasies aside—you would discover the role of the professor.

Sociologists are interested in such things because knowing an individual's statuses and understanding his or her roles reveal

---

[1]A *social structure* is made up of social statuses and roles. A *status* is a position in a social structure; a *role* is the sum total of expectations attached to a status.

a great deal about the life of that individual and how he or she is expected to behave. Sometimes living out one's statuses and playing the accompanying roles is fairly straightforward. But sociologists have identified three major problems that come up— what I call "tricky situations"—role strain, status inconsistency, and role conflict.

TRICKY SITUATION 1: ROLE STRAIN

Some statuses are accompanied by very demanding roles. Take the status of student. Expectations about how students should act—that is, the student role—can be very demanding. You may have five different professors who seem to think that their class is the only one in which you are enrolled. And they expect you not only to attend class regularly but to come to class prepared, to write papers, and to study for exams.

As if all that were not enough, any incumbent in the status of student knows that the role involves more than completing course work. It also requires "extracurricular" activities—participating in residence hall or Greek events, going to football and basketball games, and attending to a variety of other time-consuming activities. Then there is that part-time job that helps keep the student in school.

According to sociologists, when the demands of a particular role are such that the incumbent is hard-pressed to meet them all, *role strain* is likely to occur.

Many occupational statuses expose incumbents to role strain. Consider the police officer who is expected to fulfill his or her quota of traffic tickets, respond to emergencies, solve crimes, and protect the rights of suspects. At times, it must seem to the police officer that these demands are impossible!

My mother, who is not a sociologist, nonetheless had a good sense of what role strain involved. I can remember her mentioning that being a parent involved (as she put it) "wearing many hats." She not only shopped for the groceries, cooked meals, cleaned house, and washed and ironed the clothes, but also chauffeured us to music and dance lessons, was a den mother when my brothers were Cub Scouts, was my sister's Camp Fire leader, and presided over the PTA for a couple of years.

TRICKY SITUATION 2: STATUS INCONSISTENCY

It's bad enough having to cope with one particular role that is very demanding. When you realize that most of us occupy more than one status and therefore have to play more than one role, you start to imagine how tricky that can be.

The problem of status inconsistency occurs when an individual comes to occupy multiple statuses that, in combination, do not mesh with social expectations. For example, consider the case of a 50-year-old man, John Jones, who returns to college to obtain his degree. When he enrolled in school, Jones took on the status of student. The student's role is to study and to be deferential to the teachers. But Jones still retained his previous status of middle-aged man, as well as husband, father, and businessperson.

Suppose Jones has a professor who is half his age. Normally this middle-aged man expects 25-year-olds to be deferential to him. But Jones is now in a situation in which this young man (the professor) refers to him as John, and he (Jones) must address this kid as *Mr.* Smith.

Status inconsistency generally involves a situation in which a person with a particular *ascribed* status *achieves* an inconsistent status. For example, status inconsistency frequently exists when a woman (ascribed status) goes to work as a truck driver (a status traditionally achieved by men). Likewise, a man (ascribed status) who becomes a nurse (a status traditionally achieved by women) is viewed as having inconsistent statuses. So, just as with the phrase *nontraditional student* (which means students older than usual college age), when you hear the phrase *nontraditional work roles,* you can assume there is a perception of status inconsistency. The basis of this status inconsistency is the belief that the statuses that one achieves are not congruent with the statuses that others have ascribed to the individual.

There is nothing inherently contradictory about being a student and being middle-aged; nor is there anything contradictory about being a woman and a truck driver or being a man and a nurse. The inconsistency is not in the combination of statuses itself but in how people perceive particular combinations of statuses.

One very telling example of status inconsistency involved Justice Thurgood Marshall, the first African American to sit on the Supreme Court of the United States. He used to tell of one time when he was in the elevator that justices used to get to their offices. A couple of lost tourists got on the elevator and instructed Marshall to take them to a particular floor. (He did, and only later did the tourists discover that Marshall was not an elevator operator but a justice of the Supreme Court.)

TRICKY SITUATION 3: ROLE CONFLICT

Not only are some combinations of statuses perceived as inconsistent, but the actual demands of their roles can clash. Sociologists call this *role conflict.*

Consider the juvenile court judge who is also a parent. The status of judge in our society requires the incumbent to play a role in which he or she treats all defendants alike. The role of parent is different. Parents are supposed to be loyal to and love their children, and when their child gets into trouble, the parents are expected to be that child's advocate!

A serious role conflict would exist if Belinda Smith, daughter of Judge Smith, was arrested and brought into Judge Smith's court. No one would believe that Judge Smith could act as an impartial judge in such a case because of the conflict between the roles of parent and judge.

Role conflicts are not always so dramatic. Suppose you are baby-sitting some night for a 7-year-old kid. You have thus taken on the status of baby-sitter. The role expectations that accompany the status of baby-sitter are well known: watch and entertain the child and especially keep that kid out of trouble. But what if the person you are seeing calls and wants to come over to spend the evening with you. Now, the status of lover (or boyfriend or girlfriend) has its own role expectations, and these are in obvious conflict with the role demands of baby-sitting. You cannot play the roles of baby-sitter and lover at the same time. Attempting to mesh these two roles can only get you into serious trouble.

8.2 Define each of the following and give at least one example.
   a. role strain
   b. status inconsistency
   c. role conflict

Master Status

Sociologists know that most of us occupy a number of different statuses, and therefore we must play a number of different roles. But not all statuses are weighted the same in the minds of individuals (Hughes 1945).

I am a sociology professor, as is my colleague Jim. I have heard students refer to Jim as a sociology professor but refer to me as a *female* sociology professor. That is a clue to the fact that in those students' minds, my status as a woman "filters" their perception of me as a sociology professor. This suggests as well that because I am a woman professor, these students may be tempted to treat me differently than they treat Jim and they expect me to act differently than they expect Jim to act. To the degree that students see me as a woman professor, rather than simply as a professor, they are treating my gender as my *master status*. In their minds, it seems, my gender affects expectations about how I ought to and will play my role and how they ought to and will respond.

In modern society, gender is not the only master status. An individual's race or ethnicity can also be a filter through which other statuses are perceived. When you hear someone say, "He's an African American doctor," or "She's an Asian American lawyer," you can assume that racial and ethnic statuses influence people's perceptions of occupational roles.

In our society, we like to think that our achieved statuses are more important than our ascribed statuses. For this reason, when our master status is linked to a quality that is ascribed to us rather than to something that we have achieved, it can be upsetting. If I want to be taken seriously as a professor, it is annoying to be called a "professor-ette"—even if the person calling me that means no disrespect. (When I was doing research in the criminal courts of Cook County, Illinois, one of the [male] judges used to refer to any female lawyer as "little lady" but to her male counterpart as "counsel" or "Mr." As you can imagine, this mode of address really annoyed those professional women.)

Groups

A careful inspection of the list of statuses you occupy should lead you to an important sociological discovery: These statuses define who you are. Moreover, who you are (or so I predict) is frequently a result of your membership in groups: a family group, a marriage, a friendship group, some club or organization, some work group, and so on.

We do not spend our lives among random assortments of individuals. Rather, most of us live our daily lives in groups—that is, with *one or more other individuals with whom we share some sense of identity or common goals and with whom we interact within a specific social structure.* Group membership is so important to people that sociologists tend to focus almost exclusively on individuals in groups (large and small). Our assumption is that we can understand individuals' behavior only if we study individuals within the context of their own social groups.

There are, of course, many different sorts of social groups, and these vary in size and degree of intimacy among members, as well as in how open or closed they are to new members. But social groups are always something more than mere social aggregations. *A social aggregation is some collectivity of people who happen to be in the same place at the same time.* The aggregations of fans who gather at a football game or rock concert are not social groups, although the five guys who paint their faces and sit together may be a social group.

PRIMARY AND SECONDARY GROUPS

Sociologists typically distinguish between *primary* and *secondary* groups. The concept of primary group comes to us from the work of sociologist Charles H. Cooley (1864–1929). Cooley was particularly interested in how humans become *socialized*—that is, *how they are taught to be functioning members of social groups.* Cooley believed that the most important kinds of socialization took place in primary groups like the family and friendship groups. In such primary groups, said Cooley, people learn the rules of social life and cooperation.

Secondary groups are different. Your family is a primary group, but your sociology class is a secondary group. You and your best friends are a primary group, but the university is a secondary group. The distinction between primary and secondary groups is, in part, frequently a matter of the size of each group—but only because it is impossible to experience the kind of intimacy a primary group affords with large numbers of people. However, the most important difference between primary and secondary groups has to do with the kinds of relationships that exist within them. Secondary relationships, or relationships in secondary groups, tend to be means-to-an-end relationships. Other members of the secondary group view you first as a member, or a worker, or a student, and only incidentally as a person with individual needs. In a secondary group, you may be little more than a spot on the organizational chart. In other words, in a secondary group, *what is important is your status, not your personal characteristics.* Table 8.1 summarizes the key differences between primary and secondary groups.

Recalling the distinction that Tönnies made (see chapter 1), we can say that secondary groups tend to be *Gesellschaft* while primary groups tend to be *Gemeinschaft*. Here is how Cooley described the primary group. As you read his description, what sorts of groups come to mind?

> By primary groups I mean those characterized by intimate face-to-face association and cooperation. They are primary in several senses, but chiefly in that they are fundamental in forming the social nature and ideals of the individual. The result of intimate association, psychologically, is a certain fusion of individualities in a common whole, so that one's very self, for many purposes at least, is the common life and purpose of the group. Perhaps the simplest way of describing this wholeness is by saying that it is a "we"; it involves the sort of sympathy and mutual identification for which "we" is the natural expression. One lives in the feeling of the whole and finds the chief aims of his will in that feeling. (1909, 23)

Table 8.1 Primary Versus Secondary Groups

	Primary Groups	**Secondary Groups**
Examples	Family, friendship group, work group, gang	Corporation, city, university, nation, sociology class
Size	Tend to be small	Can be *very* large
Nature of Members' Attachment	Socioemotional (membership an end in and of itself); personal	Instrumental (membership often only a means to an end); impersonal
Duration	Long term	May be long term but can also be very short term
Demands on Members	Greedy; want to take in entire individual	Limited demands; only require performance of a specific role (such as worker)
Nature of Social Control	Informal	Formal
Boundaries	Relatively closed; tend to be hard to enter and exit	Relatively open; tend to be easy to enter and exit

Cooley emphasized that primary group relationships are not always "sweetness and light." In fact, he said, a great deal of competition will take place between members of a primary group:

> It is not to be supposed that the unity of the primary group is one of mere harmony and love. It is . . . usually a competitive unity, admitting of self-assertion and various appropriate passions; but these passions are socialized by sympathy, and come, or tend to come, under the discipline of a common spirit. The individual will be ambitious, but the chief object of his ambition will be some desired place in the thoughts of the others, and he will feel allegiance to common standards of service and fair play. So the boy will dispute with his fellows for a place on the team, but above such disputes will place the common glory of his class and school. (1909, 24–25)

8.3 Think of a primary group to which you belong. Which of the characteristics of primary groups (listed in table 8.1) does your primary group have?

  a. What is the name of your group (for example, "my family" or "friendship group")?
  b. How big is your group (number of members)?
  c. What is the nature of members' attachment? That is, what's your motive for staying a member of this group?
  d. How long has this group been in existence?
  e. What are the demands on individual members? That is, what sorts of things do others in your group expect of you?

STOP & REVIEW

f. What is the nature of social control? That is, if a group member gets out of line, what sorts of negative sanctions might he or she expect? Give examples.

g. What are the boundaries of the group? That is, how easy is it for a new person to join or an established member to leave this group?

FORMAL ORGANIZATIONS AND BUREAUCRACIES

The quintessential secondary group is the formal organization. Formal organizations come into being when groups of people *band together to achieve a specific goal* (for example, to make money for stockholders or to provide a specific service to the community) and *formalize their relationships with one another.* Generally, such organizations operate under some sort of charter or constitution that specifies the status positions with the organization (president, vice president, worker bee) and describes role expectations (job descriptions).

One of the most prevalent types of formal organizations is the bureaucracy. Max Weber claimed that modern life would come to be increasingly played out in bureaucracies. The bureaucracy, according to Weber, is one of the more important manifestations of the trend toward the rationalization of life.

Weber studied a number of different organizations and derived what he called the *ideal type* of bureaucracy (1920/1958). By ideal type, Weber didn't mean the *best* kind of bureaucracy but rather the *pure* form of bureaucracy. The ideal-type bureaucracy is what is left when you strip away all the parts of an organization that are not necessary to it being a bureaucracy. Real-life bureaucracies may have a lot of characteristics that are not necessary for the organization to be a bureaucracy. In the next section I have highlighted some of what Weber saw as the most important characteristics of the ideal-type bureaucracy.

IDEAL-TYPE BUREAUCRACIES

I. There is the principle of fixed and official jurisdictional areas, which are generally ordered by rules, that is, by law or administrative regulations.

People who work within a bureaucracy have specific "jurisdictional areas," or places in the division of labor. That is, areas of authority are delegated to individuals. These are the workers' "official duties." Workers must stay within their jurisdictional areas and must carry out their duties according to the rules. Thus, in the Baker Shoe Company (see figure 8.1) the vice president of sales would never try to give a command to a factory line supervisor. Moreover, individuals are expected to become experts within their own areas.

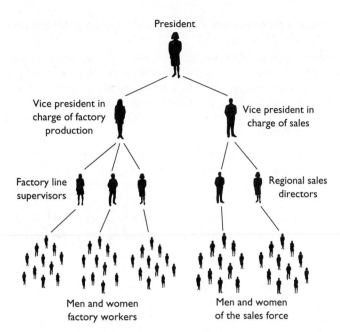

Figure 8.1 The *Baker Shoe Company*

President

Vice president in charge of factory production

Vice president in charge of sales

Factory line supervisors

Regional sales directors

Men and women factory workers

Men and women of the sales force

II. The principles of office hierarchy and of levels of graded authority mean a firmly ordered system of super- and subordination in which the lower offices are supervised by the higher ones.

Bureaucracies have strict chains of command or authority structures. Generally these are shaped like pyramids—with fewer people at the top of the bureaucracy than at the bottom. Orders or commands travel from the top of the organization to the bottom. Every worker has a known supervisor to whom he or she is responsible. Going over one's supervisor's head (to complain, or whatever) is considered inappropriate.

III. The management of the modern office is based on written documents (files), which are preserved in their original or draft form.

Every significant move the organization makes (purchases, sales, hirings, promotions, firings, and so on) is recorded in writing. Orders or commands may be given verbally, but they are officially valid only if given in writing. If a subordinate disagrees with the legitimacy of a verbal order, he or she may demand that the order be put in writing and kept on file. (The files are the organization's "memory" and help ensure continuity.)

IV. Office management usually presupposes thorough and expert training.

Hiring and promotion are based on the individual's ability to do the job (or on merit), and not on such irrelevant factors as whom the individual knows. *Nepotism* (favoring one's relatives over others) is frowned on, as is accepting bribes from job candidates. Relationships within bureaucracies are impersonal, thus ensuring equal treatment for employees as well as customers and clients.

V. Official activity demands the full working capacity of the [bureaucratic] official.

In a nonbureaucratic organization, such as a one-person shoe shop, the shoemaker will spend most of his or her time making shoes and do administrative stuff, like keeping the books, only on the side. In an ideal-type bureaucracy, however, there is a specialized division of labor (as noted in characteristic I). Administrative work is a full-time commitment.

VI. The management of the office follows general rules, which are more or less stable and more or less exhaustive, and which can be learned. Knowledge of these rules represents a special technical learning, which the officials possess.

There is an established procedure or rule covering just about every situation. Knowledge of these rules and procedures is one of the tasks of bureaucratic administrators, because having such knowledge means knowing how to do the job.

Weber thus painted the ideal-type bureaucracy as a fully rationalized organization. By *fully rationalized* I mean having an organizational structure calculated to meet organizational goals most efficiently. In a rational organization there is a specialized division of labor, people follow rules, people are arranged hierarchically, and those at the top (presumably the most qualified) give orders to those at the bottom. In a rational organization someone keeps track of what the organization is doing (by keeping files), and people are hired, fired, and promoted according to their ability to do the job.

Again, Weber was talking about the ideal-type or pure-type bureaucracy. Weber knew that in real life, bureaucracies are never so pure—that nepotism happens and that people bend the rules. But his view of the ideal-type bureaucracy gives us a standard against which to measure the degree to which a particular organization is bureaucratized.

What we find when we examine a variety of formal organizations is that some are more bureaucratic than others. And even within a particular organization, some departments may be more bureaucratic than others.

It is easier to be highly bureaucratized (for example, to follow the rule book exactly) when the environment is regular and predictable. Thus, for example, we would expect that the part of the university that is organized to bill students to be fairly bureaucratized because the work is routine and predictable.

On the other hand, academic departments, such as the department of sociology, are likely to be less bureaucratized. First, you will likely have a large number of employees with PhDs, and these folks do not take kindly to others telling them what to teach or research. In the university, faculty justify their uppity behavior by citing such values as "academic freedom." And such values tolerate only a minimum of hierarchy and interference. Moreover, the work in academic departments varies from year to year as student demand for classes ebbs and flows and as professors come and go on sabbatical or research ventures.

The impersonal nature of the bureaucracy and the reliance on following rules restricts the ability of any particular supervisor or department head to act capriciously against employees. So-called red tape, which we commonly regard as so annoying, actually helps protect employees and clients from mistreatment.

Weber was ambivalent about the fact that modern life was being taken over by bureaucracies. He saw the positive functions of bureaucracies—they were organized to achieve tasks efficiently. But he also saw that bureaucracies had dysfunctional attributes—that they could become what he called "iron cages" of modern life, in which people become so trapped in following procedures and rules that they lose sight of the reason they are working so hard. In addition, if people get bogged down by procedures, they might lose their ability to adapt to changes in social circumstances. (Bureaucracies are, in effect, the slugs of the social world.)

The sociologist Robert Merton observed as well that it is easy for people who work in bureaucracies to lose sight of their ultimate purposes. "Paperwork" exists to help to communicate orders clearly, but when finishing the paperwork becomes more important than the task itself, this can cause problems. *When the process becomes more important than the outcome,* Merton noted, organizations and individuals experience *goal displacement.* For example, when filling out patients' charts is more important to health-care professionals than actually treating the patients, that's goal displacement. When doing well on an exam becomes more important than learning the material, that's goal displacement.

Chapter Review

1. Below I have listed the major concepts discussed in this chapter. Define each of the terms. (*Hint:* This exercise will be more helpful to you if, in addition to defining each concept, you create an example of it in your own words.)

   status
   achieved versus ascribed status
   status symbol
   role

role strain
status inconsistency
role conflict
master status
group versus social aggregate
primary group
secondary group
formal organization
ideal types
bureaucracy, and "iron cage"
goal displacement

2. Sociologists distinguish between ascribed and achieved social statuses. But do these different types of statuses have different or similar origins? To what extent can we claim these for ourselves, and to what extent are they awarded or assigned by others? Select two of your ascribed statuses and two of your achieved statuses and discuss their origins.

3. At this stage of your life, what is your master status? What will be your master status in ten years? In twenty years? Describe what, if any, consequences your master status will have on how you live your life.

STOP & REVIEW

Answers and Discussion

8.1

a. Remember, ascribed statuses are those that are laid upon you; frequently they have to do with the circumstances of your birth. So, your ascribed statuses include your sex, race, and ethnicity.

b. Your achieved statuses are those that you earn through your own efforts. College student is an achieved status, as is membership in Phi Beta Kappa or the Girl Scouts.

8.2

a. Role strain exists when the demands of a specific role (that is, the behaviors attached to a specific status) are very heavy and possibly even impossible to meet. Having role strain is like trying to juggle four or five balls while people keep adding more. In the text, I used the examples of my mother (cook, clean, drive, PTA, Cub Scouts, Camp Fire Girls) and of the student role (study, work, recreate, go to class, attend football games).

b. Status inconsistency occurs when you have two or more statuses that people perceive to be at odds with one another. Several years ago, there was a television show about a brilliant 16-year-old who became a physician. He experienced status inconsistency because people found it difficult to treat a 16-year-old with the respect that a physician is accorded in our society.

c. Role conflict involves a conflict between the expectations of two or more roles (or the behaviors expected of people who hold two or more statuses). In the text, I used the example of the juvenile court judge who was also a parent. She would experience role conflict if her child were brought into court.

8.3 Your answers to this set of questions will vary depending on the primary group you choose to analyze. To illustrate, I will analyze my family as a primary group—as it was when I was in college.

a. This group included seven members: two parents and five children. (I do not include my grandparents in my primary group because they live pretty far away and we have never experienced much "intimate, face-to-face association.")

b. I am attached to this group simply because they are my family. I don't think I could escape them, even if I wanted to. (See part f.)

c. I choose to date this group from the time my oldest brother was born—in 1948.

d. They expect a lot of me. I am supposed to be a "good daughter"—which means that I show up for required family events (parental birthdays, Christmas, Thanksgiving, Fourth of July). If I can't be there, I have to have a good excuse, and I must phone. Once I got into trouble for not calling home on Labor Day—my dad didn't believe me when I later told him I didn't know that Labor Day was one of the family "biggies." If something bad happens to one of the members of the family, I am expected to return home immediately to share in the somber moments. Thus, when my father had a heart attack, I dropped out of school for a quarter and came home. Being in a primary group isn't necessarily a full-time occupation, but it is like being "on call" 24 hours a day. If you are needed, you must show up.

e. When I was younger, the negative sanctions were pretty tangible: "Because you did this, you can't watch television tonight" or "I'm taking the cost of that thing out of your allowance!" By the time I got to college, the negative sanctions were less tangible but still painful: "What do you mean you are going skiing over Christmas? *Do you want your father to have another heart attack* because he's disappointed in you?" (I hope that my mother never reads this book; otherwise, I might experience some negative sanctions for using her as a source of examples!)

f. There are very definite and rigid boundaries. No one can leave this group unless he or she dies, and no one can enter this group without being born into it or marrying into it.

STOP & REVIEW

9

SOCIETY AND SOCIAL INSTITUTIONS

Here's a story I tell students in my introductory sociology class:

> You've got about an hour before your sociology class begins and that's just enough time to pick up your scholarship check. So, you mosey on down to the administration building and wait in line in front of the comptroller's office. The line moves slowly, but finally it's your turn. The fellow working behind the counter, John Smith, tells you that your check hasn't arrived. You mutter to yourself about the inefficiency of bureaucracies as you leave the building. On your way out, you encounter Sam Johnson, the president of the university. Although you don't really know him, he waves at you and you wave back. He seems friendly enough, although you've heard many stories to the contrary. You start back through the campus to the classroom building. You pause for a moment to watch the college marching band rehearsing for Saturday's half-time show. Out of the corner of your eye you notice one of the campus parking cops is giving a ticket to a car parked illegally.
>
> As you pass the Student Union, you check your watch and find there's enough time to get something to eat before class. You enter the union and the Go-Team Café. A friend of yours, Bill Peters, makes pizza in the café, and you say hello. After taking the biggest piece of pizza you can find, you stand in line (again) to pay for it. The cashier is a woman you know from your biology class, and you chat mind- lessly with her as she gives you change from your five-dollar bill. You eat your pizza as you walk to your sociology class, gobbling the final bite as you enter the classroom. At the front of the room is Lisa McIntyre, your instructor. She's chatting with Mary Done, her teaching assistant, and several of her students about last week's quiz. One of the students, you think her name is Sylvia, seems pretty ticked off—she's speaking loudly and gesturing. You assume she's

mad about the grade she got on the quiz. Then you spot Michelle and Aaron, your best friends in the class. The three of you always sit together in the back row. You settle in for class. McIntyre starts talking about statuses and roles, and although you should be taking notes, your mind wanders as you think about calling your parents and asking them for money to tide you over until your check arrives.

Twenty-five years later: Your daughter, Elizabeth, has about an hour before her sociology class begins. That's just enough time to pick up her scholarship check, so she takes herself on down to the administration building to wait in line in front of the comptroller's office. The line moves slowly, but finally it's her turn. The fellow working behind the counter, John Williams, tells her that her check hasn't arrived. She mutters to herself about the inefficiency of bureaucracy. On the way out of the building, she encounters Lisa McIntyre, the president of the university. Although she doesn't know McIntyre, your daughter waves back when McIntyre waves to her. McIntyre seems friendly enough, but Elizabeth has heard some stories! Elizabeth starts back through campus to the classroom building, and pauses for a moment to watch the college marching band rehearsing for Saturday's half-time show. She notices that one of the campus parking cops is giving a ticket to an illegally parked car.

As Elizabeth passes the Student Union, she checks her watch and figures she's got enough time to grab something to eat before class. She walks over to the student café, chats with Maryanne, the pizza maker, and picks out the biggest piece. Her pal, Andy, is working the cash register and gives her change from her hundred-dollar bill. Elizabeth eats her pizza as she walks over to the classroom building. When she enters the room, she notices the instructor, Mary Done, chatting with her teaching assistant and some of the students. One of the students, Elizabeth thinks his name is André, is speaking loudly and gesturing. Elizabeth assumes André is probably upset with the grade he got on last week's quiz. Elizabeth spots Craig and Kyoung-Joo, her best friends in the class. They always sit together in the back of the room. As Professor Done starts talking about statuses and roles, your daughter's mind wanders as she thinks about calling you and asking for money to tide her over until her check arrives.

That night, as Elizabeth describes her day to you over her IV (interactive video), you reflect that things haven't changed much. There's a new president, new financial-aid officers, new campus cops, new cooks in the café, and new professors. But things are pretty much the same.

Amazing, isn't it? The entire population of the university has changed: new administrators and police; new faculty, staff, teaching assistants, students, new everything, *except things are pretty much the same.*

Things are pretty much the same because organizations like your college are more than just groups of people, they are social structures.

Sociologists understand that much of the enduring and repetitive nature of social life has to do with the fact that the statuses (positions in a group) and roles (the scripts that spell out the rights and duties of people in particular statuses) are enduring and repetitive. In this chapter we will examine why statuses and roles tend to be enduring and repetitive. More specifically, we will examine the nature of *social institutions*—phenomena that account for much of the fact that social structures tend to be enduring and repetitive.

Before we get to the idea of social institutions, however, we need first to consider the concept of *society*, because institutions start with society.

Society came into the English language from *socius*—the Latin word for fellowship or companion. The term *society* has a variety of uses in everyday language—sometimes people refer to the upper classes as high society; frequently, groups of people with similar interests join together as members of societies. (Spending even a minute on the Internet will demonstrate the incredible variety of these groups—National Multiple Sclerosis Society, Society for American Baseball Research, Society for Creative Anachronism, and even the International Ghost Hunters Society.)

When sociologists use the term *society*, however, generally it is to refer to *the totality of people and social relations in a given geographic space*. These days, societies tend to be coextensive with (i.e., having the same boundaries as) nation-states. Thus, for example, we speak of United States society or Canadian society. The defining characteristic of society—that is, the thing that distinguishes a society from any smaller group—is *self-sufficiency*. No group, no matter how large, qualifies as a society unless it provides the resources to answer all of its members' basic needs.

Sociologist Talcott Parsons explained the self-sufficiency criterion this way:

> Self-sufficiency by no means requires that *all* the role-involvements of members be carried on within the society. However, a society does have to provide a repertoire of [opportunities] sufficient for individuals to meet their fundamental personal exigencies [needs or requirements] at all stages of the life cycle without going outside the society, and for the society itself to meet its own exigencies. (1966, 17)

Again, what Parsons meant was that for a group to be called a society, the group's resources must be comprehensive enough to meet all the basic needs of its members (food, clothing, housing, and so forth). But Parsons suggests something else: Self-sufficiency also means that the society must have enough resources to meet its own survival needs (social control, defense, membership replacement, etc.). This requirement, Parsons notes, means that a celibate group of monks cannot be considered a society, "because it cannot recruit new members by birth without violating its fundamental norms."

Societal Needs

No matter how different their peoples and cultures, all societies (big and small) must be self-sufficient. What this means exactly bears some thinking about. What do societies need to survive? Here's a short list of societal needs:

Have a continuing supply of new members.

Socialize new members.

Deal with members' sickness and health issues.

Select members for certain jobs and tasks.

Create knowledge.

Control its members.

Defend against its enemies.

Produce and exchange goods and services.

Promote social unity and the search for higher meanings.

How does a society meet these needs? The short answer is through social institutions. In chapter 7, I defined an institution as a recognized solution to a societal problem. Here is a more detailed definition: *An institution is an accepted and persistent constellation of statuses, roles, values, and norms that respond to important societal needs.*

Consider the societal problem of membership replacement. How is that problem solved? In large part, this societal problem is solved through the institution of the family. As I illustrate in table 9.1, the family is an accepted and persistent constellation of statuses, roles, values, and norms that together respond to society's need to replace its members.

Here is an important point: The institution of the family described in table 9.1 is not the *best* type of family nor even the *normal* or average type of family in our society. But the table does represent what Max Weber would call the ideal-type family (the term *ideal type* was introduced in chapter 8). Although it may well be true that only a statistical minority of families exactly resemble the ideal-type family, the idea that families *ought* to follow the institutionalized pattern is widely accepted. Because of this, members of real-life families that depart from the ideal type may be subject to informal negative sanctions from others. For example,

Table 9.1 The Family as an Institution

Statuses	Mother, father, son, daughter.
Role expectations	Wives and husbands must be sexually faithful to one another.
	Parents protect, instruct, and nourish children. Children obey their parents, go to school, and do their chores.
Values	"All for one, and one for all." "Blood is thicker than water."
Norms	Help one another. Don't rat on family members. Parents treat children equally. Children treat parents with respect.

people who attempt to raise children without marrying will encounter both informal and formal negative sanctions (from raised eyebrows to problems with insurance companies); husbands and wives may feel a sense of shame, and children from families with single or divorced parents may be pitied as being from broken homes.

9.1 Describe the difference between a social structure and a social institution.

As shown in table 9.2, we can deduce a list of social institutions from the list of basic societal problems. Figure 9.1 shows how

Table 9.2 Basic Societal Needs and Social Institutions

Societal Needs	Social Institutions
Have a continuing supply of new members	Family
Socialize new members	Family, education, religion
Deal with members' sickness and health issues	Medicine
Select members for certain jobs and tasks	Education, labor market
Create knowledge	Science, religion
Control its members	Law enforcement, judicial system, religion
Defend against its enemies	Government, military
Produce and exchange goods and services	Economic system
Promote social unity and search for higher meanings	Education, religion, politics

Figure 9.1 *Examples of Institutional Constellations of Statuses, Roles, Values, Norms, and Related Social Structures*

Social Institution	Institutionalized Statuses	Institutionalized Roles	Institutionalized Values	Institutionalized Norms	Examples of Social Structures
Family	Grandparent, mother, father, daughter, son, other kin	Support family, do chores	"Blood is thicker than water"	Don't speak of "private" family stuff to outsiders, "leave your brother alone!"	My family, your family
Religion	Rabbi, cantor, priest, shaman, disciple, worshiper	Teach about the sacred, worship the sacred	Respect the sacred and those who represent the sacred	Attend services, follow the holy teachings, "thou shalt not ..."	Synagogues, temples, churches, prayer groups
Economy	Stockholder, employer, employee, customer, creditor, debtor	Produce goods, supervise employees, get the job done	Profit is good; the customer is always right; *caveat emptor* (let the buyer beware)	Equal pay for equal work, 40-hour work week	General Motors, Bank of America, Consumer Credit Counseling
Law	Police officer, notary, attorney, judge, citizen	Enforce the law, resolve disputes, punish lawbreakers	Innocent until proved guilty; equality before the law	Tell the truth under oath, obey the law	Law firms, courts, police departments
Politics	Citizen, voter, elected and appointed official, lobbyist	Obey the law, vote, run society, look out for constituency's needs	One person, one vote; the will of the majority prevails	Do not stuff the ballot box, do not accept bribes	Democratic party, Republican party, political action committees
Science	Scientist, researcher, administrator, journal editor	Seek and publish knowledge	Do objective and unbiased research, disseminate findings	Do not steal others' ideas, do not "fudge" your data	Universities and colleges, American Sociological Association, scientific journals

different statuses, roles, values, norms, and related social structures make up some of the basic institutions of society.

9.2 Using figure 9.1 as a guide, complete the following chart to describe some of the statuses, roles, values, and norms that are involved in the social institutions of the military, education, and health care. Then indicate some social structures (e.g., groups or organizations) that bring each of these institutions to life.

Social Institution	Institutionalized Statuses	Institutionalized Roles	Institutionalized Values	Institutionalized Norms	Examples of Social Structures
Military					
Education					
Health care					

The Nature of Social Institutions

In addition to the fact that they respond to societal needs, institutions have other attributes in common:

1. Institutions are generally unplanned; they develop gradually.

2. Institutions are inherently conservative; they change, but slowly.

3. A particular society's institutions are interdependent; because of this, change in one institution tends to bring about change in others.

4. The statuses, roles, values, and norms associated with an institution in one society frequently bear little resemblance to those in another society.

Let's take a closer look at each of these attributes.

INSTITUTIONS ARE GENERALLY UNPLANNED; THEY DEVELOP GRADUALLY

How do institutions come into being? The short answer is this: Faced with a particular problem, people try a variety of things to solve their needs. Some of these work better than others. The "best" way becomes a pattern for subsequent generations to follow.

I use the term *best* not to suggest the most efficient or even the most effective way. Institutions are constellations of statuses, roles, values, and norms. So, how a society solves its problems must fit with its existing social values and norms. For example, social control is a problem that all societies must solve. Perhaps the most effective and efficient method of social control would be to just execute everyone who violated a norm. But we don't do this because it goes against our values.

How Institutions Begin: A Hypothetical Example

A woman and a man are stranded on opposite ends of the same desert island. Finally, they happen to meet. Realizing that their chances of survival would be enhanced if they joined forces, they unite to form a group. As the days pass, they fall into a number of routines for everyday activities. Perhaps the man begins his day by chopping wood, and the woman makes the fire. Then the man spends the bulk of his mornings cooking and weaving grasses into useful domestic items, while the woman (who has a restless nature) explores the island and checks the tide pools for fish and other edibles. These routines quickly become habits and, in time, each morning begins as the one before without any great deliberation on the part of either the woman or the man. Occasional disruptions occur in their routines—one morning the man burns his fingers as he cooks the fish, so rather than weaving that day, he joins the woman on her inspection of the tide pools. But as soon as he heals, he returns to his usual routine.

Over time, then, the behavior of these two people has become *habitualized*. This habitualization would come as no surprise to a sociological observer. In their analysis of human interaction, sociologists Peter Berger and Thomas Luckmann explained the transformation of behavior into routine this way:

All human activity is subject to habitualization. Any action that is repeated frequently becomes cast into a pattern, which can then be reproduced with an economy of effort and which, *ipso facto*,[1] is . . . [seen] by its performer *as* that pattern. Habitualization further implies that the action in question may be performed again in the future in the same manner and with the same economical effort. This is true of non-social as well as social activity. Even the solitary individual on the proverbial desert island habitualizes his activity. When he wakes up in the morning and resumes his attempts to construct a canoe out of match sticks, he may mumble to himself, "There I go again," as he starts on step one of an operating procedure consisting of, say, ten steps. In other words, even solitary man has at least the company of his operating procedures. (1967, 53)

Berger and Luckmann explained that following routines provides benefits to people: Routines free up mental space for thinking about more important things. (For example, each time I sit down to eat a bowl of Jell-O, the fact that I need not think anew about

---

[1]*Ipso facto* is a Latin phrase meaning "by that very fact."

how to eat the stuff allows me time to ponder the lecture I'm going to give after lunch.)

Not all routines are institutions. Routine behavior is the way we do it, but institutionalized behavior is *the way it must be done.*

Why this is so is complicated but important: Our original islanders developed a routine that dictated that the man chops the wood and the woman builds the fire, that the man weaves and the woman fishes. They taught these routines to their children, and their children will teach them to their children. Initially, these routines need no explanation—the routines have been established, and following a routine makes life easier. The first generation of children and grandchildren knew how these routines came about (that the first woman was the restless sort and needed to walk around the island every day, while the man liked the intricacy of weaving). But among later generations, there may well be a child who asks "why must we do things this way?" His or her parents, who long ago accepted and became comfortable with the established routines (finding them effective, safe, and easy), may sense that the child needs to hear more than just "because that's the way we do things." Because the parents are invested in keeping disruption to a minimum and want the child to accept their routines, they are likely to answer in terms of the *logic* of doing things a particular way as well as the *rightness* of it.

Anthropologist Mary Douglas explained that institutions survive only if their rightness can be explained as both reasonable/logical and natural (1986, 53). Children's questions about why women fish and men weave, then, are not likely to be responded to with explanations about their great-great-great-grandparents' preferences. Indeed, the original reason for the routine may have been forgotten by then. Instead, children will be told that (1) it is reasonable to have a division of labor between men and women, and (2) the way labor is divided has to do with the fact that women, as child-bearers, have a God-given talent for dealing with nature (including fire), whereas men do not.

STOP & REVIEW

9.3 Describe the difference between behavior that is habitualized and behavior that is institutionalized.

INSTITUTIONS ARE INHERENTLY CONSERVATIVE; THEY CHANGE, BUT SLOWLY

The fact that institutions are legitimized by both logic and appeals to the nature of things makes them difficult to change, because any attempt at change seems to be an attack on nature as well as logic.

Consider the institution of the family in our own society. In recent times this institution has faced many challenges— gays and lesbians, for example, have called on the legal system to grant them many of the rights that until now have been accorded only to heterosexual partners. The obstacles faced by same-sex partners who wish to marry are great because their adversaries will call on both reason and nature to justify their opposition.

People who oppose same-sex marriage claim that it is not reasonable (logical) to grant legal rights to same-sex partnerships because such unions are not recognized as valid by law. Marriages exist to facilitate the reproduction of members (children), and it takes a man and a woman to produce children. In case that logic is not persuasive (as it might not be to someone who points out that many gay men and lesbian women are parents and that many heterosexual couples choose not to have children), opponents respond by appealing to the belief that such homosexual unions are immoral by their very nature either because they are against God's law or because they are contrary to nature.

Not surprisingly, then, when the issue of same-sex marriage first came before the courts in Minnesota (in 1971), that state's supreme court ruled that the law prohibiting same-sex marriage is based in both legal statutes and, or so the court implied, God's will:

> [The Minnesota statute] which governs "marriage" employs that term as one of the common usage, meaning the state of union between persons of the opposite sex. It is unrealistic to think that the original draftsmen of our marriage statutes, which date from territorial days, would have used the term in any different sense. The term has contemporary significance as well, for the present statute is replete with words of heterosexual import as "husband and wife" and "bride and groom." We hold, therefore, that [the Minnesota statute] does not authorize marriage between persons of the same sex and that such marriages are accordingly prohibited. . . .
>
> The institution of marriage as a union of man and woman, uniquely involving the procreation and rearing of children within a family, is as old as the book of Genesis. . . . This historic institution manifestly is more deeply founded than the asserted contemporary concept of marriage and societal interests for which petitioners [the two men who sued to get the state to allow them to marry] contend. . . .
>
> Petitioners note that the state does not impose upon heterosexual married couples a condition that they have a proved capacity or declared willingness to procreate, posing a rhetorical demand that this court must read such conditions into the statute if same-sex marriages are to be prohibited. . . . We are reminded that "abstract

symmetry" is not demanded by [the Constitution]. (Baker v. Nelson 291 Minn. 310, 191 N.W. 2d 185 [1971]).

Recent research suggests that "same-sex couples constitute 1 percent of coupled households and 0.6 percent of all households in the United States." Twenty percent of same-sex couples are raising children under the age of 18. Nearly one in ten (9.7 percent) of people involved in same-sex marriages are military veterans (Romero, et al. 2007).

Two decades after the Minnesota Supreme Court attempted to lay to rest the issue of same-sex marriage, it came up again. In 1991, three same-sex couples in Hawaii sued the state department of licensing, which had denied them the right to marry their same-sex partners. The trial court dismissed their case because, according to the judge, homosexual marriage was not a fundamental right under the state constitution. The couples appealed that decision to the Hawaii Supreme Court, which ruled that the denial of marriage licenses was unconstitutional unless that state could justify the ban. In 1996, the case was back before a trial court, and that court ruled that the ban on same-sex marriage was unconstitutional. The voters of the state responded by passing an amendment to their constitution prohibiting same-sex marriage.

The possibility that same-sex marriages might be legalized sent shock waves through the United States. By law and custom, marriages granted in one state had been given "full faith and credit" in other states. Before the Hawaii court ruled, the Defense of Marriage Act (DOMA) was introduced into and subsequently passed in the U.S. Congress: For purposes of federal law, the DOMA stipulated, marriage was defined as the union of a man and a woman. The act also said that same-sex marriages contracted in one state need not be recognized by other states.

The controversy, of course, continues. As of this writing, only ten U.S. states recognize same-sex marriage or civil unions which extend the same rights and duties to gay couples as to other married couples. (The District of Columbia does not recognize the validity of same-sex marriages performed in the District, but it does recognize same-sex marriages legally performed elsewhere.) In each case, the steps toward changing the legal definition of family have met with spirited opposition. After Massachusetts legalized same-sex marriage in 2004, for example, James Dobson, psychologist and founder of Focus on the Family, a nonprofit organization, claimed that Massachusetts was granting "death certificates for the institution of marriage" (Badgett 2004).

On the other hand, in the past fifteen years, Canada, Mexico, and South Africa, as well as eighteen European countries, have come to recognize the validity of same-sex marriages.

Given the "globalization" of the social world, some proponents of same-sex marriage are suggesting that the changes in other countries' laws may have an impact on the institution of marriage and family in the United States.

How this trend will play out in countries that have not yet recognized same-sex relationships is still up in the air. Will the United States, for instance, accommodate a major corporation's desire to have one of its top executives from Canada move here with her legal spouse? Or a domestic-partnered diplomat from New Zealand? Or an American lucky enough to find the man of his dreams while working in South Africa? Will Sir Elton John's highly publicized civil union with long-time partner David Furnish be recognized by a hospital emergency room in Las Vegas or St. Louis or Salt Lake City should one of them fall ill on a concert tour? (Ettelbrick 2006)

A PARTICULAR SOCIETY'S INSTITUTIONS ARE INTERDEPENDENT; BECAUSE OF THIS, CHANGE IN ONE INSTITUTION TENDS TO BRING ABOUT CHANGE IN OTHERS

Although institutions are inherently conservative, change does occur. Technological and economic changes, or even wars, for example, can require people to disrupt their routines and ulti-mately can cause institutional change. Once it was conventional wisdom that women—at least middle-class white women—should stay in the home and care for the children and household. In 1900, only about 5 percent of married women worked outside of the home. As a result of World War II, things started to change. Millions of men enlisted (or were drafted) into the military ser-vice, and this left U.S. factories literally unmanned just when they were gearing up to provide the goods that the country needed to wage war. Women stepped in to take men's places. When men returned to civilian life after the war, women were forced to leave the well-paying factory jobs. But the wartime experience proved that women could work outside of the home and that society would not collapse as a result. So, in the 1950s women began to respond to the needs of an expanding economy for more workers by taking jobs.

Today the evidence suggests that most married couples find it nearly impossible to survive financially unless both wife and husband work outside of the home. Indeed today, fewer than one quarter of families in the United States follow the model of the male being the only earner. This has led to changes in the kinds of child-care arrangements that parents must make, a (slight) increase in the amount of work that married men do around the home, increased pressure (including legal pressure) on employ-ers to open occupations to women that were traditionally filled by men, and pressure on the educational system to provide after-school programs for students. In addition, women's increased participation in the labor force has led to many legal changes—equal opportunity laws and laws prohibiting sexual harassment in the workplace.

9.4 Suppose that our economy became almost totally reliant on computers, nearly all goods and services were manufactured by robots, and most people did their jobs from home. Over time, what impact on other social institutions might these changes in the institution of the economy have on other social institutions—for example, on the institutions of education, family, or even religion?

THE STATUSES, ROLES, VALUES, AND NORMS ASSOCIATED WITH AN INSTITUTION IN ONE SOCIETY FREQUENTLY BEAR LITTLE RESEMBLANCE TO THOSE IN ANOTHER SOCIETY

All societies have similar needs, but the ways in which they institutionalize their responses to these needs can vary a great deal. For example, the institutional response to the need to distribute political authority (i.e., government) may be organized as a *monarchy* (rule by king or queen), *aristocracy* (rule by the best few), *tyranny* (rule by an absolute or oppressive leader), *theocracy* (rule by God or God's representatives), or *representative democracy* (rule by representatives of the people).

Likewise, a society's response to the search for higher meaning or understanding of the sacred takes a variety of institutionalized forms: the idea that a life force exists in all living beings and that people ought to live in harmony with the rest of the natural world—*animism* (as practiced by some American Indian tribes); or the belief in a single supernatural sacred being—*monotheism* (as in Judaism, Christianity, and Islam); or the belief in many gods—*polytheism* (as in the Hindu religion).

In most of Western society, a family begins with *monogamous* marriage—that is, a marriage in which there is one wife and one husband.[2] In other societies some form of *polygamous* marriage serves as the foundation of family life: either *polygyny* (several wives with one husband) or, much less frequently, *polyandry* (one wife, several husbands). And it is not just the forms of marriage that may differ; the values and norms that are the foundations of those forms can vary as well. In our society, people believe that the normal progression is to fall in love and then marry. In other societies, things proceed in the opposite direction. For example, in India most marriages are arranged by the parents of the bride and groom. Love is expected to be a result of marriage (Sprecher and Chandak 1992).

---

[2]It is frequently observed that in the United States, the institution of serial monogamy is practiced—that is, a monogamous marriage, followed by divorce, followed by another monogamous marriage, and so on.

Polygamy and Monogamy

In the 1950s, anthropologist George Murdock (1897–1985) examined 554 societies and found that most societies allowed polygamous marriages. Here are his results:

415 polygyny

135 monogamy

4 polyandry

Even where polygamous marriages are permitted, *in practice monogamy prevails* because having multiple spouses tends to be more costly than having a single spouse. Morever, in most societies it seems that the ratio of women to men is such that there aren't enough members of either sex available for many people to have multiple partners. (1957, 59, 664–697)

Social Change: The Trend Toward Increasing Specialization

Sociologists have found that as a society grows in size and complexity, its institutions tend to become more specialized. One illustration of this tendency is the fact that, in Western society, the role of the family used to be much broader than it is today. Prior to industrialization, the family had responsibility not only for nurturing children but also for seeing to both their secular (nonreligious) and nonsecular (religious) training. Moreover, the family was the basic economic unit in society; people in families worked together in their farms, shops, or trades.

Similarly, the Church's role has become much more specialized in the West. A few hundred years ago, the leaders of the Catholic Church in Europe, for example, had control of such things as taxation and legal disputes. The Church even had its own armies and courts of law.

It's important to understand the idea of institutions—the statuses, roles, values, and norms that are organized responses to important societal needs. Understanding institutions is important because much of what people do—how they fall in love, make transactions in the marketplace, respond to lawbreakers, and even how they worship—is in large part in response to institutions.

Institutions are established and accepted routines; their existence means that members of each generation need not continually find new solutions to society's needs; but by that very fact institutions also limit people's choices.

Chapter Review

1. Below I have listed the major concepts discussed in this chapter. Define each of the terms. (*Hint:* This exercise will be more helpful to you if, in addition to defining each concept, you create an example of it in your own words.)

   society (defined)
       self-sufficiency (as defining attribute of society)
   social institution
   ideal type
   habitualized action
   attributes of social institutions
   mentioned in passing:
       aristocracy
       monarchy
       tyranny
       theocracy
       representative democracy
       animism
       monotheism
       polytheism
       polygyny
       monogamy
       polyandry
       serial monogamy

2. At the beginning of this chapter, I asserted that the values on which particular institutions are based must fit with the values of the larger society. Test this assertion: Look back to chapter 7 to the box titled "What Do Americans Value?" Then pick two social institutions described in this chapter. How good is the fit between the values of that institution and the values of the larger society?

3. Sociologists have found that as societies grow in size and complexity, institutions become more specialized. That same growth in size and complexity may give rise to new institutions. Some sociologists have argued that one of the new institutions in society is the media. Do you agree that the media qualify as an institution? Explain why or why not. (*Hint:* Remember that for something to qualify as a social institution, it must *respond to a basic societal need,* have *institutionalized statuses, roles, values, and norms,* and *manifest itself in some sort of social structure.*)

STOP
&
REVIEW

Answers and Discussion

9.1 A social structure always exists as some form of group—a particular family, business, platoon, or even society. An institution is a set of ideas or beliefs about how social structures ought to be organized. Thus, *my* family is a social structure, but *the* family as an institution is made up of ideas about how the statuses, roles, values, and norms of specific families ought to be organized.

STOP
&
REVIEW

9.2

Social Institution	Institutionalized Statuses	Institutionalized Roles	Institutionalized Values	Institutionalized Norms	Examples of Social Structures
Military	Commander in chief, general, sergeant, private	Give and obey orders, kill the enemy	Duty, honor, country	Obey orders!	Army, navy, marines, air force
Education	School board member, principal, teacher, professor, student	Administrate, teach, learn	All children should be treated equally, learning is a lifelong process, academic integrity	Prepare for class, do homework, have school spirit	Preschool, elementary school, high school, university
Health care	Physician, nurse, medical researcher, patient	"First, do no harm," cure patients, discover new medicines	Give best medical care possible regardless of patient's status	Be careful, follow physician's advice, pay medical bills	Clinics, hospitals, drug stores, American Medical Association

9.3 Habitualized behavior includes any routine that you follow because that's the way you like to do things—that is, it's your personal preference. For example, it's my routine to put on both socks before I put on either shoe; other people routinely put on one sock and then one shoe, then the other sock and shoe. Institutionalized behaviors are also routines, but institutionalized routines are ones that we believe we *ought* to follow. For example, I routinely prepare my lectures before class because I believe I ought to carry out my role of professor competently.

9.4 How you answer this depends on how good an imagination you have. One thing I am sure of, however, is that such a radical change in a single institution would bring about changes in others. For example, people might begin to accept "virtual interaction"—not just in the economic arena but in a variety of situations. Virtual education and perhaps even virtual religion might become commonplace. But if all this virtual interaction did become commonplace, and if people worked, learned, and even worshiped from home—it would undoubtedly have an effect on how parents and their children interact as a family. People might come to value their privacy more than ever and build more "walls" around themselves at home. Thus, ironically, doing everything at home might lead to members of the same family spending even less quality time together. On the other hand, spending so much time at home might drive people out of their homes during their free time and result in a refocusing on community life.

10

SOCIALIZATION

A never-ending problem for every society is that people die. If a society is to survive, it must constantly replenish its membership rolls. Fortunately, humans seem to have a built-in proclivity for reproducing themselves. But the simple biological production of new members does not entirely resolve a society's problem. The society must have new members who are capable of functioning effectively within existing social structures. In other words, a society needs people who can fill positions within the social structure (statuses) and carry out the behaviors expected (roles) of status incumbents.

Sociologists refer to the process by which society molds its members into properly social beings as *socialization*. More specifically, *socialization is the process by which people acquire cultural competency and through which society perpetuates the fundamental nature of existing social structures.* Although the socialization process is most intense for young people, it is a lifelong process.

Nature and Nurture: Biological and Social Processes

To say that infants are not yet social beings is not to say that they are not human. Of course, babies are human. And, of course, heredity plays a definite role in who a baby grows up to be. The color of the skin, eyes, and hair; the adult height and weight; perhaps even the sexual orientation as an adult—all depend primarily on the baby's genetic and biological nature.

But the personal attributes that sociologists deem most important in an adult—that is, *the social self, or the values, beliefs, ideas, and decision-making strategies, and the general way in which people live their lives*—are best explained by social rather than biological factors.

The importance of social factors in the development of humans is illustrated by stories of children raised outside a real social environment. "Anna" was a child born out of wedlock, the second such child to be born to her mother. Anna spent the first six years of her life locked in an attic-like second-floor room because her mother did not wish to incur her father's wrath by bringing Anna downstairs. Though she was fed, she was not otherwise nurtured—never really cuddled or talked to. When Anna was rescued at the age of 6, she could not do any of the things we expect of 6-year-old children: She "could not talk, walk, or do anything that showed intelligence" (Davis 1940, 119). Anna died about four years later. During her four years in the social world, she had progressed only to the level of a 2½-year-old child.

"Isabelle" fared better. Like Anna, Isabelle was born to an unmarried mother and was kept in seclusion, away from most human interaction. When she was rescued at the age of 6½, she responded to people as a wild animal might. But within a couple of years, Isabelle had managed to catch up with members of her age group (Davis 1940). Why did Isabelle make more progress than Anna? One answer might be that Isabelle had better teachers. But there was another difference: Isabelle had never been cut off from human contact to the same degree that Anna had been. Isabelle was nurtured by her mother, and this early socialization seems to have made a difference—even though Isabelle's mother was a deaf-mute who communicated with Isabelle with gestures.[1]

It might be suggested that the real cause of Isabelle's and Anna's deficiencies was not a lack of social contact but rather physical factors such as malnutrition. Certainly, Isabelle suffered the effects of a poor diet when she was found to have a severe case of rickets.[2]

But other research suggests that taking good care of an infant's *physical needs* is not enough to produce a healthy child.

---

[1] A more recent case of a child raised in extreme isolation (that of "Genie") is discussed in a book by Susan Curtiss (1997).

[2] Rickets is a children's disease caused by a lack of vitamin D and, especially, inadequate exposure to sunlight. Rickets is common in the tropics, due to the swaddling of infants and the confinement of women and children to the home. It causes dysplasia (an abnormal development) of the growing child's bones and can result in spinal deformity and distortion of the skull. In extreme cases, the child may grow up to be knock-kneed or bowlegged. The term *rickets*, or *rhachitis* (a synonym), comes from a Greek word meaning "disease of the spine." In adults, the same condition is called *osteomalacia* (Greek, *osteo* [bones] plus *malacia* [softness]) (Berkow 1987, 925).

Psychologist Rene Spitz (1945) compared the progress of infants in two different settings. The first was a nursery that had been established for babies born to women in a prison; the second was a "foundling" home (orphanage). The children in both settings were clean, well fed, and attended to by health-care professionals. The only real difference between the two environments was the amount of social interaction experienced by the children. In the prison nursery the infants were cared for mostly by their own mothers. In the foundling home six nurses cared for about forty-five infants. The outcome was that the children in the foundling home did not do nearly as well. Here's part of Spitz's report:

> In the ward of the children ranging from 18 months to 2½ years, only two of the 26 children could speak a couple of words. The same two are able to walk. A third child is beginning to walk. Hardly any of them can eat alone. Cleanliness habits have not been acquired and all are incontinent [not toilet trained].

Spitz and his colleagues found a group of younger children (8 to 12 months) in the prison nursery to be an amazing contrast:

> The problem here is not whether the children walk or talk by the end of the first year; the problem with these 10-month-olds is how to tame the healthy toddlers' curiosity and enterprise. They climb up the bars of the cots after the manner of South Sea Islanders climbing palms. . . . They vocalize freely and some of them actually speak a word or two. All of them understand the significance of simple social gestures. When released from their cots, all walk with support and a number walk without it. (60)

Sociologists thus believe that without social interaction, humans find it difficult to survive. Without social interaction, humans cannot develop a *social self,* that *relatively organized complex of attitudes, beliefs, values, and behaviors associated with an individual.*

According to one of his biographers, "Cooley's life was extremely uneventful. He shunned controversy and contention; any sort of conflict upset him and cost him sleep" (Coser 1971).

How Socialization Works

How does society socialize its members? How do people acquire cultural competency? As far as sociologists are concerned, socialization does not simply happen to people; socialization is a dynamic process of give-and-take between people and others in their environment. To say that socialization is a dynamic process means that people do not receive their social selves passively. Rather, individuals help to create their selves in the socialization process.

THE LOOKING-GLASS SELF: CHARLES HORTON COOLEY

Sociologist Charles Horton Cooley (1864–1929) gave us a great deal of insight into the socialization process. Cooley emphasized that the social self arises through interaction with others. According to Cooley, based on our perception of how others see us, we develop our reflected or *looking-glass selves*. (A looking glass is a mirror.) He explained the dynamic of self-creation this way:

> As we see our face, figure, and dress in the glass [the mirror] and are interested in them because they are ours, and pleased or otherwise with them according as they do or do not answer to what we should like them to be, so in imagination we perceive in another's mind some thought of our appearance, manner, aims, deeds, character, friends, and so on, and are variously affected by it. (1902, 152)

Cooley's idea of the social self had three principal elements. First, we imagine how we look to the other person; second, we imagine that other person's reaction to our appearance; third, we have some self-feeling such as pride or shame.

Suppose it's the first day of class. I walk up to the front of the room and begin to talk. I look at my students; I imagine how I must look to them; I imagine the result of their appraisal of me—and I feel good or bad about myself, depending on what I think they think of me.

Suppose I trip as I walk into the room. Here's what's going on in my mind: "They saw me trip; they must think I am a total clod"; I am embarrassed. But suppose, as is more typical, I enter the room gracefully and spend the class period making some brilliant observations about the nature of society and the importance of sociology. I look at my students and think, "They think I am brilliant and fascinating"; I am proud.

Cooley argued that the social self is constructed as a result of this reflective process. According to Cooley, we learn to use this looking glass, and thus learn who our selves are, in the intimacy of primary groups—especially the family. Recall (from chapter 8) what Cooley said about these groups. Primary groups are

> characterized by intimate face-to-face association and cooperation. They are primary in several senses but chiefly in that they are fundamental in forming the social nature and ideals of individuals. The result of intimate association, psychologically, is a certain fusion of individualities in a common whole, so that one's very self, for many purposes at least, is the common life and purpose of the group. Perhaps the simplest way of describing this wholeness is by saying that it is a "we." (1909, 117)

Cooley believed that primary groups—family, friends, play groups, work groups—were especially potent agents of socialization. It is in the primary group, he pointed out, that we learn to read what other people are thinking and to discover what happens when we adjust our behavior according to what they are thinking. Cooley recalls observing his own daughter as she developed her ability to use the looking-glass self:

Cooley said that society is made up of people's "imaginations" about one another: "Society is an interweaving and interworking of mental selves." People must not only imagine what goes on in the minds of others but take this into account in their own behavior. This is not to say that Cooley believed that people must conform to what others think. But, said Cooley, people must take into account and acknowledge what other people think of them.

Here's one of my favorite quotations from Cooley. (My guess is that you will find the quote easier to understand if you read it aloud to yourself.)

"I imagine your mind, and especially what your mind thinks about my mind, and what your mind thinks about what my mind thinks about your mind. I dress my mind before yours and expect that you will dress yours before mine. Whoever cannot or will not perform these feats is not properly in the game." (1902)

In the case of M. I noticed as early as the fourth month a "hurt" way of crying which seemed to indicate a sense of personal slight. It was quite different from the cry of pain or that of anger, but seemed about the same as the cry of fright. The slightest tone of reproof would produce it. On the other hand, if people took notice and laughed and encouraged, she was hilarious. At about fifteen months old she had become "a perfect little actress," seeming to live largely in imagination of her effect upon other people. She constantly and obviously laid traps for attention, and looked abashed or wept at any signs of disapproval or indifference. At times it would seem as if she could not get over these repulses, but would cry long in a grieved way, refusing to be comforted. If she hit upon any little trick that made people laugh she would be sure to repeat it, laughing loudly and affectedly in imitation [of others' laughter]. She had quite a repertory of these small performances, which she would display to a sympathetic audience, or even try upon strangers. I have seen her at sixteen months, when [older brother] R. refused to give her the scissors, sit down and make believe cry, putting up her under lip and snuffling, meanwhile looking up now and then to see what effect she was producing. (1902)

Children have strong motives to learn to use the looking-glass technique well—because it assists them in the competition for affection from other members of the primary group. As children age and interact with more and more persons, the self begins to grow as a result of these interactions. To Cooley, the child or person who lives in isolation from others is not fully human. Only with social experience, he argued, do people become truly human: "In these [primary groups] human nature comes into existence. Man does not have it at birth; he cannot acquire it except through fellowship, and it decays in isolation" (Cooley).

THE "I" AND THE "ME": GEORGE HERBERT MEAD

Sociologist George Herbert Mead's (1863–1931) conception of the socialization process was similar to Cooley's but worked out in more detail. Mead said that the self actually involves two phases: the "Me" and the "I." The Me is that part of the self that is based on how one sees others as seeing oneself. The Me is what you see when you put yourself into the shoes of another and look back at yourself. (This is a tad complicated, so bear with me!) The I is the part of you that is uniquely you—your personal reactions to the situation.

The social self is a product of the ongoing interaction between the Me and the I. Consider the following interaction:

1. I am in class. Some students in the back row are making a lot of noise. (This strikes at the Me, which should be obeyed because I am the professor!)

2. I want to yell at them! (That's the I's reaction to being "dissed.")

3. But, I think, how will that make Me look? (The Me thinks about how a particular behavior will be perceived by onlookers.)

4. I am not going to yell at the noisy students because it will seem as if I am out of control.

According to Mead, this sort of dialog between the Me and the I is ongoing. The Me sees myself as an object, as others see me; the I is my response to my perception of how I think others see me in this situation.

Thus, my self is built up through the interaction of my I and my Me—the interaction between my own impulses (the I) and my understanding of other people's reactions to those impulses (the Me).

Here's another example:

1. A test is coming up in sociology class. Student X wants to do well because that's what is expected. (The wanting to do well is the Me's response.)

2. The student decides he would likely do well if he cheats. (That's the I, the impulsive response to the demands of the Me to get an A.)

3. The student says to himself, "But if I cheat, how would that make me look?" (The Me reacts with disgust.)

4. The student says to himself, "I will study and get an A. Then I will feel good about myself."

After graduating from Oberlin College, George Herbert Mead tried his hand as a grade school teacher—he lasted about four months before being fired. He was more successful with older students; Mead taught at the University of Chicago for more than 35 years.

Children are not born with the I and the Me. According to Mead, these must be developed. Early on, children develop these parts of their selves and the ability to use them through play and games.

For Mead, play was an essential part of human development. By *play* he meant *simple imitative behaviors.* The child plays at being a police officer or astronaut by pretending to take on the role of police officer or astronaut. Often the child will take on a variety

---

From: Stephanie Y.
Date: Tue Nov 7 2006 10:45 PM US/Pacific
To: Lisa J. McIntyre
Subject: Mead's I and Me

The I and Me concepts are very confusing. Is it that the I is who we are, and the Me is how others perceive us? The whole thing is very difficult to grasp for me and everyone in my soc class is confused.

From: Lisa J. McIntyre
Date: Wed Nov 8 2006 7:53 PM US/Pacific
To: Stephanie Y.
Subject: Mead's I and Me

Stephanie: I am sorry you are having trouble with the I and Me thing. Try this explanation: Mead would say that you have both an I and a Me. The I is your impulse about what to do in a particular situation; the Me represents your interpretation of what other people will think of you if you follow your impulse (i.e., if you do what the I tells you to do).

I:	I want to eat that entire box of donuts!
Me:	But that will make people think me a selfish pig.
I:	Okay, I will eat six donuts.
Me:	That will still make me look piggish.
I:	Okay, I will have one donut now and then, when no one is looking, I will eat the rest of the box.
Me:	Good, then people will think me a reasonable eater. Just don't let anyone see me eat the rest of the box.

So, the I is impulsive—it articulates what you really desire. But notice, too, that the I can learn from the Me. The Me explains to the I how it will look if the I has its way. Generally, the I listens to the Me and you end up modifying your behavior accordingly. So, the Me is not other people's expectations or opinions, but how you interpret those. The Me learns what to expect by having social interactions with others. This is why Mead concluded that one's behavior is the result of an on-going conversation between the I and the Me.
   I hope this helps!

of roles in the same play period—both police officer and criminal, both doctor and patient. As they play, children (1) *begin to appreciate the perspectives of other people* and (2) *build up a sense of themselves as something that other people look at and make judgments about.*

> I have this vivid memory of playing "church" with my siblings. On the mantle in the living room was this enameled goblet. We would take Necco wafers, a flat candy, and put them in the goblet. Then I would stand in front of the altar/fireplace and distribute these wafers to my brothers and sisters. In other words, I would assume the role of priest and they would assume the role of churchgoers. (Of course, unless they knelt in front of me, I would not give them a piece of candy!)

Play is an important phase in children's development—it is their first exposure to taking on the roles of others and seeing themselves as others might see them. In other words, play is a first step to constructing a Me. In playing the priest and administering communion to my siblings, I got a chance to imagine how a priest would see me when I went for communion.

In play, there are no official rules about how to carry out the activity; the child makes it up as he or she goes along. On one occasion, a child might use her toy truck to build roads in a pile of dirt, on another occasion, she might use her truck to smash bugs. How play is done is limited only by the child's (or the children's) imagination.

Games are different. Games have rules and specific roles (batter, pitcher, catcher, outfielder); the rules specify how the person in each role participates. In Mead's view, the roles and the rules in games are "impersonal"—they apply no matter who occupies the role.

To successfully participate in a game, one must not only know what is expected but must have the discipline to take that into account. Thus, a child who competes as part of a baseball team always has a specific role and must be mature enough to play by the rules.

Participating in games enhances children's ability to do *role-taking*—that is, *to take on the role of another and see how things look from his or her point of view.* As the child begins more and more to be able to take on the point of view of others, we say that he or she has acquired a *generalized other.* As Mead described it, "The attitude of the generalized other is the attitude of the whole community." Thus, for example, in the case of such a social group as a ball team, the team is the generalized other insofar as it enters "as an organized process on social activity, into the experience of any one of the members" (1934).

Sociologists today also see the social self as a constantly evolving thing. Socialization is not something that simply happens to children; it is a lifelong process. The self is not taken in passively. Rather, as Mead suggested with his description of the self as an interaction between the I and the Me, the self is a dynamic process.

More specifically, the self evolves continually as it interacts with a variety of *agents of socialization,* including the family, schools, peers, and the workplace.

FAMILY

The family is such a crucial agent of socialization in large part because it gets first crack at the job. In our society, until they go to school, most children are wholly dependent on their families. In this family setting, children acquire some competency in non-material culture—ways to communicate, a sense of right and wrong, basic beliefs about the nature of the world—as well as competency in the use of material culture—tying shoelaces and buttoning shirts; using forks, tissues, and telephones.

In introducing this topic, I noted that socialization is not only the process by which individuals acquire cultural competency but also the process by which society perpetuates its existing social structure. Again, the family as an agent of socialization plays an important role in reproducing existing social arrangements. At a most basic level, the family is the main source of individuals' *ascribed statuses.* (The concept of ascribed statuses was introduced in chapter 8. If you cannot remember what this concept means, now would be a good time to review the first page of that chapter.)

As I show in table 10.1, depending on their social statuses (that is, their places in the social structure of society), parents tend to expect different things of their children as they work to prepare them for adulthood. The higher the parents' social status, the more they expect behaviors of their children that would prepare them for taking on higher social statuses. Thus, for example, intellectual curiosity is more valued than being a good student by parents from higher-status backgrounds. On the other hand, parents with lower socioeconomic status are more likely to value obedience. In the real world, such findings suggest this: Intellectual curiosity is the sort of quality that is required to do well in higher-status jobs; obedience is an attribute that is required if one is to do well in lower-status jobs.

These findings are illustrative of what social scientists generally discover when they study socialization. As they raise their children, parents whose social status is relatively low typically value obedience to authority, neatness (for example, "coloring within the lines"), cleanliness, and good behavior. Middle-class parents, on the other hand, are more likely to stress such qualities

Table 10.1 U.S. Adults Who Mention Particular Qualities as One of the Three Most Desirable for a Child to Have, by Adult's Income, Education, and Occupational Prestige

	Quality Mentioned				
Adults' Status Attributes	**1 Good Sense**	**2 Obeys Parents**	**3 Considerate**	**4 Intellectually Curious**	**5 Good Student**
Income					
Less than $4,000	19%	49%	29%	19%	32%
$4,000–$13,999	32	45	35	24	22
$14,000–$34,999	49	35	40	22	14
$35,000 and over	49	25	37	26	15
Education					
Less than high school	28	54	29	15	28
High school graduate	43	36	38	23	18
Some college	45	28	40	23	9
College degree	46	26	45	27	11
More than college	58	21	45	42	17
Occupational Prestige					
Low	27	49	27	14	22
Lower-middle	41	37	39	23	18
Upper-middle	43	35	36	25	16
Upper	46	23	48	35	11

NOTE: Data drawn from a national probability sample of 1,500 adults in the United States.

SOURCE: Adapted from the *General Social Survey* (Chicago: National Opinion Research Center, 1986).

as creativity, self-discipline, ambition, independence, curiosity, and self-direction. Thus, *parents tend to pass on to their children the outlooks that are suited to their own experiences in the world.* For example, the more parents are supervised in *their* lives, the more they tend to encourage and require obedience and conformity in their children. This tendency is one way in which the socialization process helps ensure the perpetuation of the existing social structure.

SCHOOL

The school is another important agent of socialization, but the socialization experience it offers is generally quite different from what the child receives in the family. At home, parents may have worked hard to treat each child as a unique individual. But in school the first lesson one learns is that everyone can expect to be treated in the same relatively impersonal manner.

The manifest function of the institution of education is to provide students with the knowledge and skills necessary for success in the adult world. The kinds of knowledge and skills taught in school, however, go beyond the academic course work. In every schoolroom where students recite the pledge of allegiance, for example, they are being taught the value of patriotism. Part of the latent function of education (sometimes called the *hidden curriculum*) is to prepare students to accept what teachers and administrators believe will be the students' places in the social structure. In some schools, for example, students are "tracked" into special programs (such as into vocational versus college preparatory classes). Although it is frequently said that students are tracked based on their individual aptitudes, there is a fairly strong association between a student's social class background and whether that student is, for example, encouraged to apply to college. (We will discuss this phenomenon of tracking in greater depth in chapter 13.)

MASS MEDIA

There is a great deal of debate about the degree to which the media influences a variety of different behaviors. For example, does watching violent television shows and movies or playing violent video games *diffuse* children's violent urges or cause them to *act* upon them? What is not controversial, however, is the fact that exposure to media influences people's perceptions of reality. For example, research shows that "television viewing shapes viewers' conceptions of social reality. Specifically, the more one is exposed to television, the more likely one's interpretation and perceptions of social reality will reflect the television world, as opposed to the real and observable world" (Chen 1995, 22). Although television is hardly the only medium to which people are exposed, it does seem to be the most pervasive:

> By the time an average American student graduates from high school, she or he will have spent more time in front of the television than in the classroom. Viewers learn and internalize some of the values, beliefs, and norms presented in media products. Take the example of crime. Although beginning in 1991 the FBI reported *declines* in violent crime each year for a decade, the number of crime stories on news broadcasts *increased* dramatically during that period, especially during the first half of the 1990s. At the same time, there has been a considerable *increase* in the degree to which American citizens fear violent crime. (Croteau and Hoynes 2003, 14–15 *emphasis added*)

Croteau and Hoynes thereby remind us of the lesson of the Thomas Theorem: "if people define situations as real, they are real in their consequences."[3]

PEER GROUPS

Unlike the institutions of family and school, which are formally charged with the task of socialization, the manifest function of peer groups is simply to have fun. Nonetheless, the latent function of peer groups is to act as a socializing agent. For the adolescent, the influence of the peer group can loom very large. Often peer groups grow into fairly elaborate subcultures, as kids develop their own peculiar values, norms, language, and use of symbols. As children interact with others in their peer groups, they learn a great deal about how they are expected to behave. The peer group is different from either family or school because it socializes children to become independent from adult authority. Still, much of what children experience in peer groups reinforces standard cultural conventions of statuses and roles. In other words, peer groups, too, can act to reinforce the existing social structure.

For example, peer groups play a large role in socializing children into "appropriate" gender-role behavior. One researcher found that girls are labeled "slags and sluts for many forms of independent behavior, such as going places on their own and talking aggressively to boys who insult them" (Eder 1995, 11).[4] And boys do not escape the socializing influence of their peers—in fact, one researcher argued that peer groups are the most important sources of "policing masculinity" in our society:

> The boys themselves often conveyed the importance of toughness through ritual insults. Many of the names the boys used to insult each other imply some form of weakness such as "pud," "squirt," and "wimp." Other names, such as "pussy," "girl," "fag," and "queer," associate lack of toughness directly with femininity or homosexuality. These names are used when boys fail to meet certain standards of combativeness. (Eder 1995, 63)[5]

It is within peer groups that children often encounter their first experiences with status distinctions: Very early on, children begin

---

[3]If you don't recall the Thomas Theorem, review the Introduction to this book.

[4]Researchers have found that whereas more than 200 English words exists (including slang) for sexually promiscuous women and girls, there are fewer than two dozen words for sexually promiscuous men and boys.

[5]Such efforts at social control are not confined to the junior high playground; I have frequently heard college men taunt each other with such remarks as "What are you, chicken?" and "Are you a fag, or something?"

to distinguish between the kids who are valued and those who are not. In her study of adolescent culture, Donna Eder found many examples of this phenomenon in her interviews with middle-school students:

Eighth-Grade Interview (School Cafeteria)
Julie: And those kids who are poor and can't afford expensive clothes sit over there. [Points to the other side of the cafeteria]
Bonnie: Most of them . . .
Julie: [Laughs]
Donna: How does that get started? How does it get started that certain people sit over there and certain people sit at this table?
Bonnie: Like if there's a gross dirty kid that came and sat by this girl that was real clean and everything she'd go, "Oh, gross. You smell," or something like that. So they'd get up and go over there and most of those guys over there think that everybody over here is a snob and they don't want to sit by them.
Julie: Most of them are. (1995, 41)

THE WORKPLACE

Socialization in the workplace "has diverse psychological consequences, including effects on intellectual flexibility, self concept, world view, and affective states" (Miller 1988).

Socialization does not end with childhood but is ongoing throughout an individual's life. For adults, a major agent of socialization is the workplace. Sociologists have found that workplace socialization involves several steps, some of which take place before the worker even finds a job! The first step is to make a career choice, that is, to decide what you want to be when you grow up. The second step, called *anticipatory socialization,* involves learning about and even playing at a work role before entering it. Young children may play at storekeeping or teaching. Adolescents may join the Future Farmers of America to gain experience in agricultural jobs. High school and college students may do volunteer work, undertake internships, or research a particular sort of job. These activities constitute a rehearsal for the future in that they allow an individual to begin to identify with a work role and learn something about its expectations and rewards.

Finally, the individual finds employment and begins to learn the reality of the job—all of its disadvantages and advantages. This final stage can involve some difficult moments because workers generally find that no job is all that it's cracked up to be. New nurses may enter the hospital ward wanting to spend their time comforting the sick and injured but find they must spend most of their time doing administrative work and overseeing the work of nurses' aides. New college professors may expect that they will educate young adults to take their places in the world and then find that no one seems to be listening to their lectures.

Rites of Passage

Many steps in the process of socialization are marked by *rites of passage*. These are ceremonies or rituals that mark important transitions from status to status within the life cycle. Anthropologist A. Radcliffe-Brown described part of the rite of passage of boys-to-men among the people of the Andaman Islands:

> The boy kneels down and bends forward until his elbows rest on the ground in front. One of the older men . . . makes a series of cuts on the boy's back. Each cut is horizontal, and they are arranged in three vertical rows, each row consisting of from 20 to 30 cuts. When the cutting is finished the boy sits up, with the fire at his back, until the bleeding stops. During the operation and a few hours following it the boy must remain silent. (1922/1948)

In a particular society, different rites of passage may be more important than others. In ancient Greece women counted their age from the date on which they were married, not from the day they were born, thus signifying that the wedding was the start of a woman's *real* life.

Factory workers may discover that the work is tedious beyond anything they could have imagined. And so it goes. Individuals have to find ways of coping with the reality of their jobs; generally, they learn these from more experienced co-workers. So, part of the on-the-job socialization involves not merely learning to do the work but learning to *cope* with doing the work.

Sociologists have found that people tend to become heavily invested in their work. Work is not simply another role to play in the social structure; work may become one's master status. Many adults, for example, when asked to explain who they are, preface all their other remarks by noting their occupation. Here's how one observer put it:

> Work is our calling card to the rest of the world. Men and women alike use their work to identify themselves to others. Picture yourself silently circulating at a cocktail party and eavesdropping on how people introduce themselves to one another. I guarantee that you are not going to hear anything like the following: "Hi, I'm Bob, and I'm an Episcopalian"; "Hello, I'm Patty. I'm active in the Democratic Party"; "Howdy, I'm Susan, and I support Habitat for Humanity." It just doesn't happen that way. Workers describe themselves first by "name, rank and serial number," that is, by name, occupation, and title. It is only later, if at all, that they might divulge what they like, what they value, and how their lives are structured outside of work. (Gini 2000, 9)

Resocialization and Total Institutions

Most socialization processes take place in the context of everyday life—in our families and peer groups, in school, in the workplace. But in some cases, socialization takes place in what sociologists call *total institutions*. This phrase was coined by Erving Goffman, who studied such places as mental hospitals and prisons. He found that in these kinds of organizations, an intense socialization experience takes place: "[A total institution is] a place of residence and work where a large number of like-situated individuals, cut off from the wider society for an appreciable period of time, together lead an enclosed, formally administered round of life" (Goffman 1961, xiii).

In a total institution, people are cut off from the rest of society and stripped of their individuality. They are no longer persons but objects; not men or women but "inmates," "patients," or "recruits." The goal of the total institution is to take away the individual's self and give him or her a new one more in keeping with the needs of the total institution. In other words, the goal is *resocialization.*

By way of example, Goffman offered this account of the resocialization of cadets in a military academy:

> For two months . . . the swab is not allowed to leave the base or to engage in social intercourse with noncadets. This complete isolation helps to produce a unified group of swabs, rather than a heterogeneous collection of people of high and low status. Uniforms are issued on the first day, and discussions of wealth and family are taboo. Although the pay of the cadet is very low, he is not permitted to receive money from home. The role of the cadet must supersede other roles the individual has been accustomed to play. There are few clues left which will reveal social status to the outside world. (1961, 46)

Sociologist Peter Rose and his colleagues (1979) discovered a similar process in their study of Marine Corps recruits. Their account of the process reminds us that resocialization is generally begun by subjecting the individual to what sociologists call "degradation ceremonies." The goal of these is to degrade the individual, that is, take away the individual's self in preparation for giving him or her a new one.

Part of the Marine Corps resocialization began with *depersonalization.* The young men were no longer called by their names, their possessions were taken away, and they were subject to many new rules. Merging with the group was stressed: Recruits were no longer treated as individuals but had to speak, look, and act like every other recruit—or else. Uniforms and haircuts were important components of the transformation. To accomplish depersonalization, the men had to do some unlearning. It

> ### *Ponder*
>
> How might the central role of work in an individual's life increase the problems of socialization in retirement?

no longer mattered whether the recruit had been a high school football star, a talented carpenter, a big man on campus, or his parents' pride and joy. Former roles and identities simply did not count. The sooner they were forgotten, the better the recruit would get along.

It is important to understand that total institutions frequently fail to meet their goals; in fact, it is likely that no total institution has the power to completely erase its inhabitants' individuality. The process of resocialization seems to work best in instances where newcomers want to be resocialized (as in the military or religious settings). Likewise, for resocialization to be successful, the total institution must not just tear down the newcomer, but build him or her back up. Hence, military boot camp tends to be more successful in resocialization than, say, prisons because boot camp stresses pride in the identity it is offering. (Of course, the military also has the advantage of being able to discharge its failures, an option not enjoyed by prisons.)

10.1 Match the total institution on the right with the appropriate description on the left:

STOP & REVIEW

   a. for the incapable and harmless
   b. for the incapable and unintentionally harmful
   c. for the capable and intentionally harmful
   d. for the more efficient pursuit of tasks
   e. retreats from the world

     i. monasteries
    ii. prisons
   iii. boarding schools, boot camps
   iv. mental institution
    v. nursing homes

Chapter Review

1. Below I have listed the major concepts discussed in this chapter. Define each of the terms. (*Hint:* This exercise will be more helpful to you if, in addition to defining each concept, you create an example of it in your own words.)

   socialization, defined
   social self
   Charles Horton Cooley, looking-glass self

George Herbert Mead, I and Me
  play and games
role taking
generalized other
agents of socialization
  family
  school
    hidden curriculum
  mass media
  peer groups
  workplace
rites of passage
anticipatory socialization
total institution
resocialization
degradation ceremony
depersonalization

2. What is the most recent rite of passage in which you have participated (as the one making the passage)? Explain in what respects it was a rite of passage. What is the next rite of passage in which you anticipate you will participate?

3. Pick one of the following statements and discuss the extent to which a sociologist would agree with the sentiment expressed:

   a. "All children are essentially criminal" (Denis Diderot, 1713–1784).

   b. "I have never understood the fear of some parents about babies getting mixed up in the hospital. What difference does it make as long as you get a good one?" (Heywood Broun, 1888–1939).

4. I've attended many university meetings with students and noticed that whenever we go around and introduce ourselves to others in the group, students introduce themselves this way: "Hi, I'm Al, and I'm a psych major," or "I'm Tara, and I'm majoring in business." What information does knowing someone's occupation convey? Does knowing someone's major convey the same sort of information? Explain your reasoning.

STOP
&
REVIEW

Answers and Discussion

10.1

  a. nursing homes
  b. mental institutions
  c. prisons
  d. boarding schools, boot camps
  e. monasteries

11

DEVIANCE AND SOCIAL CONTROL

Deviance is one of the more intriguing topics studied by sociologists. The sociological study of deviance covers the gamut of fascinating (if occasionally despicable) behaviors: alcoholism, mental illness, gambling, murders, adultery, crime, drug use, stripping, pimping, prostitution, bulimia, suicide, pedophilia, necromancy, pornography, panhandling—to name just a few.[1] At first glance, gamblers, murderers, prostitutes, and the rest may seem like strangers among us. They aren't (as I will discuss in this chapter, the deviants are us). Moreover, because deviance is the flip side of conformity, understanding deviance contributes to our understanding of conformity. Besides, although curiosity about "perversion" may seem morbid, it's hard not to be fascinated by deviant behavior.

The Relativity of Deviance (What We Already Know)

Because of the close connection between norms and deviance, it is fair to say that we already have a great deal of sociological knowledge about deviance.

For one thing, we know that *norms vary across societies*. So, we also know that *what is considered to be deviant varies across societies*. Different societies have different expectations about how people ought to behave. A particular act may be regarded as normative

---

[1]When I was a college student, people referred to deviance courses as "the sociology of nuts, sluts, and perverts."

169

in society A but deviant in society B. In some countries (e.g., Belgium, France, Germany, Japan, Spain), it is expected that you will stop to help a stranger in trouble; fail to help and you might end up being arrested. In most places in the United States, however, the law can't touch you—even if you stand by and watch a murder.

Important: To define an act as deviant is to say nothing about whether that act is inherently good or bad, or moral or immoral. Remember, good, bad, moral, and immoral are not sociological concepts. (If you need to, review chapter 4 on that point.) To say that an act is deviant is to say only that it violates the norms of a particular group of people at a particular point in time.

Travelers to Singapore are warned that anyone caught spitting in public can be subject to a fine of more than $500 and that failing to flush a public toilet could cost you almost $100. However, a recent law does allow one to purchase chewing gum in Singapore, as long as one has a prescription. Traveling in the Netherlands, on the other hand, might be a little more relaxing—if you are at least eighteen years of age, you can stop in at a coffee shop and order marijuana with that mocha latté (one gram for about five or six dollars).

It's a shocking fact that it is impossible to find any specific act that is regarded as deviant in every culture.[2]

For another thing, we know that *norms change over time—even within a particular culture.* So, we also know that *what is considered to be deviant at one time may be considered normative at another time.* For example, in the 1950s college women were expected to wear skirts or dresses to class and men were expected to wear jackets and ties; these days things are much more casual (I occasionally see students wearing pajamas to class). One hundred years ago, it was a crime to join a labor union. Two hundred years ago, one person could own another person; today, slavery is considered very deviant.

Finally, we know that *norms vary within a particular society—that different subgroups have different norms.* So, we also know that *what is considered deviant will vary from subgroup to subgroup within a particular society.* For example, according to the norms of many groups, dancing and playing cards are respectable, normative behaviors. But in some religious subcultures, dancing and card playing are regarded as deviant. Generally, drinking alcohol is normative, as long as the drinker does not drive or become drunk. But in some adolescent subcultures, on the other hand, "drinking until you pass out" *is* normative. (You may recall from chapter 7

---

[2]Wait! You might be thinking, what about murder? Isn't murder regarded as deviant in all cultures? The trick here is that murder is not an act, but a category of acts that a society has elected to say are deviant. To put it another way, some form of killing is tolerated in nearly every society. But what sorts of killing are called murder and what sorts are not varies according to society. Similarly, what constitutes killing in self-defense varies across societies.

that one of the things that defines a subculture is that its norms vary from those of the larger society.) We also have different expectations for different kinds of people. Thus, it is considered deviant for women to chew tobacco but not for men.

11.1 Which of the following statements about deviance are true, and which are false? Explain your answers briefly.

   a. Society can be divided into people who conform and people who do not conform to social norms.

   b. People generally agree on which behaviors are deviant and which are not deviant.

   c. Most people have violated one or more important mores at some time in their lives.

   d. Most deviant behaviors are regarded as deviant in all societies and at all times.

   e. Only acts that are harmful to people are judged deviant.

Nonsociological Theories of Deviance

Deviance has long intrigued social observers. For centuries many theorized that deviance was simply a product of sin and was caused by such factors as demonic possession. By the mid-nineteenth century, however, skeptical social observers began to look for different causes. The first attempts at scientifically explaining deviance focused on biological factors. For example, Cesare Lombroso, a physician who worked in Italian prisons, argued in 1876 that deviants were, in effect, biological failures. Claimed Lombroso, "Criminals are evolutionary throwbacks," or *atavists*.[3]

But Lombroso's study overlooked a couple of important factors. First, owing to heightened scrutiny on the part of police, Italian prisoners were most likely to be Sicilian—a group of people who tended to have lower foreheads, more prominent cheekbones and protruding ears, and more body hair than the average Italian. Had Lombroso journeyed to Sicily, he would have found the same physical characteristics to be present among the general *nonimprisoned* population. British psychiatrist Charles Goring and others later probed the matter more carefully. Comparing thousands of convicts and nonconvicts, they found no evidence of

---

[3]The term *atavism* refers to a biological state with a variety of physical manifestations, including low foreheads, prominent cheekbones, protruding ears, and lots of body hair.

Deviance is relative—acts considered deviant today (smoking and other forms of air pollution) were not necessarily regarded as deviant in times past.

"Judge, my client is willing to plead guilty to bank robbery if you'll drop the charge of smoking in public."

any physical differences that would distinguish members of one group from the other.

Other researchers have attempted to identify physical characteristics typical of criminals. In the late 1940s, William Sheldon contended that a person's body shape plays a role in criminality. He distinguished three general body types: (1) *ectomorphs* (tall, thin, fragile), (2) *endomorphs* (short and fat), and (3) *mesomorphs* (muscular and athletic). After analyzing the body structures and criminal histories of hundreds of young men, Sheldon reported that criminality was linked to mesomorphy. Later researchers found merit in Sheldon's findings but argued that he had misunderstood the cause-effect relationship between body type and crime. According to these researchers, mesomorphy itself was not the cause of criminality. Rather, the way mesomorphs tended to be socialized (to be tougher and to have less sensitivity toward others) created a kind of self-fulfilling prophecy that encouraged criminality.

Another category of nonsociological theories treats deviance as a result of personality factors—especially those arising from "unsuccessful socialization." Such researchers hypothesize, for example, that people with a strong conscience (or *superego*, to use Freud's term) tend to be good, whereas people with a weak conscience tend to be bad. Psychological theorists may also posit that some forms of deviance, such as violence, are a manifestation of an "aggressive personality," whereas other forms, such as homosexuality, may be seen as an expression of "psychological dependency." These theories do not explain, however, why such a small percentage of people with aggressive personalities commit homicide or why such a small proportion of people with dependent personalities become homosexual.

Sociological Theories of Deviance: Émile Durkheim and Suicide

Sociologists tend to be much more impressed by the fact that deviance is tied to social norms. Because social norms exist outside the individual, sociologists look for causes of deviance in the same place: *outside the individual.*

THE COLLECTIVE CONSCIENCE AND STRUCTURAL STRAIN

Émile Durkheim was one of the first researchers to look for the causes of deviance in terms of social rather than individual factors. In his early research during the 1880s, Durkheim focused on the act of suicide. Suicide was an interesting choice in that hardly anything seems more personal than the decision to kill oneself. Surely the causes of suicide must be within the individual! (In point of fact, Durkheim was not really interested in individual acts of suicide. He was concerned with suicide rates and what changes in suicide rates indicated about the health of a particular society.)

As we discussed briefly in chapter 1, Durkheim's primary concern was the nature of society and social order. What sorts of factors hold a society together? What sorts of factors can destroy a society? Durkheim envisioned society as a system made up of interrelated parts. Like a well-oiled machine, a well-functioning society depends on each of its parts working together. Each part of the social system—the institutions of family, religion, and education, for example—work together to make the entire system of society run well. Because of the close connection among all the social parts, when one part of this social machine is not working properly, the entire system ceases to work well.

According to Durkheim, in some societies the social machine was maintained in smooth working order because of the strength of what he called the *collective conscience*—"the totality of beliefs and sentiments common to the average members of the same society." The collective conscience, in other words, was made up of the values, beliefs, norms, and goals shared by people in a particular society. The collective conscience was a kind of social oil that made things work smoothly.

As we also discussed in chapter 1, in the late nineteenth century, many people believed that society was in chaos and about to fall apart. For centuries society had seemed to be in a holding pattern, and social change, when it did occur, came slowly— almost unnoticed. But in the eighteenth and nineteenth centuries, social change became a fact of life. That sounds reasonable to us, because we live in a society in which change is a part of life. But a couple of hundred years ago, change was new and seemed to be undermining the very nature of what held society together. There were many prophets of doom.

To Durkheim, one of the symptoms of this "society falling apart" syndrome was the high rate of suicide. In many Western countries, the rate of suicide seemed to be increasing. Whereas many of his contemporaries were asking what was wrong with the people who were killing themselves, Durkheim started asking what it was about *society* that caused increases in the rate of suicide. Durkheim argued that changes in suicide rates could be explained not by focusing on individuals but only by focusing on different social factors.

Durkheim's study, titled *Suicide* (published in 1897), was one of the first to use statistical analysis. One finding was that the rate of suicide was higher in industrializing societies than in non-industrializing societies. This led Durkheim to suspect that suicide rates were manifestations of the amount of *structural strain* in a social system.

More specifically, as a result of his analysis, Durkheim argued that as societies grew larger, more complex, and more specialized, the things that traditionally had held people together would begin to fail. As the division of labor became specialized, people began to do different kinds of work; these differences meant that some people achieved a financial success that took them far from their original lifestyles. However, although people could technically improve their social class standing, they did not know any of the norms that accompanied their new stations in life. No longer was there a great deal of agreement on what values were most important and on which norms applied to whom.

EGOISM AND ANOMIE

Durkheim identified several sources of suicide, including *egoism* and *anomie*. Each is a manifestation of a different kind of structural strain. *Egoism occurs when people are not well integrated into society*. In a state of egoism, people lack ties to their social groups. For example, Durkheim found that unmarried people were less integrated into society than married people, who had ties to spouses, children, their children's friends' parents, and so on.

Durkheim also argued that Protestants (whose religion encouraged independent thinking) were less integrated into their social groups than Catholics (who were encouraged to look to their priests for leadership). Integration is tied to suicide rates because people who lack ties to their social groups simply have less to live for (that is, less reason not to kill themselves).

> For example, while both married and unmarried individuals may occasionally entertain suicidal thoughts, the married have more social responsibilities, which deters them from committing suicide, than do the unmarried, who have no one to worry about . . . ; Catholics are socially integrated, they experience social support (comfort, understanding, and sympathy), which deters them from committing suicide in times of despair. (Liska 1987, 30)

Increases in suicide rates, according to Durkheim, also were linked to rapid social change, which resulted in a state of social confusion he called *anomie*. The word is taken from the Greek term for "lawlessness" or "normlessness." So, anomie (or anomy, as it is sometimes spelled) is a situation in which people do not experience the constraint of social norms—either because there are no norms or because they don't know the norms. More technically, anomie is *a state wherein society fails to exercise adequate regulation of the goals and desires of individual members*. To put it yet another way, anomie exists when things like the collective conscience are not powerful enough to affect the behavior of individuals. The lack of social constraint from social norms, like the lack of integration present in egoistic states, creates a situation in which behavior is not properly regulated and suicide is thus easier.

Durkheim hypothesized that anomie and egoism were both major influences on the rate of suicide in modern society. When people lived in a state of anomie (that is, when the collective conscience was not powerful enough to regulate their behavior) or egoism (as when people were not well enough integrated), they were more likely to kill themselves.[4] In short, Durkheim came up with *structural* explanations of suicide rather than individualistic ones. Durkheim never argued that the decision to kill oneself was anything other than a private one for the individual. Durkheim was concerned only with the *rate* of suicide within a particular social group. Or, in Mills's language, Durkheim treated what many had regarded a private trouble as a public issue and thereby broadened our understanding of the phenomenon of suicide.

---

[4]Durkheim also identified other causes of changes in suicide rates. For example, he found that just as not enough moral regulation and integration would lead to an increased suicide rate, so would too much moral regulation. The lowest suicide rates require a balance between social freedom and social control.

More Structural Strain:
Robert Merton and Anomie

The American sociologist Robert Merton rediscovered Durkheim's ideas about anomie in the late 1930s. Merton was not particularly interested in the problem of suicide, but he suspected that Durkheim's conception of anomie might help us to understand other forms of deviance.

ANOMIE AND MODERN SOCIAL STRUCTURE

Merton continued in Durkheim's footsteps by focusing on structural strain as a cause of deviance. But Merton applied the concept of anomie more broadly than Durkheim had. Durkheim had implicitly assumed that once society completed its transition from preindustrial to industrial, anomie would go away. From his twentieth-century perspective, however, Merton realized that anomie was not about to go away; indeed, as far as Merton was concerned, *anomie is built into the structure of modern society.*

Merton refocused the meaning of anomie to make it speak more directly to twentieth-century society. Instead of seeing anomie as a situation in which there was a lack of norms (as Durkheim had), Merton said that *anomie occurs when the norms of a society do not match its social structure.* (This might sound complicated, but don't give up. Keep reading.)

Merton (1938) began his analysis by noticing that all social systems have two characteristics. First, they have commonly accepted *goals* for their members. These goals are simply socially valued things worth striving for. As we discovered in chapter 7, at the top of the list of things that people in the United States tend to value are achievement and success.

Second, each society establishes what it considers to be legitimate ways, or *means,* to reach these valued goals. In this society, for example, education and hard work are the legitimate and approved routes to achievement and success.

According to Merton, everything is fine in a society in which there is a good match between the culturally approved goals and the availability of legitimate means to reach those goals. In a well-structured society, everyone will understand what the goals are, and people will be able to reach those goals by following socially acceptable means.

In modern Western society, however, there tends to be a significant gap, or *disjunction,* between goals and legitimate means. Or, as Merton put it, anomie exists "when a system of cultural values extols, virtually above all else, certain common success-goals for the population at large while the social structure rigorously

Table 11.1 Adaptations to Anomie

	Culture	Social Structure
	Culturally Emphasized Goals	Institutionally Available, Legitimate Means to Goal Attainment
I. Conformity	+ accept	+ accept
II. Innovation	+ accept	− reject
III. Ritualism	− reject	+ accept
IV. Retreatism	− reject	− reject
V. Rebellion	± reject old and substitute ± new ones	

SOURCE: Adapted from Robert K. Merton, "Social Structure and Anomie," *American Sociological Review* (1938): 672–682.

restricts or completely closes access to approved modes of reaching goals for a considerable part of the same population" (1938, 211). Under such circumstances, Merton argued, "deviant behavior ensues on a large scale."

Merton understood that the American Dream (the idea that hard work will lead to success) is frequently a myth.[5] As he looked around, he saw whole segments of society whose access to legitimate means to success was highly restricted. One must have a college education to achieve the best jobs, for example, and Merton realized that a college education was out of the reach of many—no matter how smart they were or how hard they worked. This was just the sort of situation in which, Merton said, there was a disjuncture between socially approved goals (success) and means (education). This disjuncture, for Merton, represented a form of structural strain—which he called anomie. But Merton did not stop there. He noted that when there is anomie, or a disjuncture between goals and means, people may respond (or adapt) in different ways. These modes of adaptation are summarized in table 11.1.

RESPONSES TO ANOMIE

Some people in society may not experience any disjuncture between goals and means. For example, for some people hard

---

[5]Merton surely had a well-developed sociological imagination. Had it not been so well developed, he might never have come to this insight, because everything in his personal history seemed to be proof of the truth of the American Dream. Merton was born in 1910 on the "wrong side of the tracks" in north Philadelphia. He worked his way out of the slums by winning a scholarship to Temple University, where in 1931 he earned his BA Merton then won a fellowship to Harvard to pursue graduate studies, and in 1936 he was awarded the PhD in sociology.

work may indeed lead to success.[6] In other cases, even when they keep running into obstacles (as when, for example, someone can't afford to pay the costs of a college education), people may ignore the disjuncture and keep on trying. In other words, they may continue to accept the goals of success and achievement and the means of hard work even when it isn't getting them anywhere. Merton calls this adaptation *conformity*.

Other people respond to anomie in a variety of ways. Merton called the first mode of adaptation that is obviously deviant *innovation*. Innovators accept and pursue the accepted goals of society but, when confronted with a lack of legitimate means, devise new ones. For example, if in the pursuit of the accepted goal of wealth, Mary finds she has no legitimate access to wealth, she might innovate by embezzling from her employer. The innovator, then, accepts the cultural goals but rejects the legitimate means for achieving these.

Some people reject culturally approved goals but continue to pursue the means. Merton calls this apparently odd form of behavior *ritualism*. Ritualists follow legitimate means without caring about the goals. Ritualists, then, simply go through the motions. Ritualism is the deviant response sometimes chosen by petty bureaucrats who, frustrated at not being able to achieve their goals, continue to stamp papers and file them even when there is no point to doing so. To the ritualist, following the rules becomes more important than achieving the goals. The professor who shows up in class but does not put any effort into teaching is another example of a ritualist who is only going through the motions. Notice that ritualism is an invisible form of deviance. Because the ritualist goes through the motions of conforming, he or she may be viewed as a conformist.

Retreatists are noticeably different in that they reject both the goals and the legitimate means to them. For example, like ritualists, retreatists do not care about the goal of success; but unlike ritualists, neither do they care about going through the motions. Some retreatists literally drop out of society by moving, say, to the mountains of Idaho and living in huts. (A generation ago, the hippies who "turned on, tuned out, and dropped out" were splendid examples of retreatists.)

The fifth mode of adapting to anomie that Merton identified was *rebellion*. Rebels are deviant in that they reject both cultural goals and means and then substitute new ones. It is the substitution of new goals and means that distinguishes the rebel from the retreatist. And it is the substitution of new goals and means that makes the rebel

---

[6]As we will discuss more fully in chapters 13 and 14, such people tend to occupy specific places in the social structure. Upper- and middle-class people, for example, are less likely to experience the anomie of blocked opportunities (because they are less likely to experience blocked opportunities).

seem to be the greatest threat to society. The rebels' response to strain in the social structure is to tear it down and to build up a new one.

But Merton overlooked an important question: In a society in which there is a disjuncture between legitimate means and culturally approved goals, which mode of adaptation will people choose? How come some people choose to conform or to innovate? Why is it that still others choose to retreat or rebel?

LEGITIMATE VERSUS ILLEGITIMATE MEANS

Two students of Merton, Richard A. Cloward and Lloyd E. Ohlin (1960; see also Cloward and Ohlin 1959), extended Merton's analysis by suggesting that *just as legitimate means to success are unequally distributed in society, so are illegitimate means.* For example, to innovate successfully, one needs to learn certain skills. Suppose you want to be a bank robber. If your career is going to last longer than a few minutes, you need to learn how to select your targets (for example, banks located near freeway exits are much preferred to ones located on busy downtown streets). How do professional bank robbers signal to bank customers and employees that they are about to participate in a robbery and had best cooperate? How big a cut should the getaway driver be promised so that he or she won't fink to the cops?

Just as legitimate opportunity structures are unequally distributed in society, so, too, are illegitimate opportunity structures. If you are poor and illiterate, you probably will not have much of a future as a computer hacker or bank embezzler. If you are poor and want to steal, you are pretty much limited to taking on a single victim (or possibly two or three) at a time. But as an executive officer in a savings and loan, you have the unusual opportunity of swindling hundreds, if not thousands, of people.

11.2

a. Merton wrote about deviance as an adaptation to "structural strain." What was the source or nature of this strain?

b. What did Cloward and Ohlin add to Merton's theory of anomie?

Learning to Be Deviant:
Howard Becker's Study of Marijuana Use

Merton's conception of structural strain gives us some insight into *why* people might act in deviant ways, but it really does not tell us *how* people actually become deviant. Sociologists have noticed that one generally learns to be deviant through a kind of socialization—just as one learns to conform through socialization. In other words, deviance is frequently a learned social behavior.

One sociologist who made this point was Howard Becker. In addition to being a sociologist, Becker was a professional jazz musician in the 1950s, and one of the things he noticed was that jazz musicians tended to smoke marijuana—a practice that was not only deviant but illegal.

Why did people smoke marijuana? At the time, it was widely thought that there was something wrong with the personality of marijuana smokers, that people who smoked marijuana suffered from some sort of psychological maladjustment. It was believed, for instance, that people who smoked marijuana did so out of a felt need for escape or because they were insecure, lacking in self-control, immature, or simply mentally ill. Conventional wisdom, then, regarded marijuana smokers as people with distinct psychological and/or emotional problems.

As a sociologist, however, Becker suspected that to truly understand the nature of this behavior, we would have to place it in its social context. And so it was that Becker began a sociological study of marijuana use. He conducted interviews with dozens of pot-smoking musicians. From his interviews, Becker found that marijuana use did indeed have important social qualities. For example, Becker found that becoming a marijuana smoker involved three separate social processes: (1) learning to smoke (gaining proper technique), (2) learning to perceive the effects, and (3) learning to enjoy the effects.

LEARNING TO SMOKE

According to Becker (1963), the novice smoker does not ordinarily get high the first time he (Becker's subjects were primarily male) smokes marijuana. Generally, it is necessary to smoke the drug several times to achieve a high. One explanation of this is that the novice does not know how to smoke "properly"—that is, in a way that ensures a large enough dosage of the drug. Most of Becker's interview subjects agreed that the drug cannot be smoked like tobacco if the user is to get high:

> "Take in a lot of air, you know, and . . . I don't know how to describe it, you don't smoke it like a cigarette, you draw in a lot of air and get it deep down in your system and then keep it there. Keep it there as long as you can."

Unless one uses the proper technique, the effects of the drug will be minimal:

> "The trouble with people [who are unable to get high] is that they're just not smoking it right, that's all there is to it. Either they're not holding it down long enough, or they're getting too much air and not enough smoke, or the other way around, or something like that. A lot of people just don't smoke it right, so naturally nothing's gonna happen."

Becker's interview subjects also reported that learning to smoke marijuana was a social thing:

> "I was smoking it like I did an ordinary cigarette. He said, 'no, don't do it like that.' He said, 'suck it, you know, draw in and hold it in your lungs till you . . . for a period of time.' I said, 'is there any limit of time to hold it?' He said, 'no, just till you feel that you want to let it out, let it out.' So, I did that for three or four times."

Many reported that as first-time users they had been ashamed to admit their ignorance and so had pretended to already know how to inhale:

> "I came on like I had turned on [smoked marijuana] many times before, you know. I didn't want to seem like a punk to this cat. See, like I didn't know the first thing about it. I just watched him like a hawk—I didn't take my eyes off of him for a second, because I wanted to do everything just as he did it. I watched how he held it, how he smoked it, and everything. Then, when he gave it to me, I just came on cool, as though I knew exactly what the score was. I held it like he did and took a toke just the way he did."

No one Becker interviewed had become a marijuana user without first learning the technique for smoking that allowed one to inhale a sufficient dosage—one that allowed the effects of the drug to be evident.

LEARNING TO PERCEIVE THE EFFECTS

Even after the novice learns the proper smoking technique, he or she may not evaluate the results as "being high." A remark made by one smoker pointed to the next step on the road to becoming a marijuana user:

> "As a matter of fact, I've seen a guy who was high out of his mind and didn't know it." [Becker asks, "How can that be, man?"] "Well, it's pretty strange, I'll grant you that, but I've seen it. This guy got on [high] with me, claiming that he'd never got high, one of those guys, and he got completely stoned. And he kept insisting that he wasn't high. So, I had to prove to him that he was."

Becker's research suggested that getting high involves two things: (1) achieving the physiological effects of the drug and (2) recognizing and identifying these effects. Without the second element, one is not really high because one does not know one is high! Becker found that people who believed the whole thing was an illusion did not continue to use marijuana because there was no point to doing so. Thus, without social support, most people would not get beyond their first attempt. Generally, however, novice users said they had faith that eventually they would feel some real effects. Recognizing the effects of the drug frequently came as a result of interaction with more experienced users:

> "I didn't get high the first time. . . . I don't think I held it in long enough. . . . Probably let it out, you know, you're a little afraid. The second time I wasn't sure, and he [the more experienced smoker] told me, like I asked him for some of the symptoms or something, how would I know, you know. . . . He told me to sit on a stool. I sat on—I think I sat on a stool—and he said, 'Let your feet hang.' And then when I got down my feet were real cold, you know? And I started feeling it, you know. That was the first time. And then about a week after that, sometime pretty close to it, I really got on. That was the first time I got on a big laughing kick, you know? Then I really knew I was on."

One frequently reported effect of marijuana is intense hunger. One novice smoker remembers the first time he felt this:

> "They were just laughing the hell out of me because like I was eating so much. I just scoffed [ate] so much food, and they were just laughing at me, you know? Sometimes I'd be looking at them, you know, wondering why they're laughing, you know, like I'd ask, 'What's happening?' and all of the sudden, I feel weird, you know. 'Man, you're on, you know. You're on pot [high on marijuana].' I said, 'No, am I?' Like I don't know what's happening."

In essence, then, the novice smoker learns from more experienced users to experience the effects of marijuana use as a high. The ability to perceive the drug's effects must be achieved if use of the drug is to continue.

LEARNING TO ENJOY THE EFFECTS

Suppose the user has learned the proper smoking technique and has learned to identify the effects as a high. A final step is necessary before the user will continue to use the drug: He or she must learn to *enjoy the effects.* The sensations of a marijuana high are not necessarily pleasurable ones. The typical novice smoker feels dizzy, thirsty, hungry, paranoid, confused about time and space, and more. Are these responses enjoyable? As you might guess, the effects of the drug might be downright unpleasant. At best, the effects of the drug are ambiguous.[7]

---

[7]In some important respects, Becker's portrayal of becoming a marijuana user may no longer reflect the reality of this process. The active ingredient in marijuana is THC (tetrahydrocannabinol). Fifty years ago, the level of THC in marijuana was quite low, and the effects of the drug were relatively subtle. But today, the level of THC in marijuana is very high (no pun intended), and the effects of the drug are much more noticeable. This probably means that it is much easier for novices to perceive the effects of the drug but more difficult for them to perceive its effects as enjoyable.

The "taste" for sensations is in large part a socially acquired one. Remember your first sip of coffee? Yuck! What about oysters, green olives, and dry martinis? Double yuck! Yet many people begin to enjoy these. The same is true for the sensations produced by marijuana use. But it's not necessarily easy:

> "It started taking effect, and I didn't know what was happening, you know, what it was, and I was very sick. I walked around the room trying to get off, you know; it just scared me at first, you know. I wasn't used to that kind of feeling."

Another user reported:

> "I felt I was insane, you know. Everything people done to me just wigged me. I just couldn't hold a conversation, and my mind would be wandering, and I was always thinking, oh, I don't know, weird things, like hearing must be different . . . I get the feeling that I can't talk to anyone. I'll goof completely."

Over time, however, many people come to regard these sensations as desirable. As an experienced user explained:

> "Well, they get pretty high sometimes. The average person isn't ready for that, and it is a little frightening to them sometimes. I mean, they've been high on lush [alcohol], and they get higher that way than they've ever been before, and they don't know what's happening to them. Because they think they're going to keep going up, up, up till they lose their minds or begin doing weird things or something. You have to like reassure them, explain to them that they're not really flipping or anything, that they're gonna be all right. You have to just talk them out of being afraid. Keep talking to them, reassuring, telling them it's all right."

As you can see, what starts as an unpleasant experience becomes a desirable and sought-after one. In the end, with some help from one's peers, the user begins to regard being high as "fun." In simple terms, the individual not only has learned a deviant act but has learned to enjoy it as well.

The idea that deviance, like conformity, is learned behavior has added a great deal to our understanding of human behavior.

The Societal Reaction Perspective: Labeling Theory

The traditional view of deviance focuses on why and how individuals commit deviant acts. These theories tend to take for granted that some acts are deviant and others are not. One implication of this is that regardless of who commits the deviant act, they will be responded to in the same way as anyone else who commits that particular sort of deviance.

"With all that I've learned about sociology recently, establishing who's naughty and who's nice is not as simple as it used to be."

But sociologists know that this is not true. As William Chambliss (1973) found in his comparison of different youth gangs, in some cases it is not *what* you do but *who* you are. More specifically, Chambliss found that lower-class youths were more likely to be sanctioned than middle-class youths—even though the lower-class kids committed fewer deviant acts! The societal reactionist perspective in general, and labeling theory more particularly, focuses not on the one who commits the deviant act but on the response of the audience.

Labeling theorists take note of the fact that being judged and labeled deviant has significant consequences for people's behavior. The label of deviant is powerful!

Let's take the hypothetical case of Bob, who has just graduated from high school. One night Bob and three of his friends (including Melissa, his girlfriend) decide to steal a car and take it for a joyride. Actually Bob has chugged so much beer that he can barely walk, let alone go for a ride. But after listening to his friends cluck and call him a chicken, he goes along. As soon as he gets into the car, however, he throws up and passes out.

Meanwhile, John, the guy who's driving, has had a few too many beers himself and wanders all over the road. This catches the attention of the police in a patrol car, which comes up behind the stolen car with lights flashing. This strikes John as rude, and so he decides to speed up and outrun the cops. Inevitably, John's poor coordination lands them all in a ditch. The other three (who are relatively sober) take off and manage to outrun the cops. But Bob is still unconscious in the back seat—and the police are happy enough to arrest him as a reward for their crime-fighting efforts.

Bob is taken to jail, fingerprinted, and photographed. A few days later, Bob is brought to court to be arraigned. Being the upstanding fellow that he is, Bob refuses to fink on his friends, and so the court throws the book at him. He's found guilty of grand-theft-auto (a felony) and sentenced to ninety days in jail, with another nine months suspended.

Bob serves his summer in jail, but his real sentence is much longer. First, he loses his college scholarship. However, that hardly matters because Bob's only interest in college was so that he could go on to law school and become an attorney. Bob knows that convicted felons can't become lawyers, so what's the point?

Bob's girlfriend, Melissa, still loves him, but her parents forbid her to date him. After all, Bob is a convicted criminal, and they don't want their daughter hanging out with an ex-con. His other friends are sympathetic, but they go off to college and lose touch. Bob tries to find a job, but every time he fills out an application, he has to deal with the question "Have you ever been convicted of a felony?"

Bob is the same guy he was before he went along on the joyride—but this Bob has an entirely different life than the old Bob. So what if he drinks too much now and gambles away what little money he has. It's not like he has any hope of leading a normal life.

Bob is a truly pathetic case, and I've exaggerated his circumstances to make a point: The label of deviant can trigger a self-fulfilling prophecy. If you treat people as deviant and cut off their opportunities to be anything other than deviant, you increase the chances that they actually will become deviant.

Sociologists would refer to Bob's initial foray into crime (his joyriding) as an instance of *primary deviance*. Primary deviance may be committed for all sorts of reasons, including, as in Bob's case, a desire to fit in with the group. Social labeling theorists seek to explain the acts of deviance that take place after the individual has been labeled as a deviant. These subsequent acts of deviance are called *secondary deviance*. Edwin Lemert explained the difference this way:

> Primary deviance is assumed to arise in a wide variety of social, cultural and psychological contexts and at best has only marginal implications for the psychic structure of the individual; it does not lead to symbolic reorganization at the level of self-regarding attitudes and social roles. . . . Primary deviation, as contrasted with secondary, is polygenetic, arising out of a variety of social, cultural, psychological and physiological factors. . . .

> Secondary deviation is deviant behavior [that results] as a means of social defense . . . or adaptation to the . . . problems created by the societal reaction to primary deviance. . . . Secondary deviation refers to a special class of socially defined responses which people make to problems created by the societal reaction to their deviance. (Lemert 1967, 17, 40)

Erving Goffman's work on social identity helps us to make sense of the power of labels. Goffman argued that the stigma[8] of negative social labels can work to spoil a person's identity. According to Goffman, a stigma is "any attribute that discredits a person or disqualifies him or her from 'full social acceptance'" (1963, 3).

Goffman identified three types of stigma. First, there are *abominations of the body*—clearly visible physical marks (deformities, scars, disfiguring injuries). Second, there are *blemishes of individual character*—labels of mental disorder, dishonesty, alcoholism, or bankruptcy. Finally, there are *tribal stigmas*—or being discredited for membership in a particular racial, religious, or ethnic group or subcultural group. In other words, a stigma can be either ascribed or achieved.

Goffman argued that a stigma can affect one's social interactions in two ways. When a stigma is visible or known, it can result in a *discredited identity*. Like Bob, who because he lived in a small town was publicly labeled as a criminal and treated as such people with discredited identities have a tough time being nondeviant even if they want to be.

Frequently, however, individuals are able to hide attributes that, if visible, would stigmatize them. In other words, stigmatized individuals may try "to pass"—that is, to camouflage the attribute that would get them labeled as deviant. Successfully passing means that the individual is not discredited. But because the person is vulnerable to being found out, he or she is *discreditable*—that is, in danger of feeling the full force of the stigma.

Goffman observed that the results are the same regardless of whether the person achieves a stigma or has it ascribed to him or her: "In all of these various instances of stigma the same sociological features are found: an individual who might have been received easily in ordinary social intercourse possesses a trait that can intrude itself upon the attention and turn those of us whom he meets away from him, breaking the claim that his other attributes have on us" (1963, 18).

Others have found that a negative label, or a social stigma, can easily become a person's master status (the concept of master status was introduced in chapter 8). Criminologist Edwin Schur noted, for example, that such negative social labels as drug addict, homosexual, prostitute, or juvenile delinquent "will dominate all other characteristics of the individual. Good athlete, good conversationalist, good dancer, and the like are subordinated to or

---

[8]The term *stigma* comes from ancient Greece and Rome, where runaway slaves and criminals were branded with a hot iron or needle as a sign of their disgrace. These brands were called stigma, from the Greek verb *stizein*, meaning "to tattoo." When the word became part of the English language in the late sixteenth century, it was used as it had been by the ancients—to refer to visible signs of disgrace.

negated by this trait, which is immediately felt to be more central to the 'actual' identity of the individual" (1971, 9).

11.3 Explain the difference between *primary* and *secondary* deviance. Why do some sociologists think it is important to distinguish between the two types?

STOP

&

REVIEW

The Functions of Deviance: Maintenance of the Status Quo and Social Change

According to conventional wisdom, society would be much better off if it could get rid of crime and deviance. Durkheim started changing at least sociologists' minds about this. His reasoning was this: If people continue to violate norms, their behavior must offer some benefit to society. What benefit do crime and deviance confer on society? Well, for one thing, criminals and deviants represent social enemies, and hating these social enemies can help unite society. Thus, Durkheim argued,

> crime brings together upright consciences and concentrates them. We have only to notice what happens, particularly in a small town, when some moral scandal has just been committed. They stop each other on the street, they visit each other, they seek to come together to talk about the event and to wax indignant in common. (1893/1933, 102)

Sociologist Kai T. Erikson extended Durkheim's idea that crime could be functional by noting that deviance *clarifies* society's norms and moral boundaries. Typically a group's norms are pretty vague, but societal reaction to rule breakers helps to clarify the limits of normative (appropriate) behavior:

> The reaction to some people as rule violators functions to clarify the meaning of the norm. Others learn "how far they can go." Consider the rule, "do not cheat on examinations." What does it mean for specific examination situations? In the case of a take-home examination, it clearly means that a student should not copy another student's answer. Does it also mean that students should not work together or talk over the assignment at all? How does the rule apply to term papers? Does it mean that students should not seek assistance from other students or other professors? Does it mean that one term paper should not be submitted in two classes? When some

---

Ponder

Generally speaking, the stigma that results from conviction for a white-collar crime is less than the stigma that results from conviction for a street crime. Why do you think this is so?

students "go too far" and exceed the academic community's boundaries or tolerance limits, the community reacts, and that reaction
defines specific situational meanings of the rule. (Quoted in Liska
1987, 40)

Finally, deviance encourages social change. Durkheim noted
that deviant people are sources of social change of the sort that
can benefit society. As proved by the American revolutionaries
of the eighteenth century, today's deviance may become tomorrow's morality, today's deviant may become tomorrow's hero.

A CAUTION ABOUT CRIME DATA

Sociologists who study crime and deviance use data from a variety of sources. It's important to be careful when interpreting
these data. Suppose, for example, you came across table 11.2. This
table shows, among other things, that in the year 2000 more than
half (57.9 percent) of all people in state prisons for drug offenses
were black. This statistic is made all the more startling given that
blacks make up only about 12 percent of the U.S. population.

A sociologically naive person might conclude that blacks are
more likely to use drugs than whites or Hispanics.

A close inspection of table 11.3, however, would show how
wrong-headed that conclusion would be. The data in table 11.3
look at the people who are regular drug users. It shows that if
we look at all regular drug users, we find that the percentage of
each group is fairly close to their percentage in the United States.
In other words, whites make up about three-quarters of the U.S.
population and close to three-quarters of those who regularly use
illegal drugs.

Table 11.2 Racial Composition of those Incarcerated for Drug Offenses
in U.S. State Prisons, 2000–2005.

Race/Ethnicity of Prisoner	Year		
	2000	2003	2005
White	23.2%	25.9%	28.5%
Black	57.9	53.0	44.8
Hispanic	17.2	20.0	20.2
Other	1.7	1.1	6.5
Total	100%	100%	100%
(N)	251,100	259,900	253,300

SOURCE: Adapted from Marc Mauer, 2009. *The Changing Racial Dynamics of the War on Drugs.*
Washington, DC: The Sentencing Project.

Table 11.3 Racial Composition of the United States and of Regular Illegal Drug Users in the U.S., 2000–2005.

Race/Ethnicity of Drug User	Percent of Total Population	Year		
		2000	**2003**	**2005**
White	76%	74.8%	71.0%	69.2%
Black	12	11.5	12.3	14.0
Hispanic	9	9.1	12.2	12.4

SOURCE: Adapted from Marc Mauer (2009), and *Drug Use Among Racial/Ethnic Minorities*, Revised Edition, National Institute on Drug Abuse, Department of Health and Human Services, National Institutes of Health. 2003.

The question is, why are regular drug users who are black or Hispanic more likely to go to prison? One might be tempted to say that perhaps black or Hispanic drug offenders commit more serious drug offenses (i.e., selling as opposed to possession of drugs). Unfortunately, there are no reliable data on this point; however, "Persons who use drugs . . . generally report that they purchased their drugs from someone of their own race" (Mauer 2009, 8).

The differences in incarceration rates is probably explained by a number of factors. In recent decades, the criminal justice system has specifically targeted the use of "crack" cocaine[9] with enhanced sentences. Because crack is relatively cheap, it is attractive to low-income users. Blacks are more likely than whites to have low incomes and live in communities with "limited access to treatment and alternative sentencing options" like diversion programs (Mauer and King 2007, 18).

11.4 In 1955 Rosa Parks, an African American woman, disobeyed an Alabama state law by not giving up her seat to a white person (as the law insisted). Parks was arrested, convicted, and fined $10 plus $4 court costs. What function did her deviance play?

STOP & REVIEW

Deviance Is Not Immutable[10]

Deviance is an inevitable part of social life. According to Emile Durkheim, it is impossible for a society to exist without deviance: Societies create norms and, inevitably, some people will violate them.

---

[9]Crack cocaine is a kind of cocaine that is produced by dissolving cocaine in water, mixing it with common household chemicals, and boiling the mixture until "rocks" appear.

[10] Immutable means unchanging and unchangeable.

Figure 11.1
Percentage of American Adults Who Say that Sex between Two Adults Is "Always Wrong," or "Not Wrong at All" (1973–2010).

SOURCE: Smith, 2011.

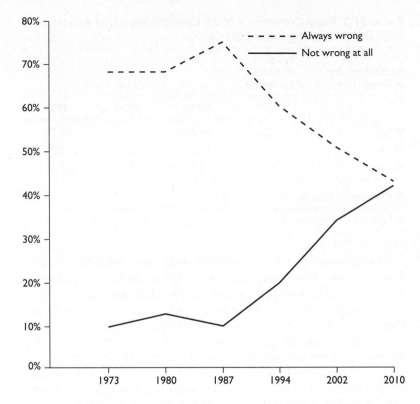

No act, however, is inherently deviant. Any particular behavior is deviant only if people in a society have rules against that behavior. Moreover, as people change, rules may change and different behaviors may be defined as deviant (or not).

Traditionally, if a student enrolled in a social problems or a sociology of deviance class, one of the topics listed on the syllabus would be homosexuality. There was little question that homosexual behavior was deviant.

Indeed, until the early 1960s, homosexual acts, called *sodomy* or *crimes against nature*, were felonies in all state jurisdictions in the United States. Things began to change in the 1960s and 1970s, but—as late as 1986, half of the states still had laws prohibiting sodomy.[11] As shown in figure 11.1, in the 1980s, most Americans believed that homosexual behavior was "always wrong" and most court decisions reflected that belief. For example, in 1982, Michael Hardwick was arrested in his bedroom with another man and charged with violating Georgia's law against sodomy. Over the course of the next four years, the case found its way to

---

[11]Technically, sodomy includes any sexual intercourse that does not involve a penis and a vagina—whether it involves same sex or different sex partners. However, I can't find any record of different sex partners being prosecuted.

the U.S. Supreme Court, where five of its nine members found that people who wished to engage in same sex sexual acts have no constitutionally protected right to do so.

However, in the new century, people's attitudes began to change. Then, in 2003, the Court was presented with another sodomy case. In *Lawrence v Texas* (2003) a six-to-three majority ruled that sodomy statutes were unconstitutional violations of American's right to privacy.

Did this mean that sodomy laws were taken off the books? No. At this writing, some fourteen states' laws criminalize sodomy, and in many of these states there continue to be prosecutions or, at least, legal harassment of gays.[12]

A year after the *Lawrence* case was decided, in 2004, the Massachusetts Supreme Court ruled that the state's constitution equal protection clause required that same-sex couples be allowed to marry. At this writing, same sex marriage is legal in Connecticut, Iowa, Maine, Maryland, Massachusetts, New Hampshire, New York, Vermont, and Washington State (and Washington D.C.).

Same sex marriage is allowed in several other countries: Argentina, Belgium, Canada, Iceland, Netherlands, Norway, Portugal, Spain, South Africa, and Sweden.

Gays in the Military

The 1916 Articles of War prohibited homosexuals from serving in the military. In World War II, "the military developed procedures for spotting and excluding homosexual draftees from service: recruits were screened for feminine body characteristics, effeminacy in dress and manner and a patulous (expanded) rectum."[13] During the Vietnam War, some draftees claimed homosexual tendencies in order to avoid service. "It didn't always work: in 1968 Perry Watkins, a 19-year-old man, "was drafted despite checking the 'yes' box in the category 'homosexual tendencies' during his pre-induction physical examination. After 16 years of service, the

---

[12]In the following states, sodomy is outlawed for both gays and straight people: Alabama, Florida, Idaho, Louisiana, Michigan, Mississippi, North Carolina, Virginia, South Carolina, and Utah. In Kansas, Montana, Oklahoma, and Texas, sodomy is only a criminal act if involves same-sex couples.

[13]Unlike their male counterparts, lesbians had little difficulty serving in the military in WWII. For one thing, those seeking to serve were not asked about their sexual orientation—partly because it was contrary to social norms to ask women such questions and partly because women service members who displayed male tendencies were considered to probably "be perfectly normal sexually and excellent military material"(Berube, 1990, 29). After the war, however, women were placed under greater scrutiny, requiring lesbians, like gay men, to work harder to hide their sexuality if they wanted to continue to serve.

military discharged [Sergeant] Perry Watkins for his sexual orientation; he promptly filed a lawsuit" (Webley, 2010). Perry won the lawsuit and the court awarded him retroactive pay, an honorable discharge, and promotion from staff sergeant to sergeant first class.

In 1993, the United States Congress passed the Military Personnel Eligibility Act, informally known as "Don't Ask, Don't Tell." The act barred the military from asking those seeking to serve about their sexual orientation. However, contrary to the common understanding of the law, the act continued to allow the military to investigate the sexual lives of serving personnel. As a result, between 1994 and 2010, "more than 12,000 service members" were dismissed from the military for their sexual orientation" (Webley 2010).

In 2010, The U.S. Congress passed the "Don't Ask, Don't Tell Repeal Act." The act removed all restrictions against homosexuals serving in the military. While surveys suggested most Americans (about 60 percent) were in favor of allowing gays to serve, there was opposition. In 2009, for example, more than 1,000 retired admirals and generals published a statement saying that "Repeal . . . would undermine recruiting and retention, impact leadership at all levels, have adverse effects on the willingness of parents who lend their sons and daughters to military service, and eventually break the All-Volunteer Force" (quoted in Belkin, et al., 2012).

A year after repeal, research suggested that the pessimistic predictions about allowing gays to serve openly in the military were wrong: The repeal of DADT has had no overall negative impact on military readiness or its component dimensions, including cohesion, recruitment, retention, assaults, harassment or morale" (Belkin, et al., 2012, 4). In June, 2012, Secretary of Defense Leon E. Panetta celebrated "Pride Month" with a video statement thanking "gay and lesbian service members and lesbian, gay, bisexual and transgender civilians for their dedicated service to the nation" (U.S. Department of Defense, http://www.pentagon-channel.mil/Home.aspx).

Chapter Review

1. Below I have listed the major concepts discussed in this chapter. Define each of the terms. (*Hint:* This exercise will be more helpful to you if, in addition to defining each concept, you create an example of it in your own words.)

   relativity of deviance
   normative behavior

nonsociologial approaches to deviance
    demonic possession as a theory of deviance
    Cesare Lombroso's theory of atavism
    William Sheldon (ecto-, endo- and mesomorph)
Émile Durkheim, collective conscience
    structural strain
    anomie and egoism
Robert Merton and anomie
    responses to anomie (conformity, innovation ritualism,
        retreatism, rebellion)
Richard Cloward and Lloyd Ohlin
    differential opportunities to deviate
Howard Becker
    deviance as learned behavior
societal reaction/labeling theory
Edwin Lemert
    primary and secondary deviance
Erving Goffman
    stigma
    discreditable versus discredited identity
functions of deviance

2. Review Merton's typology of adaptation to anomie. Create an example of each type of adaptation (conformity, innovation, ritualism, and rebellion) and explain how each of your examples fits the definition of that type of adaptation. (Don't use examples given in the chapter; make up your own.)

3. Durkheim suggested that deviance can be a source of social change. Give an example of someone who, during your life-time, was judged to be deviant or criminal but nonetheless brought about social change.

4. The relationship between conformity to norms and deviance is frequently a complicated one. Describe a situation in which conformity to the norms of some smaller group would result in nonconformity to the norms of the larger society. Then, discuss what implications this sort of conflict of norms might have for sociologists who want to understand why people deviate.

Answers and Discussion

11.1

    a. False—society *cannot* be divided into people who conform and people who do not conform to social norms. If we tried to make such a division, everyone would be on the same side of the line. Everyone deviates sometimes, and most people conform most of the time. (Even chainsaw murderers usually eat dinner with a fork and use toilet paper in the socially prescribed manner.)

b. False—people generally do *not* agree on which behaviors are deviant and which are not deviant. In fact, there is a great deal of disagreement in society about what is deviant and what is not. It varies among subcultures and across time. However, within a particular society, there may be general agreement on the most important norms (for example, there is usually pretty solid agreement on what constitutes taboo behavior).

c. True—most people have violated one or more important mores at some time in their lives. You may be the exception, but most of us will violate an important norm at least occasionally.

d. False—most deviant behaviors are *not* regarded as deviant in all societies and at all times. As I tried to emphasize, it is very difficult to identify a particular behavior that is deviant everywhere.

e. False—it is *not* merely acts that are harmful to people that are judged to be deviant. There are many acts that really do not harm anyone but that are still regarded as deviant. It would be accurate, I think, to say that all deviant behaviors are offensive (if only in the sense that deviant acts offend social norms). Talking with your mouth full of food, for example, or picking your nose doesn't harm anyone, but these behaviors certainly do offend people.

11.2

a. For Merton, the structural strain that led to anomie was the contradiction between socially approved goals and socially approved means. In our society, earning lots of money is a socially approved goal. But there are not enough socially approved/legitimate means for everyone to achieve this goal. This contradiction leads some people to deviate.

b. Their contribution was to point out that just as not all people have the same access to socially approved/legitimate means, not all people have the same access to illegitimate means.

11.3 Primary deviance is deviance that people commit—on a whim or owing to particular circumstances. If they are caught and sanctioned for this act, they may be led to perform secondary deviance. Secondary deviance is deviance that people perform as a result of being labeled as a deviant.

11.4 She said that she did it because her feet were tired, but when Parks refused to give up her seat to a white person and was arrested for this "crime," she became a symbol that helped launch the civil rights movement.

12

STRATIFICATION AND INEQUALITY

Inequality is an inevitable fact of social life. In all societies, people are evaluated on the basis of some characteristic (or set of characteristics) and placed into higher- or lower-ranking groups. People in higher-ranking groups tend to receive disproportionately larger shares of valued social stuff (such as wealth, power, and respect). People in lower-ranking groups tend to receive correspondingly smaller shares of these social rewards.

Sociologists refer to this evaluation-ranking-reward system and its results as *social stratification*. The term *stratification* is one that we borrowed from the earth sciences because it conveys the fact that society is made up of social layers, or *strata,* that are arranged in a hierarchy. As figure 12.1 shows, like rocks in the earth, some people are at the bottom of society, some are in the middle, and some are at the top.

Be careful: The analogy between social strata and geological strata can be a little misleading. Yes, groups of people are arranged by strata in society just as rocks are in the earth. But geologists do not value a kind of rock simply because it is found in the top stratum. In every type of *social* stratification system, however, the people at the top are considered better than the people at the bottom. Sometimes, as I will describe shortly, *better* can mean purer, or smarter, or braver. But it always means more of something that is valued in that society (Barber 1968).

Although every society has some form of stratification, the forms vary from society to society. Notwithstanding their differences, all stratification systems have three related things in common. First, the systems tend to persist for a long time. Second, the systems are resistant to change. Third, each system is bolstered by widely accepted *legitimating rationales.* These rationales help

Figure 12.1
Perspectives on Stratification. Sociologists use the term stratification to refer to the different social strata that exist in society. People in higher strata receive greater rewards than do people in lower strata.

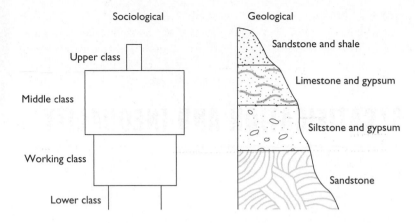

to account for the persistence of particular social stratification systems.

In the most general sense, legitimating rationales are widely accepted beliefs that something is fair and just. With respect to stratification, then, legitimating rationales are widely accepted beliefs that the inequalities that exist in a particular society (differences in power, wealth, prestige, and so on) are essentially "right and reasonable" (Della Fave 1980). In other words, the rationales that legitimate stratification systems reflect people's beliefs about why some people are ranked higher than others and why this is fair. To the degree that stratification systems differ across societies, we would expect them to have different legitimating rationales. Understanding these rationales will help us to make sense of people's acceptance of the kind of stratification that exists in their society.

Though there are perhaps as many forms of stratification as there are societies, sociologists generally group these into three major categories: caste, estate, and class.

Caste Systems

In a *caste system*, one's rank is determined at birth. In other words, one's position in a caste system is based on ascribed characteristics. Caste membership generally determines a person's prestige, occupation, and residence, as well as the nature of his or her social relationships.

The most frequently cited example of a caste system is the one that originated in India some 4,000 years ago. When Portuguese explorers visited India in the mid-sixteenth century, they were very impressed by the fact that each person was born into a particular subgroup and was more or less allowed to interact only with people from the same subgroup. The many prohibitions on interaction led the Portuguese explorers to call the subgroups *casta*—a Portuguese word meaning "pure" or "something that ought not be mixed." What the word reflects, then, is the sense the explorers had that the boundaries between the subgroups in India were so very strong that it was as if the people in different castes belonged to different races.[1] In 1908 Célestin Bouglé, a French social scientist, defined *caste* this way:

> The caste system divides the whole society into a large number of hereditary groups, distinguished from one another and connected together by three characteristics: *separation* in matters of marriage and contact, whether direct or indirect; *division* of labour, each group having, in theory or by tradition, a profession from which their members can depart only within certain limits; and finally *hierarchy*, which ranks the groups as relatively superior or inferior to one another. (Paraphrased in Dumont 1970, 21)

In a caste system, no one is allowed to wed, eat food cooked by, or drink from the cup of anyone from a lower caste. Many kinds of contact are judged to defile (contaminate) the higher-caste person. At one time, for example, members of the lowest castes were forbidden to move about in public during the daylight hours merely because of the possibility that their shadows might fall upon an upper-caste person.

The caste system of India finds its legitimating rationale in the Hindu religion. This rationale begins with the Hindu idea of *transmigration* (or what many Westerners would call *reincarnation*). It is generally believed that each person is born into a particular caste as a result of his or her actions and thoughts in a previous life. This has to do with the concept of *karma*—a Sanskrit word meaning "work" or "fate."[2] Those who subscribe to the Hindu faith view karma as the *inexorable application of the law of cause and effect.* That is, people who lead a good life, carefully follow the rules of the religion, and fulfill their *dharma,* or caste-based duties, will inevitably be born into a higher caste in the next life. But those who fail to carry out their dharma will lose caste in the next life (Smith 1958).

According to the Hindu religion, human beings *"do not start life with a clean slate. The soul of every newborn infant formerly inhabited some other body. Sometimes the soul came from another human being, sometimes from an animal. Wherever it had been before, it accumulated karma. Karma is a little like dust: it collects on the soul just through the process of living. Only a very wise and good individual, aided by ritual purification, can avoid accumulating a lot of it"* (McNeill 1987, 153).

According to the Hindu religion, there are four *varnas,* or "colors" or "grades of being." As told by the Hindu creation story found in the Rig Veda (an ancient religious text), the universe was born from the sacrifice of the male/female entity Purusha.

---

[1]It was in this sense that Charles Darwin, in his *On the Origin of Species,* referred to different castes of insects.

[2]Sanskrit is the sacred language of the Hindu religion.

Purusha was dismembered by the gods, and the detached parts became the stuff from which the entire universe was fashioned. More specifically, from the different parts of Purusha's body came the four *varnas:* (1) the *brahmans,* or priests, seers, and philosophers; (2) the *kshatriyas,* or warriors, royalty, and administrators; (3) the *vaishyas,* or producers, merchants, farmers, artisans, and other skilled workers; and (4) the *shudras,* or peasants and unskilled workers. A final group of people, the *scheduled castes,* or untouchables, complete India's stratification system, though for thousands of years they were deemed too impure to be part of the caste system itself.[3]

"Thousand-faced Purusha, thousand-eyed, thousand footed—he, having pervaded the earth on all sides, still extends ten fingers beyond it. Purusha alone is all this—whatever has been and whatever is going to be. . . . He is the lord of immortality and also of what grows on account of food.

When they divided Purusha, in how many different portions did they arrange him? What became of his mouth, what of his two arms? What were his two thighs and his two feet called?

His mouth became the brahman; his two arms were made into the [kshatriyas]; his two thighs the vaishyas; from his two feet the shudra was born."

—Rig Veda

Within each *varna,* or grade of being, are castes (*jatis*) numbering in the thousands. As with their *varna,* people's membership in a *jati* begins at birth and lasts until death. Each *jati* is associated with a particular occupation (for example, shoemaker, teacher, animal herder, or leather worker). However, it is no longer the case that all the members of a *jati* necessarily work in that occupation—especially in urban areas.

In 1949 the concept of untouchables was outlawed in India, and in 1950 the Constitution of Independent India outlawed the entire caste system. Did this mean the end of the caste system in India? No. Systems of inequality are institutions and, like all institutions, very difficult to change. The changes in law had very little effect. Because of its tie to important religious beliefs, the caste system has retained much of its strength and is still enforced by very strong informal norms and sanctions. Recently, as some of the former untouchables have sought to claim their legal rights, these informal sanctions have tended to be quite violent. In the city, it's possible to get past some of the constraints of the caste system because of the anonymity of urban life. In the countryside, however, everyone knows who belongs to each caste, and the caste system still has a great deal of power. This is a good example of how enduring and how difficult to change social

[3]During his tenure as the great modern leader of India, Mohandas Gandhi (1869–1948), nicknamed Mahatma ("the Great Soul"), made some concessions to bring the untouchables into mainstream society in India. Mahatma called the untouchables the *Harijan* (sons of Hari). *Hari* is the name commonly used to refer to Vishnu, an important Hindu deity. In other words, Gandhi was renaming the untouchables "creatures of God." Many former untouchables rejected the renaming as just a cosmetic change, however. Today, members of this casteless group prefer the less euphemistic term "scheduled caste" (a term used in the Constitution). Others prefer the name *dalit*—meaning "crushed" or "broken down" in Marathi—a language spoken in central India.

institutions are. It seems that social institutions will resist changes as long as participants believe in legitimating principles.

Estate Systems

As in a caste system, a person's place in the hierarchy of an *estate system* is determined at birth. Contacts between members of different estates are permitted, though generally this contact is fairly impersonal (as between a boss and an employee). So, for example, marriage between people of different estates is generally forbidden by law. The feudal system that prevailed in Western Europe during the Middle Ages is frequently cited as a good example of an estate system of stratification.

In England, as in much of the rest of Europe, there were three estates, or social strata. The highest stratum, the first estate, was made up of the aristocracy or nobility. The first estate, which persisted nearly into modern times in England, came into power after William the Conqueror (also known as William the Bastard) came from Normandy to proclaim himself king of England (in 1066 C.E.). William and his soldiers eventually confiscated most of the property owned by the original English (the Saxons). To show his appreciation, William granted these lands (or *feuds*) to the men who had helped him to conquer England. The earliest members of this first estate, then, were those with distinguished records of loyalty and military service to William (and later, to subsequent kings). Originally, royal land grants were more like land loans, and in theory, when the individual grantee died, the lands reverted to the king, who could then grant them to someone else. Over time, it became customary for the king to regrant the lands to the heirs of the previous owner. In this way membership in the first estate came to be inherited, or ascribed.

The clergy made up the second estate. Like the members of the first estate, the church had a great deal of power, in large part because it owned a great deal of land. Membership in the second estate was not based on ascribed characteristics. But the highest-ranking churchmen (and churchwomen) came from the ranks of the first estate, and the lowest-ranking from more common stock.

Originally the third estate included only the peasants (sometimes called *villeins*, or serfs). These were the people who were tied legally to specific parcels of land. So, when the king granted a piece of land to a member of the first estate, the aristocrat—or lord of the manor—got the people, too! The lord–peasant relationship was supposed to be for their mutual benefit. The lord of the manor pledged to protect his peasants from outside threats and keep the peace. In return, the peasants pledged their labor and loyalty.

A Year in the Life of the Peasant

"From the 29th of September until the 29th of June he must work two days a week, to wit on Monday and Wednesday; and on Friday he must plough with all the beasts of his team; but he has a holiday for a fortnight at Christmas and for a week at Easter and at Whitsuntide. If one of the Fridays on which he ought to plough is a festival or if the weather is bad, he must do the ploughing on some other day. Between the 29th of September and the 11th of November he must also plough and harrow half an acre for wheat, and for sowing that half-acre he must give of his own seed the eighth part of a quarter: Whether that quantity be more or less than is necessary for sowing the half-acre he must give that quantity, no more, no less: and on account of this seed he is excused from one day's work. At Christmas time he must make two quarters of malt and for each quarter he is excused one day's work. At Christmas he shall give three hens and a cock or four pence and at Easter ten eggs. He must also do six carryings in the year within the county between the 29th of June and the end of harvest at whatever time the bailiff shall choose, or, if the lord pleases, he shall between the 29th of June and the 29th of September work five days a week, working the whole day at whatever work is set him, besides carrying corn, for he shall carry but four cartloads of corn for a day's work. If at harvest time the lord shall have two or three 'boon works,' he shall come to them with all the able-bodied members of his family save his wife, so that he must send at least three men to work" (Pollock and Maitland 1898/1968, 267).

Vocabulary

bailiff: overseer

boon works: days of work the lord could require of a peasant as a favor

carrying: transporting crops

fortnight: 14 days

harrow: cultivate

malt: barleywater or barley added to water (the first step in beer making)

plough: plow

quarter: 8 bushels (8 gallons or 4 pecks)

sow: plant seed

Whitsuntide: Whitsunday/Pentecost (a Christian holiday celebrated in spring)

Each lord of a manor likewise owed duties to the king or some other overlord. Typically, these duties could be discharged by paying off any taxes assessed by the king. But some duties were different:

> A Kentishman was required to "hold the King's head in the boat" when he should cross the Channel. Even more peculiar was the case of a certain [minor lord] obliged every Christmas to make before his lord, *unum saltum et siffletum et unum bumbulum* ("a leap, whistle and audible gaseous expulsion"). (Bishop 1968, 111)

In time, the third estate came to include merchants and craftsmen as well as peasants. When they were few in number, the merchants and craftsmen were regarded as free men and existed on the periphery of the estate system. But, beginning in about the twelfth century, the nobles came to fear the growing power of these ambitious individuals. To keep them in their place (that is, below the first estate), the aristocrats enacted laws officially designating merchants and craftsmen as members of the third estate. In this way, the third estate came to be the estate of commoners.[4]

What beliefs legitimated the feudal system? Early on, the privileges that came from being a member of the first estate were justified because of the personal qualities of each aristocrat—his military prowess, bravery, loyalty, and so on. When rank in society (and land ownership) became hereditary, of course, even the proverbial 90-pound weakling could become lord of the manor. In time, people came to believe they belonged to the estate that suited them. As far as the people were concerned, social rank was assigned by God. As one historian explained, members of the aristocracy were perceived to be "noble," and "everyone else was judged 'ignoble' or 'churlish'"—that is, rude and ill-bred:

> The gentleman or nobleman was a man set apart to govern. He was independent and leisured: he derived his income without having to work for it, that income made him free from want and from being beholden to or dependent upon others, and he had the time and leisure to devote himself to the arts of government. He was independent in judgment and trained to make decisions. Not all gentlemen served in the offices which required such qualities (justice of the peace, sheriff, militia captain, high constable, etc.). But all had this capacity to serve, to govern. (Morrill 1984, 297)

As industrialization came to Europe, the estate system broke down. Industry created new jobs and pulled people away from the land. Still, remnants of the estate system can be found even

In the fifteenth-century, Lady Luliana Berners wrote about 'the common conviction that Seth and Abel, sons of Adam and Eve, were gentlemen, but Cain a churl and ancestor of the churls of the world. Christ [she said] was a gentleman on his mother's side.'"

—Morris Bishop (1968, 115)

---

[4]Occasionally, people speak of the fourth estate. This refers to the members of the media/press. The "term has its source from a reference to the reporters' gallery of the British Parliament whose influence on public policy was said to equal that of the Parliament's three traditional estates, the clergy, nobility, and commons" (Black 1979, 591).

today. For example, membership in the upper house of the English Parliament, the House of Lords, is open to all holders of hereditary *peerages,* or noble rank—these are the *Lords Temporal.*[5] Moreover, the upper house includes the *Lords Spiritual*—the archbishops and the most senior bishops of the Church of England (other religions are not officially represented in Parliament). At the same time, membership in the lower house of Parliament, the House of Commons, is limited to commoners—no one of noble birth can stand for election to the House of Commons without repudiating (giving up) his or her title.

Class Systems

The social class system of stratification was made possible by industrialization and urbanization. Workers moved from farms and agricultural occupations to cities and factory positions. Geographic mobility and industry presented many more opportunities to change one's life circumstances. A class system seemed to be an inevitable result.

Recall that in the estate system it was commonly believed that God placed the best people in the highest ranks. In the *class system,* by contrast, it is commonly thought that the best people work their own way into the highest ranks. In theory, at least, a true class system is supposed to turn on achieved rather than ascribed characteristics. Those who are smart, talented, and hard-working (and a little lucky) can rise to the top of the class system. Of course, people who are not as smart, talented, or hard-working (or who have bad luck) can just as easily sink to the bottom. In brief, this is the sort of belief that justifies class-based stratification systems as fair and just. To paraphrase James Kluegel and Eliot Smith, the class system is legitimated by the principle that the opportunity to get ahead is available to all. According to this logic, the position you reach in the class system is the direct result of your own efforts, traits, and abilities, and *not* the result of economic or social factors. That your efforts determine where you end up means that you are personally responsible for the rewards you receive. Thus, the logic of the class system regards inequality as legitimate because, after all, people end up where they deserve to be (1981, 29–32).

---

[5]This group does not include those lords who are not yet 21 years of age or who are disqualified owing to being foreign-born, bankrupt, or in prison for a felony or treason. Since 1963 women of noble rank have been allowed to sit in the House of Lords. The *Act of Lords* in 1999 ended the right of hereditary peers to pass their seats to family members. Since then, members are mostly appointed by a special committee.

Theoretical Conceptions of Class

What it is, exactly, that determines one's place in a class system has been a matter of great debate. One of the first to take a stand on this matter was Karl Marx. According to Marx, the most important thing about any society was its economic system, especially the means by which it produced the stuff that people needed to survive. In the earliest days of humanity, the *means of production* was hunting and gathering; in the Middle Ages, it was agriculture; in modern times, it is industry. Marx said that to understand an individual's resources, personality, values, and beliefs, we need to understand where he or she stands relative to the means of production.

From Marx's perspective, people in a fully developed capitalist society fall into one of two classes: the proletariat and the bourgeoisie. The proletariat are those whose place in the means of production is to labor; they have only their labor power to sell. The bourgeoisie are those who own the means of production—the factories and other large production facilities.[6]

Marx called the capitalist/owner stratum the *bourgeoisie*— a French word meaning "shopkeeper." In the Middle Ages, the bourgeoisie were relegated to the third estate. But, as Marx observed, as the means of production changed from agriculture to industry, the landowning aristocrats lost power to the spirited entrepreneurial shopkeepers who had risen up to become the factory owners.

Marx called the worker stratum the *proletariat*—from the Latin *proletarius*, a term that was used to refer to the lowest class of citizens in ancient Rome.

Max Weber had a different take on the nature of modern stratification. First, he said, Marx's conception of economic class was too narrow. The crucial thing was not where one stood in relation to the means of production (that is, whether one was an owner

---

[6]In the Middle Ages, the bourgeoisie were relegated to the third estate. But, as Marx observed, the means of production changed from agriculture to industry, the landowning aristocrats lost power to the spirited entrepreneurial shopkeepers who had risen up to become the factory owners. Marx also discussed a class he called the *petite* (or petty) *bourgeoisie* (small bourgeoisie)—owners of small stores and crafts people. The petit bourgeoisie, Marx predicted, would eventually disappear owing to the competition from large factories and retailers who could produce and market goods more cheaply. The petty bourgeoisie "sink gradually into the proletariat, partly because their diminutive capital does not suffice for the scale on which modern industry is carried on, and is swamped in the competition with large capitalists, partly because their specialized skill is rendered worthless by new methods of production. (Marx & Engels, 1848/1964, 70-71).

Ponder

Economist Simon Kuznets suggested that the graphic relation-ship between the means of production and the level of social stratification is a parabolic one (that is, one shaped like ∩). I've illustrated this relationship in figure 12.2.

Given your understanding of the different kinds of stratifica-tion systems, why do you think that industrial societies might have more equality than agrarian societies (that is, those based on agriculture)?

Figure 12.2 *Kuznets's Curve—Social Stratification and Technology*

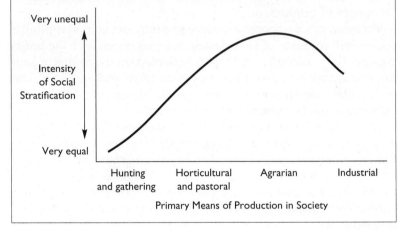

or a worker), but where one stood in the market situation. Weber defined class this way:

> The term *class* refers to any group of people . . . [who have the same] typical chance for a supply of goods, external living conditions, and personal life experiences, insofar as this chance is determined by the . . . power . . . to dispose of goods or skills for the sake of income in a given economic order. . . . *Class situation* is, in this sense, ultimately *market situation*. (Weber 1920/1958, 180)[7]

Marx's version of class would place major-league baseball players (for whom, in 2009, the minimum salary is $400,000, while more than half of the players make in excess of $1 million dollars) in the same class as secretaries who earn less than $35,000

---

[7]Weber distinguished between lifestyle and life chances: *Lifestyle:* distinctive ways in which people consume goods and services; the social customs associated with each class. Lifestyle differences tend to reflect people's financial and social resources. *Life chances:* phrase coined by Max Weber to indicate the probabilities concerning the fate an individual can expect in life. Life chances include the probability that the individual will obtain good health, education, autonomy, and a long life.

a year, because they all earn a living by selling their labor. But from Weber's point of view, baseball players would be in a much higher economic class than secretaries owing to the differences in their respective market situations.

Furthermore, according to Weber, Marx's emphasis on economic factors to the exclusion of all else was misguided. For Weber, social stratification was *multidimensional,* and economic situation was only one dimension of social position. For example, a college professor who earns less than $60,000 a year still has a higher social standing than the building contractor who makes $70,000.

Weber argued that to truly understand the nature of social stratification, sociologists had to take into account not only economics (market system) but also the dynamics of power and status in society. As Weber defined it, *power* "is the probability that one actor within a social relationship will be in a position to carry out his own will despite resistance." Thus, according to Weber, power is the ability to impose one's will or to get one's way even when faced with opposition from others.

Weber distinguished between different types of power. Legitimate power (which he called *authority*) is power that is seen as justified. For example, when a police officer stops a bank robber and takes her loot, this is a legitimate use of power. When a mugger stops a pedestrian and takes his wallet, this is an illegitimate use of power. According to Weber, the extent to which people have power (especially authority or legitimate power) has a big impact on their overall position in the stratification system.

Frequently, money and power are related, but not always. A local district attorney, for example, will earn less money than the executive officer of a large corporation, but the DA can exercise the power of her office to prevent the corporate officer from breaking the law.

Finally, Weber said, we must also take into account the degree to which people have social *status.* In this context status has to do with prestige—or the degree to which an individual has social honor.[8] Most research on social status or prestige has focused on occupations. As illustrated in table 12.1, sociologists have found that people in different occupations fairly consistently receive different amounts of social honor.[9]

---

[8]This may seem confusing to you because in chapter 8 I defined *status* as "a position that a person occupies on a social structure." Weber used the word *status* differently—to specify the degree to which a position in the social structure is respected or deferred to.

[9]Occupational prestige is usually determined by asking survey respondents to rank a number of occupations on a scale of 0 to 100. The average score given an occupation determines its prestige rating.

Table 12.1 Occupational Prestige Rankings of Selected Occupations in the United States

Occupation	Prestige Score	Occupation	Prestige Score
Physician	86	Bookkeeper	47
Lawyer	75	Machinist	47
College professor	74	Mail carrier	47
Architect	73	Secretary	46
Chemist	73	Photographer	45
Aerospace engineer	72	Bank teller	43
Dentist	72	Tailor	42
Secret Service agent	70	Welder	42
Clergy	69	Farm owner	40
Psychologist	69	Telephone operator	40
Pharmacist	68	Carpenter	39
Registered nurse	66	Radio/TV repair	38
Secondary school teacher	66	Security guard	37
Accountant	65	Brickmason	36
Athlete	65	Childcare worker	36
Electrical engineer	64	File clerk	36
Elementary school teacher	64	Hairdresser	36
Veterinarian	62	Baker	35
Computer programmer	61	Bus driver	32
Sociologist	61	Auto mechanic	31
Reporter	60	Sales clerk	30
Police officer	60	Cashier	29
Actor	58	Assembly line worker	29
Dietician	56	Garbage collector	29
Radio/TV announcer	55	Taxi driver	28
Librarian	54	Waitress or waiter	28
Aircraft mechanic	53	Bellhop	27
Fire fighter	53	Bartender	25
Dental hygienist	52	Farm laborer	23
Social worker	52	Household maid	23
Electrician	51	Door-to-door salesperson	22
Funeral director	49	Janitor or cleaner	22
Realtor	49	Shoe shiner	9

SOURCE: Adapted from *General Social Survey, Cumulative Code Book, 1972–1990* (Chicago: National Opinion Research Center, 1990).

Here's an important point: In view of what I have just stated, to refer to our stratification system as one based on class is rather misleading. So, you should firmly implant the following fact in your brain: When sociologists use the word *class*, they tend to mean more than economic factors. Most sociologists follow Weber's example in treating social class as a multidimensional thing. Thus, for example, when sociologists use the word *class*, they frequently mean *socioeconomic standing*, or SES. Measures of SES look at people's income, education, occupational prestige, and wealth and provide some overall assessment of people's place in the social stratification system.

12.1 Mary Beth inherited her parents' small farm. Her profits range from $25,000 to $35,000 annually.

Elizabeth graduated from Harvard Law School. Now she works as an in-house counsel (attorney) for General Motors. She brings home about $145,000 a year.

  a. According to Marx, who occupies the higher class position—Mary Beth or Elizabeth? Why?
  b. What would Weber say about who occupies the higher class position? Why?
  c. Suppose the stock market crashes, times are really tough economically, and people stop making major purchases. Who is more economically vulnerable—Mary Beth or Elizabeth? Why?

STOP & REVIEW

Some Words About Slavery

Although slavery is a major source of inequality everywhere it exists, I have not included it as a system of stratification in and of itself. The reason for this is that slavery can exist (and has done so) within caste, estate, and class systems. Slaves are people whose function is to serve others and who have no political rights of their own—no right to own property, to sign legal contracts (and then go to the courts to get their contracts enforced), to legally marry, or to maintain legal custody of their children. Slaves may be given certain freedoms by their masters, but these are dependent on the goodwill of the master. In the most extreme form of slavery, slaves are treated as if they were the property of their masters, in much the same way as goats or cattle. This extreme type of slavery is called *chattel slavery*—*chattel* being a legal term for "movable property" (like farm animals) as opposed to "real property" (like land). This is the sort of slavery that existed in southern states prior to the Civil War.

Slavery is most frequently found in societies that are heavily agricultural (as opposed to industrial). Depending on the society, people can be enslaved in a number of ways. The earliest forms of slavery involved people who had been captured in war or kidnapped. In many societies, people have been enslaved because they could not pay their debts (or the debts of a family member). Often, criminals have been sentenced to slavery. In some societies, children are sold into slavery by their parents (frequently as an alternative to infanticide, or infant killing, which usually involves only girl babies). Finally there is *self-enslavement*, which occurs when people sell themselves into slavery as a way to overcome serious economic insecurity.

Historian Orlando Patterson (1982) found that regardless of how groups of people originally find their way into the position of being slaves, if slavery persists in a society for more than a couple of generations, it tends to become hereditary. In other words, there is a tendency for slavery to change from being an achieved to an ascribed status.

Some social scientists have suggested that a slave system is just like a caste system and that slaves are simply the outcastes. They have a point—but Patterson argues that there are important differences between slaves and outcastes:

> There was never any marriage, or even illicit sexual relations, between the outcaste group and ordinary persons, whereas such relations were common between "free" males and slave women. . . . Slaves universally were not only sexually exploited in their role as concubines, but also in their role as mother-surrogates and nurse-maids. However great the human capacity for contradiction, it has never been possible for any group of masters to suckle at their slave's breasts as infants, sow their wild oats with her as adolescents, then turn around as adults and claim that she was polluted. (1982, 50)

Moreover, slaves can be freed, or manumitted[10]—but outcastes cannot lose their caste status. Finally, in a variety of societies, slaves were drawn from even the highest caste. "Indeed, in order to perform the various duties imposed on domestic servants, to be permitted to cross the threshold of an owner's dwelling, it was imperative for the slave to enjoy a degree of ritual purity conferred only by membership in certain castes." Thus, for example, in Nepal "even Brahmins were enslaved without losing caste" (Patterson 1982, 51).

---

[10]Manumission was a formal process by which a slave was made free. The term comes from the Latin *manu* (hand, power) and *mitter* (to let go).

Social Mobility and Open
Versus Closed Systems

At the most abstract level, sociologists distinguish between *open* and *closed* stratification systems. The distinction depends on the amount of *social mobility* that the system allows.

Sociologists also distinguish between different types of social mobility. *Horizontal* mobility refers to movement, say, from one occupation to another in the same stratum. *Vertical* mobility refers to movement up or down in a stratification system (for example, from lower to middle class). A truly open system of stratification will have a great deal of both horizontal and vertical mobility. A truly closed system will have neither.

Sociologists further distinguish between *inter*generational and *intra*generational mobility. *Intergenerational* mobility refers to changes in position in the stratification system by different generations of family members. When a son attains a higher (or lower) class than his father, the son has experienced intergenerational mobility. *Intragenerational* mobility—or *career* mobility—has to do with the mobility that occurs within a person's lifetime. For example, a woman who starts her life in poverty and grows up to be a justice of the Supreme Court has experienced intragenerational, or career, mobility. In an open system of stratification, we would expect to see a great deal of intragenerational or career mobility—people should have opportunities to work their way up (or down). And we would also expect a great deal of intergenerational mobility—if a system is truly open, where you start out (such as poor or rich) should not determine where you end up.

A word of caution is in order here. Recall from chapter 8 Weber's concept of the ideal type. The ideal type of a thing is that thing considered in its *pure form*. As we discussed in chapter 8, the ideal-type bureaucracy is a step removed from real bureaucracies, because real bureaucracies often are not pure. The concepts of open and closed stratification systems are also ideal types. No known system of stratification is either totally open or totally closed. Table 12.2 lists some of the major differences between ideal-type open and closed systems.

It is fairly easy to see where each of the major systems of stratification—caste, estate, and class—would fit in this classification. The caste system is the most closed system. In India the differences between people in different *varnas* and even *jatis* are perceived to be related to differences in the purity of the individual's soul. This means that there is no real chance of changing one's caste (or the caste of one's children) during one's lifetime.

The estate system is also mostly closed, but there is some room for advancement. As noted previously, one could change one's

Table 12.2 Attributes of Ideal-Type Open and Closed Systems of Stratification

Open Systems	Closed Systems
Boundaries between strata are permeable (open).	Boundaries between strata are impermeable (closed).
Positions within the system are achieved.	Positions within the system are ascribed.
The opportunity to change ranks exists.	No opportunity to change ranks exists.
The law permits exogamy (marriage outside of a stratum), but informal norms promote endogamy (marriage within a stratum).	The law requires endogamy.

estate by joining the church. Even men without religious vocations could at least hope for advancement because "here and there little men became big through astuteness, prowess, or royal favor. Valiant fighters were knighted on the field of battle." At the same time, some not-so-valiant "knights sank into the peasantry or lived as robbers" (Bishop 1968, 115). In general, however, distinctions between the estates were seen as fixed by God.

The class system is the closest thing to a truly open stratification system. As I suggested, one's class is supposed to be determined by what one does, not by who one's parents are—that is, by achieved rather than ascribed characteristics. In a class-based system, then, we would expect to see a great deal of all kinds of mobility—vertical and horizontal, intragenerational and intergenerational. The degree to which that is true in real life (as opposed to theory) is something we will examine in the next two chapters.

12.2 Give two examples of each of the following:
   a. vertical mobility
   b. horizontal mobility
   c. intragenerational mobility
   d. intergenerational mobility

Chapter Review

1. Below I have listed the major concepts discussed in this chapter. Define each of the terms. (*Hint:* This exercise will be more helpful to you if, in addition to defining each concept, you create an example of it in your own words.)

   stratification
   legitimating rationale

caste system, in India
  transmigration
  karma
  dharma
  varna
  jatis
  brahmans, kshatriyas, vaishyas, shudras, dalits (scheduled
  castes)
estate system, medieval Europe
  feudal
  estates, first, second, third
  villeins
  fourth estate
Marx's conception of class
  bourgeoisie, proletariat
Weber's conception of class
  lifestyle versus life chances
Kuznets's curve
power versus authority
status and prestige
socioeconomic status
chattel slavery
manumission
social mobility
  horizontal and vertical
  inter- and intragenerational
open system versus closed system
exogamy and endogamy

2. Suppose that your much younger brother or sister (a 7-year-old) has just watched a television show about poverty in the United States that featured many clips of children dressed in shabby clothes and looking hungry. Your little brother or sister poses a question to you—"How come some people are so poor and others have so much money?" Explain how you would respond.

3. Something terrible happens, and you have to drop out of college. The only job you can find pays $7.50 an hour. Create a budget for how you would spend that money—for rent and other necessities. Would you be able to live a "comfortable" life? (Check the local paper to find out about rent, visit a grocery store to discover what different foods cost.)
    Then assume that on the same level of wages, you had to support two children. What would their lives be like?

4. Describe the differences in the kinds of rationales or principles that justify caste, estate, and class systems.

STOP

&

REVIEW

Answers and Discussion

12.1

a. Marx would say that Mary Beth, the owner of the plumbing firm, has a higher class position than Elizabeth, the attorney. The reason is that Mary Beth owns (part of) the means of production, while Elizabeth makes her living selling her labor.

b. Weber would say that Elizabeth has the higher class position, because her salary puts her in a better position with respect to the marketplace. She can purchase more stuff than Mary Beth and increase the quality of her life chances and lifestyle.

c. This could be argued either way, but in my opinion, it's possible that Elizabeth is the more economically vulnerable. During depressed economic times, General Motors might have to downsize. And given that lawyers are not necessarily central to the business of General Motors, they might be the first to be laid off. Unless she has other sources of wealth, without a regular paycheck coming in, Elizabeth could experience some financially stressful times. Mary Beth, on the other hand, is less vulnerable to economic disaster because even in economic times, people will still need farm produce.

12.2

a. Vertical mobility occurs when someone goes up or down the "occupational ladder." A promotion from typist to executive secretary is vertical mobility, as is a demotion from executive vice president to sales representative.

b. Horizontal mobility is movement in which someone changes jobs but not necessarily for the better or worse. If I quit my present teaching job and moved to a new university, this would probably be a horizontal move. Sociologists and other observers of the modern labor market predict that the current generation of workers will change careers more than a half dozen times in their lifetimes. Many of these changes will be horizontal.

c. The prefix *intra* means "within." So, intragenerational mobility is career mobility, or mobility within the lifetime of a person. Movement from graduate student to instructor, to assistant, to associate, and then to full professor is intragenerational mobility.

d. The prefix *inter* means "between." So, intergenerational mobility is mobility between generations. Suppose your dad was a blue-collar worker and you became a physician. You would have experienced intergenerational mobility. (Of course, it could be that your mom was a physician and you became a bum. That would be intergenerational mobility, too.)

13

INEQUALITY AND ACHIEVEMENT

Social Class

When I introduce students to the concept of stratification, they often react as if it's a topic that is relevant only to other societies. More specifically, I have observed in my students a tendency to believe that in the United States, there are no such things as social classes, let alone social class differences.

My students are not unusual in this respect. Many researchers have reported that people in the United States are reluctant to admit the existence of class. This was something that Paul Fussell discovered early on when he was writing his *Class: A Guide Through the American Status System.* The subject of class, he concluded, is "always touchy":

> You can outrage people today simply by mentioning social class, very much the way, sipping tea among the aspidistras [a kind of lily] a century ago, you could silence a party by adverting too openly to sex. When, recently, asked what I am writing, I have answered, "A book about social class in America," people tend first to straighten their ties and sneak a glance at their cuffs to see how far fraying has advanced there. Then, a few minutes later, they silently get up and walk away. . . . It is as if I had said, "I am working on a book urging the beating to death of baby whales using the dead bodies of baby seals." Since I have been writing this book I have experienced many times the awful truth of [economist] R. H. Tawney's perception, in his book *Equality* (1931): "The word 'class' is fraught with unpleasing associations, so that to linger upon it is apt to be interpreted as the symptom of a perverted mind and a jaundiced spirit." (1983, 15)

Why *is* class such a touchy issue in the United States? It's touchy because asking questions about social class violates an important social myth: that people in the United States are pretty much equal. As one respondent to a survey explained to

Figure 13.1
*Distribution of
Income in the United
States, 1774, 1860,
2011*

SOURCE: Weissmann 2012.

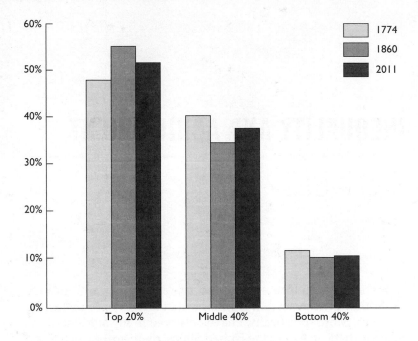

In 2010, the most
affluent (wealthiest)
1 percent of
Americans owned
34.5 percent of
the nation's wealth.
The top ten
percent owned
74.5 percent of
the nation's wealth
(Levine 2012, 4).

sociologist Richard Scase, "Class is not as important as it used to be, most people are middle class nowadays" (1992, 1). Indeed, study after study has found that most everyone (well, anyway, at least 80 percent) in the United States will describe him- or herself as a member of the middle class. So, when you ask people about class and class differences, they will typically respond that such differences do not exist—at least not where they come from.

> Being told that there are no social classes in the place where the interviewee lives is an old experience for sociologists. "'We don't have classes in our town' almost invariably is the first remark recorded by the investigator," reports Leonard Reissman, author of *Class in American Life* (1959). "Once that has been uttered and is out of the way, the class divisions in the town can be recorded with what seems to be an amazing degree of agreement among the good citizens of the community." (Fussell 1983, 17)

How much inequality is there in the United States? When it is measured in terms of income, we find that there is a great deal of inequality. Examine figure 13.1. It shows that if we divide the U.S. population into five groups, the highest fifth (the top earning 20 percent of the people) receives half of the money that is paid out in income each year.

Figure 13.2 shows that the level of inequality of wealth is even more striking. The top fifth (the richest 20 percent of society) owns more than 80 percent of the wealth. That means that the remaining four-fifths of the U.S. population share one-fifth of the wealth.

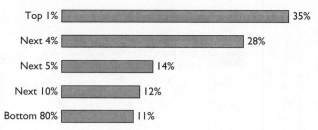

Figure 13.2 *How the Nation's Wealth Is Distributed (2010)*
Sᴏᴜʀᴄᴇ: *Domhoff, 2012.*

Thus, there is inequality in terms of both income and wealth, but more inequality in wealth. What is the implication of this? _Income_ is the amount of money that an individual or family group receives in wages, salaries, investments, and so on. _Wealth_ is the total value of the assets owned by an individual or family group, minus the amount of debt they have. Wealth, then, is special. It tends to be more enduring and provides more access to what Weber called _"life chances"_:

> Wealth signifies the command over financial resources that a family has accumulated over its lifetime along with those resources that have been accumulated across generations. Such resources, when combined with income, can create the opportunity to secure the "good life" in whatever form is needed—education, business, training, justice, health, comfort, and so on. *Wealth is a special form of money not used to purchase milk and shoes and other life necessities. More often it is used to create opportunity, secure a desired stature and standard of living, or pass along class status to one's children.* In this sense the command over resources that wealth entails is more encompassing than is income or education, and closer in meaning and theoretical significance to our traditional notions of economic well-being and access to life chances. (Oliver and Shapiro 1997, 2 *emphasis added*)

Still, the existence of inequality does not necessarily mean that class is all that important. And, in fact, for many Americans, class is not seen as very important because most people believe that regardless of social class, everyone has about the same chance to get ahead in society. As we observed in chapter 12, what really justifies the U.S. stratification system is the notion of "equality of opportunity." Ask people and they will tell you: What matters is how hard you work and how smart you are. Because of our socialization, such reasoning is compelling to Americans. Even young children understand and believe this logic—at least, that is what sociologists Scott Cummings and Del Taebel discovered from their survey of school children. Here's how one of their young respondents explained the logic of the American stratification system:

> "People are rich because they have the know-how and the opportunity, and to an extent most of them are wealthy because of some type of motivation that causes them not to settle at one step or one degree; they wanted to reach higher heights. . . . People are poor

Figure 13.3
Intergenerational Mobility: The Probability of Reaching a Given Income Quintile for Children Born to Parents in the Bottom and Top Quintiles
SOURCE: Isaacs, Sawhill, and Haskins, 2008.

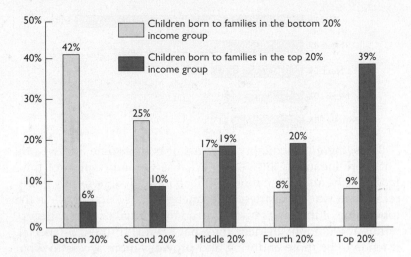

because they are not educated enough to know that there is something for them out there; that they can make money. . . . They are ignorant and uneducated; a lot of them just don't care. . . . They are happy the way they are. . . . *If you really want to have some money, you can get it no matter how poor you have been.*" [emphasis added]. (1978, 207)

If equality of opportunity does exist, an individual's class origins should not determine the level of his or her economic and social achievements. That is, if there is equality of opportunity, neither poverty nor wealth should be necessarily intergenerational; people who grew up in poor families should be no more likely to be poor as adults than people who grew up in nonpoor families.

One of the most ambitious attempts to test the validity of this rationale began in 1968 with the Panel Study of Income Dynamics, in which researchers followed 5,000 families and their children over the course of 20 years. As sociologist Margaret Corcoran discovered, where one begins does have a big effect on where one ends up. Consider figure 13.3—the data presented there suggest one thing: It matters if one's parents are poor, and *"it matters a lot"* (Corcoran 1995).

Social scientists have extensively documented that parents' social class has a tremendous effect on their children's life chances. Simply put, people have a greater chance of succeeding in life if their parents are not poor. In what respects are people's life chances affected by their class origins? We can focus on four areas in particular:

"Nobody cares more about free enterprise and competition and about the best man winning than the man who inherited his father's store or farm."

—C. Wright Mills (1959)

1. *Health:* Parental class position has long-term health consequences for children. In general, mortality (death) rates and morbidity (sickness) rates are negatively related to social class. For example, studies have demonstrated that poverty is related to delays in children's physical development. "Physically underdeveloped and ill children might become less healthy and hence less employable as adults, a process

The Matthew Effect

As figure 13.4 suggests, the advantages that come with wealth tend to endure even during troubled economic times. The figure shows that during the 1980s and 1990s, the rich got richer while the not-so-rich got poorer. This dynamic is one example of what some people call the *Matthew effect* (from the passage in the Gospel of Matthew that says, "For whosoever hath, to him shall be given, and he shall have more abundance: but whosoever hath not, from him shall be taken away . . ." [13:12]).

Economist Lester Thurow explained it this way: "Once wealth is accumulated, opportunities to make more money multiply, since accumulated wealth leads to income-earning opportunities that are not open to those without wealth" (1996, 243).

Figure 13.4 *Changes in Share of Nation's Wealth (net worth), 1983–2001*

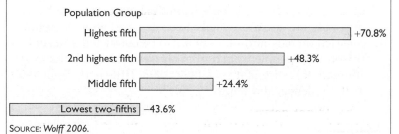

Population Group

Highest fifth +70.8%

2nd highest fifth +48.3%

Middle fifth +24.4%

Lowest two-fifths −43.6%

SOURCE: *Wolff 2006.*

Most households (63 percent) experienced a loss in net worth between 2007 and 2009. The median percentage decrease in wealth among these households was 45 percent. The broad-based downward shift of the wealth distribution between 2007 and 2009 was reflected by reductions in median and mean summary measures. The drop in *median* net worth (23 percent) was greater than the drop in *mean* net worth (19 percent), which suggests that *households in the lower half of the wealth distribution were more adversely affected by the 2007–2009 recession than those further up the distribution.* (Levine 2012, 5–6).

perhaps arising from the inadequacies of the physical environment that poverty affords or from inadequate treatment of children's ailments directly due to lack of economic resources or indirectly to parental inattention or resignation: better to ignore things that you cannot alter" (Corcoran 1995, 262–263). Poor children are also more likely to suffer from serious psychological distress (Braun 1995; Johnson et al. 1991; McLeod and Shanahan 1993; Nelson 1992).

2. *Education:* Parental income has an effect on whether children finish high school and attend and graduate from college. Poverty has an especially strong impact on very young children. In

1986, for example, only about 25 percent of poor children were enrolled in a preschool program, compared to 40 percent of children from more affluent families (Entwisle and Alexander 1993). Children who did not attend preschool have fewer skills (color identification, counting, etc.), and are disadvantaged compared to kids who did attend preschool; they are more likely to be identified by their teachers as having educational problems and this label is as strong as reading- and math-readiness scores in predicting success (Duncan et al. 1998).

3. *Working life:* Men who grew up in poor families tend to work many fewer hours per year and to earn less per hour than men who grew up in middle-class homes. Growing up in poor families reduces men's annual earnings by more than 40 percent (Corcoran 1995).

4. *Crime and justice:* Poor people are more likely to be victims of all kinds of crime. People from the lower classes who break the law are more likely to be arrested, less likely to be released on bail, and more likely to be convicted and sent to prison than people from higher classes who break the law (Bureau of Justice Statistics 1992, 1993; Tittle and Meier 1990; Tittle, Villenez, and Smith 1978).

STOP
&
REVIEW

13.1

a. What are some other examples of the Matthew effect?
b. Examine the data in table 13.1. Do they reflect another example of the Matthew effect?

Explaining Social Stratification

Most people end up in a class position that is the same as or close to the one occupied by their parents. Another way to state this is to say that members of each new generation tend to reproduce

Table 13.1 Who Goes to College, by Family Income and High School Performance

High School Performance	Student's Family Income	
	Low-Income	High-Income
Highest achievers	78%	97%
Second highest achievers	63	90
Third highest achievers	50	85
Lowest achievers	36	77

SOURCE: Gerald and Haycock, 2006.

the class structure in which they were raised. When sociologists try to explain the dynamics that underlie this reproduction of the class structure, they typically draw on one of two sorts of perspectives: cultural or structural.

CULTURAL EXPLANATIONS

Cultural explanations of the reproduction of the class structure hinge on two assumptions. First, people in different social classes have different patterns of values, beliefs, and behavioral norms, which they pass on to their children through the socialization process. Anthropologist Allison Davis, writing in the late 1940s, was an early proponent of this sort of cultural perspective. According to Davis, "Social class patterning of the child's learning, as exerted through the family, extends from the control of the type of food he eats and the way he eats it, to the kinds of sexual, aggressive and educational training he receives" (1948, 12). The second assumption of the cultural perspective is that the values, beliefs, and behavioral norms of lower classes are not very compatible with success in society.

Probably the most famous advocate of the cultural perspective on the reproduction of the class system was anthropologist Oscar Lewis. Based on his studies of the lower classes in a variety of societies, Lewis coined the term *culture of poverty*. According to Lewis and others who have followed in his footsteps, the culture of poverty turns poverty into a vicious cycle. Once it comes into existence, he said, the culture of poverty "tends to perpetuate itself from generation to generation because of its effects on the children" (1966, 50). Lewis argued that "by the time slum children are age six or seven they have usually absorbed the basic values and attitudes of their subculture. Thereafter they are psychologically unready to take full advantage of changing conditions or improving opportunities that may develop in their life time" (1966, 7).

Most proponents of the cultural explanation emphasize that it is not so much that the values, beliefs, and behavioral norms of poor people are bad; more to the point is the degree to which these values, beliefs, and behavioral norms are out of whack with those of mainstream society. Social psychologist Morton Deutch argued, for example, that

> we know that children from underprivileged environments tend to come to school with qualitatively different preparation for the demands both of the learning process and the behavior equipments of the classroom. There are various differences in the kinds of socialization experiences these children have, as contrasted with the middle class child. The culture of their environment is a different one from the culture that has molded the school, its educational techniques and theories. (1964, 172)

STRUCTURAL EXPLANATIONS

Structural explanations of the reproduction of the class system reject the notion that the best way to understand poverty is to look at cultural attributes of the poor. Proponents of the structural point of view argue that it is much more appropriate to focus on the limited access to opportunities that poor people have compared to the more affluent. They suggest that the differences in the values, beliefs, and behavioral norms that seem to exist are better explained as the *consequences* of poverty rather than as the causes. Sociologist Elliot Liebow, who explored the life of the urban poor in great depth, explained the significance of what might *seem* to be cultural differences between rich and poor this way:

> The streetcorner man *does not appear as a carrier of an independent cultural tradition* [emphasis added]. His behavior appears not so much as a way of realizing the distinctive goals of his own subculture, or of conforming to his [values and beliefs], but rather as his way of trying to achieve many of the goals and values of the larger society, of failing to do this, and of concealing this failure from others and from himself as best he can. (1967, 222)

Again, the structuralist point of view is that it is not their culture but the lack of opportunities open to the poor that holds them back. For example, the important thing is not that poor children tend to be less prepared for the realities of school than middle-class children, but that the schools themselves are inadequate.

More recently, educator Jonathan Kozol compared schools in poor neighborhoods to those in more affluent ones. The differences he found are reflected in the title of his book—*Savage Inequalities: Children in America's Schools.* Here he quotes a teacher who works in an inner-city high school:

> "Very little education in this school would be considered academic in the suburbs. Maybe 10 to 15 percent of students are in truly academic programs. Of the 55 percent who graduate, 20 percent may go to four-year colleges . . . another 10 to 20 percent may get some kind of higher education. An equal number join the military." (1991)

It is hard to blame cultural factors when even the most highly motivated students have a tough time getting an education in such schools. One young woman told Kozol,

> "I don't go to physics class, because my lab has no equipment. . . . The typewriters in my typing class don't work. The women's toilets . . . " she makes a sour face. "I'll be honest," she says, "I just don't use the toilets. If I do, I come back into class and I feel dirty." (1991)

13.2 Recently a student shared with me an example of his experiences with the stratification system in the United States:

> *"In high school I was an all-American basketball player even though I played in a ghetto school. . . . I got letters from coaches from top college programs saying, 'I've heard you are a great player, are you going to any camps?' The point was that they didn't want to come to my school to watch me play because it's in a rough place. They were willing to come see me if I could go to camp. But I wasn't able to afford to go to any of the camps."*

In your informed judgment, which point of view on the reproduction of class does this student's experience support—the *cultural* or the *structural?* Why? In your answer, summarize the two points of view—cultural and structural.

Kozol observed that things were bad all around at that school and are not likely to get better in the foreseeable future:

> The science labs . . . are 30 to 50 years outdated. John McMillan, a soft-spoken man, teaches physics at the school. He shows me his lab. The six lab stations in the room have empty holes where pipes were once attached. "It would be great if we had water," says McMillan. . . .
>
> Teachers are running out of chalk and paper, and their paychecks are arriving two weeks late. The city warns its teachers to expect a cut of half their pay until the fiscal crisis has been eased. (1991)

The situation in suburban schools tends to be quite different. Typical was one school where Kozol found, for one thing, that members of the faculty were not so worried about chalk and paper:

> According to the principal, the school has 96 computers for 546 children. The typical student, he says, studies a foreign language for four or five years, beginning in the junior high school, and for a second language (Latin is available) for two years. Of 140 seniors, 92 are now enrolled in AP [advanced college placement] classes. Maximum teacher salary will soon reach $70,000. (1991)

When Kozol asked students at this high school how they felt about their privileged positions, he found that students not only understood their advantages but accepted them as just:

> "I don't think that busing students from their ghetto to a different school would do much good," one student says. "You can take them out of the environment, but you can't take the environment out of *them.* If someone grows up in [the inner city], he's not going to be prone to learn." His name is Max and he has short black hair and speaks with confidence. "Busing didn't work when it was tried," he says. I ask him how he knows this and he says he saw a television movie about Boston.
>
> "I agree that it's unfair the way it is," another student says. "We have AP courses and they don't. Our classes are much smaller." But, she says, "putting them in schools like ours is not the answer. Why not put some AP classes into *their* school? Fix the roof and paint the halls so it will not be so depressing." (1991)

Jennifer, whose family had recently moved up from a poorer neighborhood, agreed. She pointed out to Kozol that although her family had managed to bring itself up, some people simply weren't prepared to do what it takes to be mobile:

> "It has to be the people in the area who want an education. If your parents just don't care, it won't do any good to spend a lot of money. Someone else can't want a good life for you. You have got to want it for yourself." Then, she adds, however, "I agree that everyone should have a chance at taking the same course." (1991)

According to proponents of the structural perspective, the cultural theories of poverty themselves may be contributing to the problem.

By stressing the inadequacies of poor people, they seem to encourage a cover-up of the inadequacies of the structure in which those poor people live. Sociologist William Ryan called the kind of reasoning implicit in the cultural perspective a form of "blaming the victim" (1971). For proponents of the structural point of view, then, blaming poor people's culture for their poverty is like blaming the rape victim because she wore provocative clothing; such blame is simply misplaced. Just as the rapist is the major cause of rape, the major cause of poverty is a lack of opportunities.

> To what extent do these theories obscure more basic reasons for the educational retardation of lower status children? To what extent do they offer acceptable and desired alibis for educational default: the fact that these children, by and large, do not learn because they are not being taught effectively and they are not being taught because those who are charged with the responsibility of teaching them do not believe they can learn, do not expect that they can learn, and do not act in ways which help them to learn. (Clark 1967, 130–131)

Public education in the United States is supposed to prepare children to compete with one another in the real world; the famous educator Horace Mann (1796–1859) called the U.S. public school system "the great equalizer." Research by Kozol and others suggests that when it comes to schools, the playing fields are not all that equal.

Even within the same school, the playing field is likely to be uneven. This unevenness manifests itself in the practice of tracking. In *Keeping Track: How Schools Structure Inequality*, Jeannie Oakes defined tracking this way:

> Tracking is the process whereby students are divided into categories so that they can be assigned in groups to various kinds of classes. Sometimes students are classified as fast, average, or slow learners and placed into fast, average, or slow classes on the basis of their scores on achievement or ability tests. Often teachers' estimates of what students have already learned or their potential for learning

Beyond Academics

In 2004, *USA Today* compiled data from 27 states on who won state championships in 10 team sports between January 1999 and December 2003. The schools were divided into four groups according to the income of people who lived in the neighborhoods in which the school was found.

The results were startling to anyone who thinks that sports championships are won strictly according to the talent and hard work of the athletes who compete: "Public schools in the wealthiest neighborhoods win state team championships at more than twice the rate of schools in the least wealthy neighborhoods."

A number of factors are associated with the differences illustrated in figure 13.5. "Schools in wealthier neighborhoods often have booster clubs that raise money beyond what is budgeted by school districts and that can be used for any number of wish-list functions. 'Think about coaches, equipment, weight rooms, and places to play,' says Bruce Weber, publisher of *Scholastic Coach and Athletic Director* magazine. 'All those things that money can buy.'" Athletes who live in wealthy neighborhoods are likely to have a personal advantage as well: wealthy parents. "As high school athletes become more specialized and increasingly play one sport year round, wealthier parents are more able to afford summer camps and travel teams." One parent of a talented softball player told reporters, "I figure it costs me about $5,000 per year for each of my girls" to play softball at this level. "But it is well worth it" (Brady and Sylwester 2004, 1, 4A).

Figure 13.5 *Percentage of State Team Championships (Boys and Girls) Won by Schools by Neighborhood Wealth**

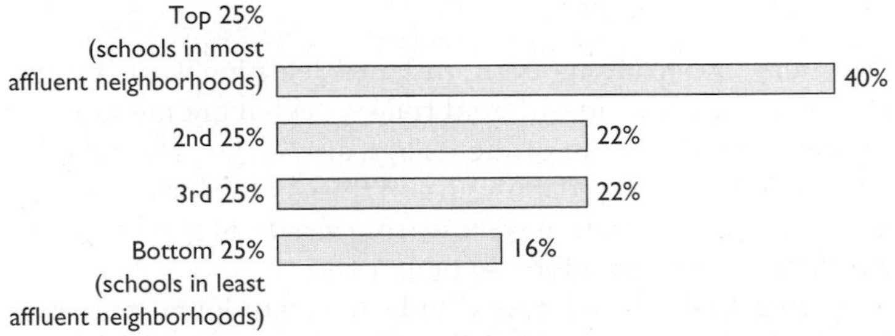

Top 25% (schools in most affluent neighborhoods) 40%
2nd 25% 22%
3rd 25% 22%
Bottom 25% (schools in least affluent neighborhoods) 16%

*Excludes private schools. Only in Rhode Island did schools in the wealthiest neighborhoods not win more championships than other schools.
SOURCE: Brady and Sylwester, 2004.

determine how students are identified and placed. Sometimes students are classified according to what seems most appropriate to their future lives. Sometimes, but rarely in any genuine sense, students themselves choose to be in "vocation," "general," or "academic" programs. (1985, 3)

Although some schools claim that they do not track their students, Oakes and others have found that most, if not all, schools have some mechanism by which they divide their student populations into groups of students who are "alike": "In fact, this is exactly the justification some schools offer for tracking students. Educators strongly believe that students learn better in groups with others like themselves. They also believe that groups of similar students are easier to teach" (Oakes 1985, 4).

What are the consequences of tracking? Sociologist Maureen Hallinan studied research on tracking and summed up the evidence this way:

> The general conclusion that can be reached from this research is that tracking and ability grouping have a negative effect on the achievement of lower track or ability group students, a negligible effect on students in the middle groups, and a weak to modest positive effect on high track and ability group students. . . . Moreover, the research reveals a considerable number of disadvantages of tracking and ability grouping for students in the lower groups in terms of the development of negative attitudes and behaviors related to learning.
>
> In addition to these immediate consequences of tracking and ability grouping for student achievement, the practice has been shown to have important consequences for future course selection and placement and for educational aspirations. . . . The research shows that placement in a college preparatory track has positive effects on a number of educational outcomes, including academic achievement, measure by grades and standardized test scores, measures of motivation, and educational aspirations and attainment. And this positive relationship persists even after family background and ability differences are controlled for. (Hallinan 1988, 260; see also Thernstrom 1992)

Teachers' expectations and students' learning vary by track. Oakes asked teachers in different tracks, "What are the most critical things you want your students to learn?" Then she asked students, "What was the most important thing you learned in school this year?" Representative quotes from teachers and students in the different tracks are given in table 13.2.

On what basis do schools divide their students into tracks? School officials report that their tracking systems reflect students' academic abilities and aptitudes. Yet kids from lower-class backgrounds are disproportionately placed in lower tracks, whereas kids from more affluent backgrounds are disproportionately placed in upper tracks. Often the tracks in which kids are placed have less to do with their abilities than with their parents' social class. A parent from a higher stratum, for example, can ensure that his or her child is placed on a fast track even if the kid hasn't been doing all that well in school. Of course, when that happens,

Table 13.2 High School Teachers' Goals and Students' Learning Experiences, by Track

What teachers say are their most important goals for their students

High Track	Low Track
Ability to reason logically, in all subject areas.	That they know that their paychecks will be correct when they receive them. Punctuality, self-discipline, and honesty will make them successful in their jobs. They must begin and end each day with a smile....
Logical thought processes. Analysis of given information.	
Ability to understand exactly what is asked in a question.	
That their own talents and thoughts are important.	Properly planning to ensure favorable performances.
Development of imagination. Critical thinking.	How to fill out insurance forms, income tax returns.
To gain some interpretive skills. Scientific reasoning and logic.	Content—minimal. Be realistic about goals. Develop ones they *can* achieve. Practical math skills for everyday living. A sense of responsibility.

What students report is the most important thing they have learned in class during the school year

High Track	Low Track
To understand complex concepts and ideas and experiment with them. Also to work independently.	I have learned that I should do my questions for the book when [the teacher] asks ...
The most important thing that I have learned in this class is the benefit of logical and organized thinking; learning is made much easier when the simple processes of organizing thoughts have been grasped.	To learn how to listen and follow the directions of the teacher.
	To be a better listener in class.
I have proved to myself that I have the discipline to take a difficult class just for knowledge, even though it has nothing to do with my career plans.	The most important thing I have learned in this class is to always have your homework in and have materials ready whenever [the teacher] is ready.
	Learn to get along with the students and the teacher.

SOURCE: Jeannie Oakes, "More Than Misapplied Technology: A Normative and Political Response to Hallinan on Tracking," *Sociology of Education.*

it means there is one less place on the fast track for a less affluent child who is doing well. The result is a highly stratified school—and the stratification within the school tends to reproduce the economic stratification outside of it.

> I have this rather vivid memory of the first day of school in the ninth grade. Mr. Mullen, my teacher, warned us to watch our step—now that we were in the high school, our every move would be noted and

would become part of our PERMANENT RECORD. Whatever we did from that day forward would have a big impact on our success in high school and beyond. It was scary to realize that one could have such a thing as a permanent record. But Mr. Mullen had implicitly conveyed a more comforting message as well—at least, I remember feeling relieved that my permanent record had not started earlier without anyone warning me.

I am glad that I didn't know it at the time, but most kids' trajectories are set as soon as or even before they enroll in the first grade. And by the time they get to high school, it has practically been set in stone.

> Entering the first-grade classroom is a big step for a child. It can be a glowing or a devastating experience. The teacher smiles at the children, looking at them to see what the year will bring. The well-groomed white boys and girls will probably do well. The black- and brown-skinned ones are lower-class and will have learning problems unless they look exceptionally clean. All the whites who do not look tidy and need handkerchiefs will have trouble. If the teacher sees a preponderance of lower-class children, regardless of color, she knows her work will be difficult and unsatisfying. The teacher wants her children to learn, all of them, but she knows that lower-class children do not do well in school, just as she knows that middle-class children do do well. All this she knows as she smiles at her class for the first time, welcoming them to the adventure of first grade, measuring them for success or failure against the yardstick of middle-classness. The children smile back at her, unaware as yet that the first measurements have been taken. The yardstick will be used again when they speak to her, as she hears words spoken clearly or snuffled or stammered or spoken with an accent. And later they will be measured for readiness for reading or intelligence. Many times that first year the children will be examined for what they are, for what they bring with them when they come to school. (Oakes 1985, 47)

But surely a child's actual performance is more important than the teacher's expectations? So what if the teacher assumes that little Johnny will have trouble learning? Can't little Johnny simply prove her wrong? Possibly. But students' performances most often prove teachers' expectations right. Does this mean that teachers have especially accurate intuition? Or could it be that teachers' expectations influence the way children perform in school?

STOP & REVIEW

13.3

    a. In your own words, summarize the major differences between teachers' expectations for high- and low-track students.

    b. In your own words, summarize the major differences between the expectations of high- and low-track students.

The Pygmalion Effect:
The Power of Expectations

In the 1960s, sociologists Robert Rosenthal and Lenore Jacobson conducted an experiment to test the existence of the Pygmalion effect in schools.[1] These researchers hypothesized that teachers' expectations influenced children's performance. The design of their experiment was simple but elegant: Rosenthal and Jacobson administered a special test to all the students in a school. The teachers were told that the results of this test could predict how students would do in school during the coming academic year. When teachers were given their class lists for the new school year, each of them found that about 20 percent of their students were labeled as being on the threshold of "spurting" or "blooming" academically. But the "special test" was actually a little-known version of an intelligence test—it could not predict future achievement. Rosenthal and Jacobson had simply *randomly* assigned one out of every five children to the spurter/bloomer group. They said nothing at all about the other children in the class. Really, all these researchers did was to create an impression in the teachers' minds that great things could be expected of some of their students in the coming year. Then they sat back and waited to see what would happen.

At the end of the year, Rosenthal and Jacobson retested the students using the same intelligence test they had used the year before. Most of the students showed some gains in points on the test (just as we would expect of children as they get older). But as figure 13.6 shows, *the kids who were expected to spurt made larger gains than nonspurters.* On their report cards, the kids who had been labeled as spurters showed even more improvement compared to the kids who hadn't been labeled. Figure 13.7 shows the grade point changes for reading. Similar increases for spurters compared to nonspurters were found in arithmetic grades.

13.4 What might account for the fact that the differences between spurters' and nonspurters' *grade increases* were larger than the differences between the spurters' and nonspurters' *scores* on the intelligence test?

---

[1]According to Greek legend, Pygmalion was the king of Cyprus who sculpted a beautiful woman out of ivory. He fell in love with the statue (Galatea) and prayed to the goddess Aphrodite to bring it to life. Aphrodite granted his wish, and Pygmalion married her. In 1913, the George Bernard Shaw play *Pygmalion* was a big hit (and in 1956 was adapted as a musical called *My Fair Lady*). In his version, Shaw's male protagonist, Professor Henry Higgins, created a fine English lady out of a streetwise Cockney girl, Eliza Doolittle. The Pygmalion effect, then, refers to situations in which some piece of raw material (ivory, Cockney girls, elementary school students) are molded by their creators into something finer.

Figure
13.6 *Spurters' and Average Students' Gains on Intelligence Test Performance*

SOURCE: Adapted from Robert Rosenthal and Lenore Jacobson, *Pygmalion in the Classroom: Teacher Expectations and Pupils' Intellectual Development* (New York: Holt, Rinehart & Winston, 1968).

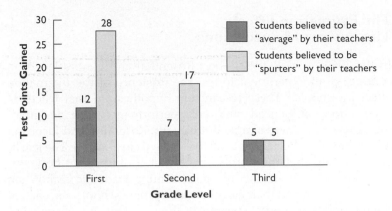

Figure
13.7 *Spurters' and Average Students' Gains or Losses in Reading Grades (Assigned by Teachers)*

SOURCE: Adapted from Robert Rosenthal and Lenore Jacobson, *Pygmalion in the Classroom: Teacher Expectations and Pupils' Intellectual Development* (New York: Holt, Rinehart & Winston, 1968).

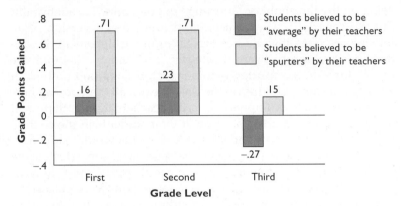

The Fallacy of Hard Work

It is important to recognize that while everyone faces significant obstacles, some people's obstacles loom quite large. For many people, this is a very difficult concept to accept because they are so socialized into the "work hard and you can succeed" theory of social life. I am reminded of this periodically when students tell me what they think about sociological approaches to stratification. Last semester a student explained her point of view this way:

> "I'm sorry, I just don't agree. People do have opportunities, it's just that some people aren't willing to work hard and take advantage of them. Look at me—my parents can't afford to pay my way through college, so I work two jobs part time to support myself. If I can do it, anyone can!"

Her point was a reasonable one. She *is* putting a lot of effort into staying in college. I agreed that not everyone would be so willing to put in the time and effort, and I congratulated her on working so hard to achieve her goals. However, I also suggested to her that

---

Ponder

Alexis de Tocqueville (1805–1859) was a French historian, political scientist, and lawyer. After touring the United States in the early 1830s, Tocqueville published his thoughts about Americans in a book titled *De la Démocratie en Amerique,* or *Democracy in America* (1835). Here's one thing he had to say about the American class system:

> I am aware that among a great democratic people there will always be some members of the community in great poverty and others in great opulence; but the poor, instead of forming the great majority of the nation, as is always the case in aristocratic communities, are comparatively few in number, and the laws do not bind them together by ties of hereditary [poverty]. . . .
>   As there is no longer a race of poor men, so there is no longer a race of rich men; the latter spring up daily from the multitude and relapse into it again. Hence, they [the rich] do not form a distinct class which may be easily marked out. . . . Between these two extremes . . . stands an innumerable multitude of men almost alike, who, without being exactly rich or poor, possess sufficient property to desire the maintenance of order, yet not enough to excite envy.

In your own words, summarize Tocqueville's view of the American class system. Then, given what you have read in this chapter about the nature of social inequality in the United States, specify the degree to which you agree or disagree with Tocqueville, and state why.

---

even though she has to work hard, she still has some advantages that other people do not.

Willingness to work hard is no guarantee that one will succeed in our competitive social system. In fact, willingness to work hard doesn't even guarantee that one can get into the race. Researchers Katherine Newman and Chauncy Lennon (1995) studied low-wage job opportunities in inner-city neighborhoods. Focusing on minimum-wage jobs at places like McDonald's or Burger King, they found that "the ratio of applicants to hires is approximately 14 to 1." Moreover,

> among those people who applied but were rejected for fast-food work in early 1993, 73% had not found work of any kind a year later, despite considerable effort. Even the youngest job-hunters in our study (16- to 18-year-olds) had applied for four or five positions before they came looking for these fast-food jobs. The oldest applicants (over 25) had applied for an average of seven or eight jobs. . . . (Newman and Lennon 1995, 66)

Perhaps the rejected applicants were not as qualified as those who actually got hired? Newman and Lennon suggest that even in competitions for the lowest-paying jobs, qualifications are not the only things that count:

> The rejection rate for local applicants is higher than the rate for similarly educated individuals who live farther away [that is, not in the inner city]. Other studies in the warehouse and dockyard industries report the same results. These findings suggest that residents of poor neighborhoods are at a distinct disadvantage in finding minimum-wage jobs near home. (1995, 67)

According to Newman and Lennon, "it is simply not the case that anyone who wants a low-wage job can get one. As is true for almost any glutted labor market, there is a queue [line] of applicants and employers can be fairly choosy." In the inner city, they conclude, people are "locked into a fierce struggle for scarce opportunities at the bottom."

Social Mobility, Social Structure, and Social Change

Those who study social stratification and mobility in the United States agree that most people do not experience vertical social mobility either between or within generations. For the most part, people who start out in blue-collar jobs tend to stay in them their entire working lives; people who start out in white-collar jobs tend to stay in them their entire working lives. In other words, most people do not experience either intergenerational or intragenerational mobility.

Nonetheless, social mobility is not exactly rare in this country. Overall, there has been a great deal of upward social mobility in the United States and in many European countries over the past century. But this mobility generally involves short steps rather than long leaps. Most occupational mobility, for example, tends to be between closely related occupations.

One crucial fact: Sociologists have found that most of the mobility that has occurred over the past century can be better explained by *social factors* than by individual effort. For example, early industrialization created a number of new jobs—jobs that allowed people to move away from the farm. As industrialization and technology continued to evolve, larger numbers of the new jobs were higher paying. Most of the social mobility that took place in the twentieth century can be accounted for merely by the increases in good jobs.

Class differences in birth rates have facilitated social mobility as well. People in the upper classes traditionally have tended to marry later and have fewer children than people in the lower classes. This has meant that when new jobs opened up toward the top of the occupational structure, the children of the upper classes couldn't fill them all. The difference in birth rates, then, has been another social fact that has drawn people up the occupational ladder.

Finally, immigration has played a role. As new residents settle in this country, they tend to be relegated to the lowest rungs on the occupational ladder. This pushes nonimmigrants out of the lowest jobs and into higher ones (or it does when better jobs exist).

Sociologists refer to mobility that results from such social facts as changes in the occupational structure, immigration, and birth rates as *structural mobility*. Structural mobility has little or nothing to do with changes in the quality of individuals; structural mobility has to do with changes in the social structure of society.

Most sociologists agree that structural factors will continue to be crucial determinants of mobility rates. But evidence suggests

Measuring Inequality

One way of measuring how much inequality exists is to use what's called the *Gini Coefficient* (or *Gini Index*)—invented by the Italian statistician and sociologist Corrado Gini (1884–1965).

The Gini Coefficient ranges from 0 to 1: If one person in a group earns all of the income, the Gini Coefficient is 1. If each person in the group has the same amount of income, the Gini Coefficient is 0. In other words, the higher the coefficient, the more inequality.

Table 13.3 shows Gini Coefficients for ten countries; larger coefficients indicate more inequality. Table 13.4 shows how the degree of inequality in terms of income and wealth has changed over time in the United States.

Table 13.3 Gini Coefficients for Family Income, Various Nations

Country	Gini Coefficient
Belgium	.28
Canada	.32
Denmark	.24
France	.27
Germany	.38
Japan	.38
Mexico	.48
United Kingdom	.34
United States	.45
Haiti	.59

SOURCE: *CIA World Factbook*, May 2009.

Table 13.4 Gini Coefficients for U.S. Income and Wealth, 1989–2007

Year	Income	Wealth (net worth)
1989	.54	.78
1992	.50	.78
1995	.51	.78
1998	.53	.79
2001	.56	.80
2004	.54	.80
2007	.58	.81

SOURCE: Kennickell 2009.

that the upward trend may not continue. Since the 1970s, for example, technological change has tended to make obsolete the lower- and entry-level positions in the occupational structure—as when robots replace factory workers and computers replace accountants—while not opening up higher-level ones. In the 1960s and 1970s, most of the newly created positions in the occupational structure paid fairly decent salaries; in the 1980s and 1990s, however, most of the newly created positions paid close to minimum wage. If this trend continues, we may well see a great deal of downward structural mobility in the twenty-first century.

Chapter Review

1. Below I have listed the major concepts discussed in this chapter. Define each of the terms. (*Hint:* This exercise will be more helpful to you if, in addition to defining each concept, you create an example of it in your own words.)

   effects of parent's social class
   income
   wealth
   Matthew effect
   cultural explanations of inequality
   Oscar Lewis, "culture of poverty"
   structural explanations of inequality
   "blaming the victim"
   tracking, in schools
   Pygmalion effect
   structural mobility
   Gini Coefficient

Table 13.5 College-Bound Seniors' SAT Test Scores by Annual Family Income, 2011[a]

| | Average Scores on SAT Sections[b] | | | |
Annual Family Income[c]	Critical Reading	Mathematics	Writing	Total
More than $200,000	568	586	567	1721
$160,000–$200,000	543	557	536	1636
$140,000–$160,000	538	552	529	1622
$120,000–$140,000	540	544	520	1594
$110,000–$120,000	526	539	515	1580
$80,000–$100,000	515	527	503	1544
$60,000–$80,000	502	512	489	1503
$40,000–$60,000	487	499	475	1461
$20,000–$40,000	464	480	454	1398
$0–$20,000	434	460	429	1325
All test takers[c]	497	514	489	1500

[a]In 2011, 1,647,123 students took the test.

[b]SAT scores range from 200 to 800 for each section of the test (total scores range from 600 to 2400). SAT used to be called "Scholastic Aptitude Test," then it became "Scholastic Assessment Test"; today, the Educational Testing Service (which owns and administers the test) says "SAT is not an initialism."

[c]As a point of information, the chief executive officer of the Educational Testing Service, Kurk Landgraf, recently admitted that his test score on the SAT was 1060 out of a possible 1600 (Evans and Glovin 2006).

SOURCE: College Board, 2011 *College-Bound Seniors, Total Group Profile Report,* 2012.

2. As a potential college graduate, you are poised to join an important American minority group—college graduates. How did you come to be so fortunate?

   a. Create a (brief) cultural explanation of your status as a potential college graduate.
   b. Create a (brief) structural explanation of your status as a potential college graduate.
   c. Briefly describe which explanation you find more believable and why.

3. Study the data presented in table 13.5. Then answer the questions posed below.

   a. Briefly describe the relationship between the variables shown in that table.
   b. Then indicate, in your informed judgment, whether these data tend to lend support to a cultural or to a structural explanation of social class differences? Explain your reasoning.

Answers and Discussion

13.1

a. I first read about the Matthew effect in a book by Robert Merton titled *Sociological Ambivalence and Other Essays* (1976). At one point in the book, Merton made reference to the Thomas theorem. (As you may recall from the Introduction, the Thomas theorem is "If people define situations as real, they are real in their consequences.") Then Merton attached the following footnote:

> What we may call the Thomas Theorem appears just once in the corpus [body] of W. I. Thomas's writing: on page 572 of the book he wrote with Dorothy Swaine Thomas entitled *The Child in America*. I ascribe the theorem to W. I. Thomas alone rather than to the Thomases jointly not because of his gender or great seniority but only because Dorothy Thomas has confirmed for me what many have supposed: that the sentence and the paragraph in which it is encased were written by him. There is thus nothing in this attribution which smacks of "the Matthew Effect," "[as] in which cases of collaboration between scholars of decidedly unequal reputation has us ascribe all credit to the prominent scholar and little or none to the other collaborator(s)." (1976, 175 n. 20)

b. Table 13.1 shows that the chance of going to college has as much to do with the student's family income as it does with his or her academic performance in high school. More specifically, for students at each level of academic achievement, those who come from high-income families are more likely to go to college than those who come from lower-income families. In fact, as I have highlighted in table 13.1a, the lowest-achieving students from high-income families attend college at almost the same rate as the highest-achieving students from low-income families.

How to account for this? As you know, college is expensive and, as I show in table 13.6, a majority of students end up borrowing a great deal of money to finance their educations. On average, students who borrow tend to end up with similar

Table 13.1a Who Goes to College, by Family Income and High School Performance

High School Performance	Student's Family Income	
	Low-Income	High-Income
Highest achievers	78%	97%
Second highest achievers	63	90
Third highest achievers	50	85
Lowest achievers	36	77

SOURCE: Gerald and Haycock, 2006.

Table 13.6 Percent of Bachelor's Degree Recipients Who Borrowed and Median Amount Borrowed, by Family Income, 1992–1993 and 1999–2000

Family Income of Dependent Students	Percent Who Borrowed		Median Amount Borrowed	
	1992–1993	1999–2000	1992–1993	1999–2000
Less than $25,000	71.1	72.6	$10,557	$15,000
$25,000–$49,999	58.0	69.3	$10,096	$16,000
$50,000–$79,000	34.8	66.7	$9,384	$17,000
$80,000 or more	23.0	49.9	$8,909	$16,165
Total	49.3	65.4	$9,502	$16,500

SOURCE: American Council on Education, 2004. *Debt Burden: Repaying Student Debt.*

amounts of debt; however, the anticipation of such amounts no doubt seems daunting to students from lower-income backgrounds.

13.2 The cultural explanation essentially holds that lower-class people do not advance because their cultural situation does not prepare them to advance. The structural explanation suggests otherwise: that there are social structural obstacles facing people in the lower classes that don't hinder people in the more affluent classes. This student seems to have had the talent and willingness to succeed at basketball; what stood in his way was a structural obstacle (the fact that he lived in a scary place and didn't have enough money to go to camp and thereby showcase his talents for college coaches).

13.3

a. The teachers' expectations of the lower-track students are quite low; it is as if they expect the students to learn only to be obedient, to be respectful of authority, and to do their work—period. They expect much more from the higher-track students—they want them to use higher-order thinking, to learn to work independently and creatively, and to ask questions. (One can almost imagine that if a kid in the lower track started doing the things that the kids in the higher tracks were doing, he or she would get into trouble!)

b. Not coincidentally, the students' experiences are closely related to their teachers' expectations. Higher-track students report that they learned to work independently and think abstractly; lower-track students report that they learned to be obedient little students.

Here's an interesting question to ask yourself: Looking back at table 10.1, do you see any correspondence between the data presented in that table and the information presented in table 13.1? (You should!)

13.4 What we might be seeing is another example of the power of the teachers' expectations. The test provides an objective measure of the students' gains in IQ. The presumption here is that the spurters advanced more because they were treated differently by the teachers. The reading scores, because they are assigned by the teachers, are subjective measures of not only students' advances but also the teachers' perceptions of the degree to which students advanced.

INEQUALITY AND ASCRIPTION

Race, Ethnicity, and Gender

"Citizens, you are brothers, but God has made you differently. Some of you have the power to command, having been made of gold; others, of silver, to be assistants; and others, of brass and iron, to be farmers and craftsmen."

—Plato, *Republic*, c. 400 B.C.E.

References to social inequality are scattered throughout the writings of Western philosophers and political thinkers, from the ancients to the moderns. In the olden days, however, the issue of stratification didn't provoke so many questions. And why should it? It made about as much sense to question why, say, Richard Fitzhugh was noble and John Smith common as it did to wonder why a seed would grow in fertile soil and not in barren sand. That was simply the way things were.

Centuries later, of course, industrialization changed everything, making traditional understandings of the social hierarchy obsolete. As industrialization proceeded, the political powers of the old landowning aristocracy were undercut by the financial resources of the capitalistic entrepreneurs. At the same time, the legal and customary restrictions that had kept even the most talented and determined individuals from being socially mobile gradually eroded. The principle that "all men are created equal" made the class system more of an open competition. In modern industrial society, the highest positions in the stratification system were to be won by the most talented and determined individuals. Money was money, and whoever earned the most of it would come out ahead—notwithstanding any snobby pretensions to aristocracy.

In chapter 13, however, we found that the social system is not as open as it might seem. If the stratification system is like a foot-race, some people are given a boost by their parents and get to start a lap or two ahead of others. Of course, if someone can run *really* fast, he or she might still beat the racers who started in front.

237

Why a Dollar Is Not Always a Dollar

Take a dollar bill out of your pocket and look at it. You would think that your dollar bill is the same as anyone else's dollar bill—right? After all, your dollar cost you the same amount as it cost anyone else to own a dollar—4 quarters, 10 dimes, 20 nickels, or 100 pennies. Your dollar will buy the same amount of stuff as anyone else's dollar. Everybody knows that, and that's why money is believed to be the great equalizer.

Although it is the basis of the conventional understanding of capitalism, the idea that a dollar is a dollar is misleading. In reality, *some people's dollars cost more and buy less.*

Take education, for example. Many people think of education as an investment. Students (and their parents) are willing to go into debt to pay tuition because they expect that down the road the investment will pay off in better jobs that, among other things, pay higher salaries.

The fact of the matter is, however, that education pays higher dividends for some people than for others. Look at table 14.1. The data show that on average the payoff of a college degree is greater

Table 14.1 Median Annual Total Earnings for Those 25 Years or Over by Gender, Educational Attainment, Race, and Hispanic Origins, 2007

	Educational Attainment			
Demographic Group	High School Graduate	Some College (no degree)	Associate's Degree	Bachelor's Degree
Men				
Asian	$31,545	$41,068	$40,716	$50,048
Black	29,474	32,425	37,398	50,079
Hispanic[a]	29,098	35,372	37,485	45,706
White	35,765	40,864	45,982	60,458
Women				
Asian	21,816	25,434	31,643	41,828
Black	21,641	27,853	30,152	40,197
Hispanic[a]	21,018	26,465	29,788	36,117
White	22,593	27,172	30,606	38,641

NOTE: These figures exclude workers with less than a high school degree as well as workers with a graduate degree.

[a]Hispanic may be of any race.

SOURCE: U.S. Census Bureau, *Current Population Survey, Annual Social and Economic Supplement, 2008.*

Table 14.2 Median Weekly Earnings of Full-Time Wage and Salary Workers by Occupation and Sex, 2011[a]

	Men	Women	Ratio[b]
All full-time workers	$832	$684	82¢
Management, professional, and related occupations	*1,269*	*941*	*74*
Marketing and sales managers	1,660	1,127	68
Purchasing managers	1,386	1,026	75
Food service managers	734	599	82
Professional and related occupations	*1,211*	*919*	*76*
Social workers	902	798	88
Lawyers	1,884	1,631	87
Physicians and surgeons	1,935	1,527	79
Service occupations	*551*	*433*	*79*
Police and sheriff's patrol officers	948	938	99
Chefs and head cooks	601	502	84
Janitors and building cleaners	514	418	81
Sales and office occupations	*738*	*602*	*82*
Cashiers	411	373	91
Dispatchers	728	629	86
Computer operators	853	651	76

SOURCE: Household Data Annual Averages, Table 39. Median weekly earnings of full-time wage and salary workers by detailed occupation and sex, 2011. U.S. Bureau of Labor Statistics.
[a] These data exclude self-employed workers.
[b] Ratio of women's to men's earnings (number of cents women earn for every dollar earned by men).

for whites than for Asians, blacks, or Hispanics and higher for men than for women.

Recent research shows that the pay gap begins early in a young person's career. As shown in Figure 14.1, Corbette and Hill found significant differences between what women and men earn just one year after graduating from college. This is so even for women and men who chose the same college majors. "Among business majors, for example, women earned just over $38,000, while men earned just over $45,000". Table 14.2 suggests that being female depresses women's income throughout their careers.

The next point is this: Even if you have money in hand, it will buy more or less depending on who you are. For example, in the early 1990s, the Federal Reserve (the government agency charged with overseeing the banking industry) found that banks distinguished between loan applicants based on criteria other than money. As figure 14.2 shows, at all levels of income, whites found it easier to obtain mortgage loans than blacks and Hispanics.

Being fortunate enough to obtain a mortgage does not necessarily resolve the problems faced by minority borrowers. One of

Figure 14.1 *Average Annual Earnings One Year after College by Undergraduate Major and gender.*
SOURCE: Corbette and Collins, 2012.

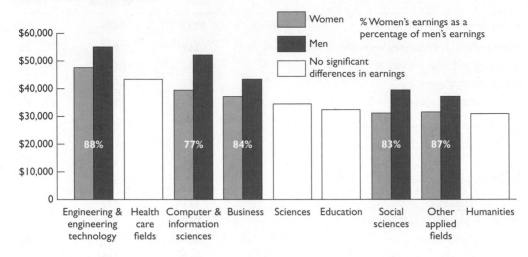

Figure 14.2 *Percentage of Applicants Who Are Denied Mortgages, by Income Level and Race/Ethnicity*
SOURCE: Federal Reserve Board 1990; Michael Quint, "Mortgage Race Data Show Gap. Fed Has Apprised Bankers of Disparity in Loan Approvals," New York Times, October 14, 1991.

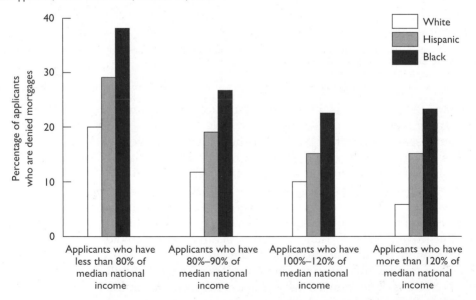

the major advantages of owning a home is building equity (that is, the market value of the property minus the value of the mortgage yet to be paid off). Equity is a form of wealth, something that can be turned into cash either by selling the property outright or by refinancing the mortgage.

When it comes to refinancing, some people find that the dollar amount of the equity they have invested in their homes doesn't amount to what it would have had someone else been doing the investing. More specifically, certain borrowers (i.e., people of color) are given less advantageous loans—even when their credit history qualifies them to borrow at better interest rates. These less advantageous loans, known as subprime loans, are frequently a result of a process known as "reverse redlining."[1]

Research has shown "pervasive racial disparities in subprime lending"; such loans tend to "reflect what a lender or broker thought they could get away with, rather than any careful assessment of actual credit risk" (Acorn 2000, 6):

> Lower-income African Americans received 2.4 times as many subprime loans as lower-income whites, while upper-income African Americans received 3.0 times as many subprime loans as did whites with comparable incomes.
>
> Lower-income Hispanics receive 1.4 times as many subprime loans as do lower-income whites, while upper-income Hispanics receive 2.2 times as many of these loans.

The pattern of subprime lending has continued into the present century. Beginning in 2004, all mortgage lenders were required by the Home Mortgage Disclosure Act to report the full costs of subprime home loans, as well as information about the people who obtained these mortgages. Analyses of these data show that African American and Latino borrowers are 30 percent more likely to receive higher-rate loans than white borrowers with similar credit histories and income (Bocian, Ernst, and Li 2006).

Moreover, women are more likely to receive subprime mortgages than men with similar incomes; in fact, "women with the highest incomes have the highest disparities relative to men with similar incomes than women at lower income levels"—even though women tend to have "slightly higher credit scores than men" (Fishbein and Woodall 2006). Along with a higher monthly

---

[1]This terminology may be confusing. A *subprime loan* is one with higher than usual interest rates. Ostensibly, such loans exist to make loans available to "credit impaired" individuals, but research has shown that they are frequently offered to people with decent credit histories who happen to be unsophisticated in their knowledge of financial matters.

Redlining was the (now illegal) practice of financial institutions that refused to lend money to people who wished to buy property in certain neighborhoods (inevitably, minority neighborhoods) as if a red line had been drawn around those neighborhoods on the bank's map. *Reverse redlining* is the practice of aggressively offering subprime loans to people in formerly redlined neighborhoods. In the most egregious cases, these loans are structured in ways that are calculated to force borrowers to lose their homes—by setting them up in ways that the lender knows will cause the borrower to fail.

payment, some predatory mortgage lenders "enhance" their profits with the following sorts of dubious tactics:

Failing to post monthly payments received from borrowers so that additional fees may be collected;

Using so-called "suspense accounts" to hold the loan payments which can also result in additional fees and penalties;

Delaying credits and adjustments to the homeowner's escrow account, which results in an unnecessary increase in the homeowner's monthly escrow payment;

Conducting multiple, unnecessary "drive-by" property inspections when the homeowner is not in default and then imposing a charge for each "inspection"; and

Improperly calculating interest on open-ended lines of credit or variable rate loans. (Hull 2009, 304)

Subprime loans were developed for people who present greater risk for lenders; the idea is that lenders hedge the risk of lending to people with bad credit by charging them higher interest rates. However, race and gender discrimination has led to a situation in which many people who would have qualified for regular "prime" mortgages were sold subprime mortgages. Higher interest rates—and, hence, higher monthly payments—made these homeowners more likely to default and lose their homes because of the recession. As two law professors observed, "these subprime loans typically begin with a reasonable interest rate, but then skyrocket, or, as the banking industry euphemistically says, 'adjust,' to a far higher rate, causing the borrower's monthly payments to soar. As monthly payments increase, many borrowers quickly fall into default on their mortgages and eventually fall victim to foreclosure" (Aleo and Svirsky 2008, 1).

"RACIAL SURTAX" ON MORTGAGES

Between 2010 and 2012, U.S. mortgage lenders paid more than half a billion dollars to settle lawsuits brought by the U.S. Department of Justice on behalf of African-American and Hispanic consumers. Thomas Perez, assistant attorney general for the Civil Rights Division of the Justice Department, said that the mortgage brokers where charging what he called a *racial surtax:*

Between 2004 and 2009, Wells Fargo discriminated by charging approximately 30,000 African-American and Hispanic wholesale borrowers higher fees and rates than non-Hispanic white borrowers because of their race or national origin rather than the borrowers' credit worthiness or other objective criteria related to borrower risk. What did this mean in reality? It meant that an African-American wholesale customer in the Chicago area in 2007 seeking a $300,000 loan paid on average $2,937 more in fees than a similarly qualified white applicant. And these fees were not based on any objective factors relating to credit risk. These fees amounted to a racial surtax. A Latino borrower in the Miami area in 2007 seeking a $300,000 loan paid on average $2,538 more than a similarly qualified white applicant. The racial surtax for African Americans in Miami in 2007 was $3,657. (Perez 2012)

Ian Ayres and Peter Siegelman (1995) found more evidence for the differential value of a dollar. Armed with extensive knowledge of the value of cars and techniques of negotiating, a team of researchers visited a number of car dealerships in a large midwestern city. Table 14.3 shows what happened. The left-hand column lists the average initial offers made by the dealer to different types of buyers. White men were offered the best deals—$1,019 over the dealer's cost. Of course, the dealer's initial offer is only the beginning of the process; it's a place from which to start negotiating. But the final outcomes of negotiation were different depending on who the buyer was, as you can see in the middle column of table 14.3. Again, whites, and especially white males, were offered the better deals. More recent investigations suggest that racial differences in the value of the dollar continue in the car-buying arena. Since 2001, several major automobile companies (including Ford, Daimler-Chrysler, Honda, General Motors, Nissan, and Toyota) have been found guilty of subjecting African American purchasers to more costly loans than those given to whites with similar credit histories—adding hundreds and even thousands of dollars to the cost of cars. By way of example, Mark Cohen, a professor of economics at Vanderbilt University, described the cases of two women who purchased Nissan Sentras in 2000. "Both women were in [the] first credit tier and were thus qualified to borrow at 8.25 percent. The first, who was white, borrowed $15,093 over five years at the preferential rate of 3.9 percent, with monthly payments of $277.73. The second, who is black, borrowed only $14,787 over five years, but she was charged a dealer markup of one percentage point, for a total interest rate of 9.25. Her monthly payment was $309.94"

Table 14.3 Average Car Dealer Profits, by Race and Gender of Purchaser

Purchasers	Initial Offer	Final Offer	Average Markup
White males	$1,019	$564	5.18%
White females	1,127	656	6.04
Black males	1,954	1,665	14.61
Black females	1,337	975	7.2

SOURCE: Adapted Ayres and Siegelman, 1995. Ayres 2008.

(Reuters News Service, 10 February 2004). It seems almost paradoxical: People who on average earned the least money were asked to pay the most for their cars.

The same sort of relationship between how much money people have and how much they have to pay to purchase consumer goods holds for less expensive items. Of course, rich and poor alike will pay $1.99 for some doodad in Smithville's Bigco Shopper store. But the price of milk in the inner-city stores where the less affluent shop will tend to be noticeably higher than in the suburbs where many of the more affluent shop. Want a quick burger? If you live in a neighborhood that's 50 percent African American, you'll pay more at the fast-food place (Graddy 1997).

Moreover, suppose you want to purchase a refrigerator or television or even a mattress set. If you use a credit card, you can expect to pay the cost of the item and anywhere from 15 to 20 percent interest on top of that. But what if you don't have a credit card? If you don't have the cash, you might go to a rent-to-own store and buy one—because rent-to-own stores will sell you the item and let you pay for it over time. But renting-to-own costs a lot: In 1997, the U.S. Public Interest Research Group found that more than half of rent-to-own stores charged at least 100 percent annual interest, and some charged as much as 275 percent. What if you want to buy a refrigerator that costs $739.95? If you use your credit card, that refrigerator will cost you an additional 20 percent or so, or about $120 in interest. But for the same refrigerator in a rent-to-own store, a consumer would pay annual interest of 87 percent, or $620.05, in addition to the refrigerator's listed price. Because the rent-to-own stores technically do not extend credit but rather rent their products to consumers, they aren't required to follow laws—such as those contained in the Truth in Lending Act and the Consumer Leasing Act—that exist to protect consumers. As a result of their investigation, the researchers concluded that "purchasing appliances, furniture, computers, jewelry or other merchandise from rent-to-own stores costs two to five times as much as buying those items at department or discount stores" (reported in *The New York Times,* June 13, 1997).

This sort of differential treatment of people based on their gender or race is not only unfair but, according to basic economic theory, irrational and (supposedly) self-defeating. Let's say there are two doodad factories—A and B. The owner of factory A pays fair wages to all her workers. The owner of factory B pays less than fair wages to some of his workers.

Common sense suggests that the best workers will apply for employment at factory A. These workers will produce more and better doodads. On the other hand, the only workers willing to work at factory B will be those who could not get hired at factory A. These will be the less qualified/less productive workers who produce doodads of dubious quality. Because of the difference in quality, consumers will be more likely to buy the doodads from factory A than from factory B. The owner of factory A will thus make higher profits than the owner of factory B. In time the owner of factory B will not be able to compete successfully and will go out of business. That's the way the free market works—or is supposed to work.

Overcharging consumers is likewise irrational. If store C charges more for milk than store D, then people will choose to shop at store D. Eventually store C will either have to lower its prices or go out of business.

The theory is simple: To compete successfully in the marketplace, one must pay one's workers fair wages and charge one's customers fair prices. There is no need for governments to regulate the market; the market regulates itself.

The reality seems to be more complex than the theory. In fact, businesses do survive even when they pay some of their workers less than others for the same job (see table 14.2). Likewise, some retailers seem to be able to charge some customers more than others. This suggests that some social facts are complicating the more straightforward economic facts. What's going on?

Prejudice

The roots of the word *prejudice* can be traced to the Latin term *praejudicium*, which means "prejudgment." Strictly speaking, then, a prejudice involves a prejudgment—or a judgment of some thing, person, or situation on the basis of prior experience with similar things, persons, or situations. There is nothing inherently wrong with prejudgment. In fact, prejudgment underlies the whole principle of learning by experience.

Prejudice has a different flavor from mere prejudgment, however. As social psychologist Gordon W. Allport pointed out in his book *The Nature of Prejudice*, the difference between prejudice and prejudgment has to do with the fact that prejudice is based on inaccurate information and/or illogical arguments. To put it another way, *a prejudice is an unjustified prejudgment;* that is, prejudice involves not only *pre*judgment but *mis*judgment.

Allport pointed out that one of the things that helps us to distinguish prejudgment from prejudice is the fact that people tend to hold onto their prejudices even in the face of

Prejudice is a negative and persistent judgment based on scant or incorrect information about people in a group. Prejudice involves beliefs and attitudes. More technically, we might define it this way: Prejudice is a negative or hostile attitude toward a person who belongs to a group, simply because he or she belongs to that group and is therefore presumed to have the objectionable qualities ascribed to the group.

contradictory information. By way of example, Allport cited an imaginary conversation between Mr. X (who is prejudiced against Jews) and Mr. Y (who is annoyingly persistent in his nonprejudice):

> *Mr. X:* The trouble with Jews is that they only take care of their own group.
> *Mr. Y:* But the record of the [United Way] campaign shows that they give more generously, in proportion to their numbers, to the general charities of the community, than do non-Jews.
> *Mr. X:* That shows they are always trying to buy favor and intrude into Christian affairs. They think of nothing but money; that is why there are so many Jewish bankers.
> *Mr. Y:* But a recent study shows that the percentage of Jews in the banking business is negligible, far smaller than the percentage of non-Jews.
> *Mr. X:* That's just it; they don't go in for respectable business; they are only in the movie business or run night clubs. (1954, 13–14)

Thus, as Allport concludes, prejudices have a way of "slithering around" the facts in order to find ways of justifying ill feelings toward members of another group.

Prejudice is sustained by *stereotypes*—oversimplified generalized images about members of a particular group. Stereotyping essentially categorizes all members of a particular group as having a specific set of characteristics. Stereotypes deny the existence of individual differences among the members of a specific social category.

Discrimination

It is crucial to distinguish between prejudice and stereotypes on the one hand and discrimination on the other. Prejudice and stereotypes involve attitudes and beliefs; *discrimination involves behavior.* Moreover, there is no guarantee that prejudiced attitudes will manifest themselves in discriminatory behaviors:

> What people actually do in relation to groups they dislike is not always directly related to what they think or feel about them. Two employers, for example, may dislike Jews to an equal degree. One may keep his feelings to himself and may hire Jews on the same basis of any workers—perhaps because he wants to gain goodwill for his factory or store in the Jewish community. The other may translate his dislike into his employment policy, and refuse to hire Jews. Both men are prejudiced, but only one of them practices *discrimination.* (Allport 1954, 14)

Sociologist Robert K. Merton added another wrinkle to our understanding of the links between prejudice and discrimination. As figure 14.3 shows, Merton suggested that just as not all people

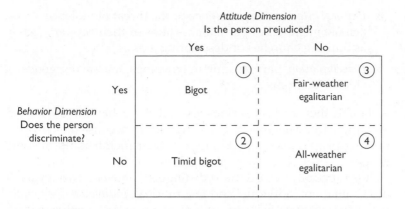

Figure 14.3
*A Typology of
Prejudice and
Discrimination*

SOURCE: Adapted from
Robert K. Merton,
*Sociological Ambivalence
and Other Essays*
(New York: Free Press,
1976).

who are prejudiced practice discrimination, not all people who practice discrimination are prejudiced.

Cells 1 and 4 represent the people whose behavior is consistent with their beliefs. Cell 1 represents that person who is prejudiced and does discriminate—no matter what. Cell 4 represents the unprejudiced person who does not discriminate—no matter what.

But cells 2 and 3 represent people whose behavior is not necessarily consistent with their beliefs. Cell 2 represents the person who is prejudiced but will not discriminate unless it is convenient to do so. So, for example, the store owner who is prejudiced against minorities but who needs their business may not discriminate against minorities. Merton calls this person a "timid bigot."

Cell 3 is the final case. This person is not prejudiced but does discriminate when it's convenient to do so. Suppose you work at Benny's Food Shack as a waiter or waitress. Your boss tells you to do all that you can to discourage minorities from eating in the restaurant (provide really slow service, mix up their orders, overcharge them, and so on). You don't want to do this because you aren't prejudiced. However, your boss makes it clear that you will either do things her way or be fired. You really need this job, so you go along. Under these circumstances, you are a "fair-weather egalitarian."

There are many types of discriminatory behaviors. Allport identified five general categories that range, as he put it, "from the least energetic to the most":

1. *Verbal rejection* ("antilocution"): using derogatory nouns ("epithets") to refer to people in particular groups; telling jokes that put down entire groups of people

2. *Avoidance:* avoiding interaction with people from particular groups

3. *Active discrimination:* acting to exclude members of particular groups from education, employment, housing, political, or recreational opportunities

4. *Physical attacks:* using violence or the threat of violence against members of particular groups or their property, such as burning churches or desecrating graves

5. *Extermination:* participating in lynchings, massacres, genocide, or pogroms

Although they vary in seriousness, all the behaviors associated with these five categories are discriminatory because they involve treating people unequally because of their membership in some group.

It is especially important to distinguish between two levels of discrimination: individual and institutional. *Individual discrimination occurs when an individual discriminates against another individual* (or group of individuals). The apartment house owner who refuses to rent to someone because of his or her race, religion, or whatever is practicing individual discrimination.

Institutional discrimination involves a denial of opportunities and equal rights to individuals and groups that results from the normal operation of society. This term was introduced in the 1960s by political activist Stokely Carmichael and his co-writer Charles Hamilton (1967). Their intent was to distinguish between the outcomes of the practices of individuals (say, members of the KKK) and the outcomes of the practices found in everyday society that lead, for example, to the deaths of young African American children. As Carmichael and Hamilton pointed out, institutional discrimination is "built into" the usual operations of society. Unlike individual discrimination, institutional discrimination can occur even when people have "no intention of subordinating others because of color [or other ascribed characteristic] or are totally unaware of doing so" (Downs 1970, 5).

Here are two examples of institutional discrimination:

Height requirements in a police or fire department that are geared to the average height of white males—thereby systematically excluding most women and male members of some minority groups—even when height has no bearing on one's ability to do the job. (The average Asian, for example, may be judged too short to work as a fire fighter in many U.S. cities; yet who does the fire fighting in Asia?) Preferences given to children of alumni ("legacies") for admission to prestigious universities (including law and medical schools)—thereby discriminating against worthy individuals not fortunate enough to be born into wealthy families.

14.1 Define *prejudice* and *discrimination*, and explain how they differ.

14.2 Explain the difference between *individual* and *institutional* discrimination.

Discrimination and "Isms"

A particular act of discrimination may be more or less injurious depending on the social context. Many sociologists group particularly potent kinds of discrimination into one of the "isms" categories: ageism, anti-Semitism, heterosexism, racism, sexism.

"Isms" are different from ordinary discrimination. For example, ageism is not simply age-based discrimination; nor is racism the same as race-based discrimination, nor sexism the same as sex-based discrimination. The suffix *ism* is generally applied to acts of discrimination that occur at the institutional level or, when they occur at the individual level, are consistent with institutional patterns of discrimination. When an African American tells an anti-white joke, it is as discriminatory as when a white person tells an anti–African American joke. But, because the patterns of institutional discrimination in our society tend to be against African Americans, only the anti–African American joke falls into the racism category. From the sociological perspective, the *ism* is used to signal the differences in potency of different types of discrimination. More generally, then, discriminatory acts are "isms" when their source is a member of the dominant group and their target is a member of a minority group in society.

Why make such a distinction? Why not categorize all race-based discrimination as racism and all sex-based discrimination as sexism? These are crucial questions. We make the distinction because, as sociologists, we know that when we take into account the larger social context, the impact of discriminatory acts is different for minorities than it is for members of the dominant group.

Sociologist Michael Schwalbe came to a similar conclusion as a result of his study of the "men's movement" in the United States:

> To [some of the men] any word of disparagement by members of one sex for another was an example of sexism. Women's joking about men's foibles or atrocious behavior was thus supposedly just as sexist, and just as unacceptable, as anything some men might do to demean or oppress women. . . . There was blindness here to power differences. Women as a group do not have the institutional power to demean, oppress, or exploit men as a group. In the context of male supremacy, women's verbal criticism of men is an act of *resistance*, not sexism. Similarly, blacks may think of whites as evil, and may even be "prejudiced against" whites. But it is perverse to call this racism, since blacks as a group do not have the institutional power to hurt white people. In fact, when blacks do disparage whites, they must do it in the safety of their own communities, lest they become victims of truly racist retaliation. (1996, 266 n. 13)

Understanding the difference between race discrimination and racism, or sex discrimination and sexism, involves taking into account the institutionalized relationships that exist between members of different groups. We can begin by examining the concepts of *minority* and *dominant groups.* What do those terms mean? Sociologist Louis Wirth explained them this way:

> We may define a minority as a group of people who, because of their physical or cultural characteristics, are singled out from the others in the society in which they live for differential and unequal treatment, and who therefore regard themselves as objects of collective discrimination. The existence of a minority in a society implies the existence of a corresponding dominant group enjoying higher social status and greater privilege. *Minority status carries with it the exclusion from full participation in the life of the society.* Though not necessarily an alien group, the minority is treated and regards itself as a people apart. (1945, 347)

Any person may be the target of discrimination—or of unequal treatment because of his or her group membership. On the playground, little girls may exclude boys from their jump rope game just as little boys may place a "NO GIRLS ALLOWED" sign on their tree house. But overall, the experience of discrimination is different for members of the dominant group than it is for members of minority groups.

For a member of the dominant group, being the target of discrimination is not only upsetting but shocking as well! After all, the defining characteristic of dominant-group membership is that one enjoys greater privilege. David Gates (1993), a reporter for *Newsweek*, provides a series of revealing quotes in this context. Tom Cole, a retired marketing executive in Chicago, claims, "The white male is the most persecuted person in the United States." Tom Williamson, president of the National Coalition of Free Men, "complains that Clinton 'has brought in a feminist administration that has no conception of men's problems. They are self-serving and self-pitying. We're going to be in for it.'" A white male firefighter says of minorities, "They stole my pay, they stole my promotion, and I couldn't say I didn't like it. White guys are being pushed around big time to make up for past wrongs. If you're black and belong to a black group, you're an activist. If you're white and you belong to a white group, you're an asshole. Nobody supports the KKK—*I* don't. But there's nothing for a white guy to join." Then there is Steve, age 29, who "sold his Jeep CJ7 to put himself through the police academy. . . . He was a finalist for a job in a rural northern California town, but got bumped down the list by three women he says didn't go through the same application process. 'When they take the chance that I had and allot it to three women just because they're female, that burns me up,' he says. 'I got shot out of the saddle.'"

When *Newsweek* polled white American men in 1993, it found that a majority believed they were losing influence in American society. More to the point, the survey found that the average white male felt that he was losing his *advantage* in terms of jobs and income.

Research suggests that when rights and privileges are extended to members of minority groups, members of the dominant group perceive their *loss of advantage as discrimination*. Moreover, the cost to dominant groups tends to be exaggerated by them. It is in this context that we can make sense of statements like "the white male is the most persecuted person in the United States"—a nonsensical statement in the light of empirical reality:[2]

> It's still a statistical piece of cake being a white man, at least in comparison with being anything else. White males make up just 39.2 percent of the population, yet they account for 82.5 percent of the Forbes 400 (folks worth at least $265 million), 77 percent of Congress, 92 percent of state governors, 70 percent of tenured college faculty, almost 90 percent of TV news directors. They dominate just about everything but NOW and NAACP; even in the NBA, most of the head coaches and general managers are white guys. (Gates 1993, 49)

Generally members of minority groups tend not to be as shocked when confronted with discrimination—frequently it's part of their daily lives. Here's how a black student at a mostly white university described the feeling he had as he walked home each night from a campus job to his apartment:

> "Even if you wanted to, it's difficult just to live a life where you don't come into conflict with others. Because every day you walk the streets, it's not even like once a week, once a month. It's every day you walk the streets. Every day you live as a black person you're reminded how you're perceived in society. You walk the streets at night; white people cross the streets. I've seen white couples and individuals dart in front of cars to not be on the same side of the street. Just the other day, I was walking down the street, and this white female with a child, I saw her pass a young male about 20 yards ahead. When she saw me, she quickly dragged the child and herself across the busy street. What is so funny is that this area has had an unknown white rapist in the area for about four years. [When

---

[2]The phenomenon that *loss of advantage* is experienced as discrimination can be found in other cultures. In India, to help integrate members of scheduled castes and tribes (the *dalit*) into the mainstream of society, the government instituted a policy of "protective discrimination," or affirmative action, in which some university scholarships and a certain percentage of government jobs are reserved for the *dalit*. Sociologist Lelah Dushkin (1979) found that upper-caste members tended to exaggerate both the costs they were paying (for example, in terms of lost jobs) and the benefits that the *dalit* were receiving.

I pass] white men tighten their grip on their women. I've seen people turn around and seem like they're going to take blows from me. The police constantly make circles around me as I walk home, you know, for blocks. I'll walk, and they'll turn a block. And they'll come around me just to make sure, to find out where I'm going. So, every day you realize [you're black]. Even though you're not doing anything wrong; you're just existing. You're just a person. But you're a black person perceived in an unblack world." (Feagin 1991, 111–112)

Being bombarded by discriminatory behaviors can take a big toll on people. Sometimes it may seem to members of the dominant group that minorities take "small slights" and blow them out of proportion, because they are "just too sensitive." Here is one middle-class black woman's account of the time that she "overreacted":

"We had a new car . . . and we stopped at 7-11 [store]. We were going to go out that night, and we were taking my son to a babysitter. . . . And we pulled up, and my husband was inside at the time. And this person, this Anglo couple, drove up, and they hit our car. It was a brand new car. So my husband came out. And the first thing they told us was that we got our car on *welfare*. Here we are able-bodied. He was a corporate executive. I had a decent job, it was a professional job. . . . But they looked at the car we were driving, and they made the assumption that we got it from welfare. I completely snapped; I physically abused that lady. I did. And I was trying to keep my husband from arguing with her husband until the police could come. . . . And when the police came they interrogated them: they didn't arrest us, because there was an off-duty cop who had seen the whole incident and said she provoked it." (Feagin 1991, 112)

Sociologist Joe Feagin found that most white Americans believe that these days middle-class blacks can live their lives substantially untouched by race discrimination. He wanted to find out whether this was true. In his research, he found evidence that race discrimination against even middle-class blacks is fairly widespread. It may lack the crudity of the era when blacks encountered "No Negroes Served Here" signs in restaurants, but it is noticeable. One of Feagin's respondents, a female black professor at a predominantly white university in the Southwest, explains how she copes when she encounters the police:

"When the cops pull me over because my car is old and ugly, they assume I've just robbed a convenience store. Or that's the excuse they give: 'This car looks like a car used to rob a 7-11 [store].' And I've been pulled over six or seven times since I've been in this city—and I've been here two years now. Then I do what most black folks do. I try not to make any sudden moves so I'm not accidentally shot. Then I give them my identification. And I show them my university I.D. so they won't think that I'm someone that constitutes a threat, however they define it, so that I don't get arrested." (114)

She explained the overall effect of daily encounters with race discrimination this way:

> "[One problem with] being black in America is that you have to spend so much time thinking about stuff that most white people just don't even have to think about. I worry when I get pulled over by a cop. I worry because the person that I live with is a black male, and I have a teenaged son. I worry what some white cop is going to think when he walks over to our car, because he's holding on to a gun. And I'm very aware of how many black folks accidentally get shot by cops. I worry when I walk into a store, that someone's going to think I'm in there shoplifting. And I have to worry about that because I'm not free to ignore it. And so, that thing that's supposed to be guaranteed to all Americans, the freedom to just be yourself, is a fallacious idea. And I get resentful that I have to think about things that a lot of people, even very close white friends whose politics are similar to mine, simply don't have to worry about." (114)

Feagin explained that "particular instances of discrimination may seem minor to outside white observers when considered in isolation. But when blatant acts of avoidance, verbal harassment, and physical attack combine with subtle and covert slights, and these accumulate over months, years, and lifetimes, the impact on a black person is far more than the sum of individual instances" (115). Feagin refers to the cumulative impact of encounters with racist behavior as having a *pyramiding effect*. Another of his respondents explained it this way:

> ". . . if you can think of the mind as having one hundred ergs of energy, and the average man uses fifty percent of his energy dealing with the everyday problems of the world—just the general kinds of things—then he has fifty percent more to do creative kinds of things that he wants to do. Now that's a white person. . . . A black person also has one hundred ergs; he uses fifty percent the same way a white man does, dealing with what the white man has [to deal with], so he has fifty percent left. But he uses twenty-five percent fighting being black, [with] all the problems of being black and what it means. Which means he really only has twenty-five percent to do what the white man has fifty percent to do, and he's expected to do just as much as the white man with that twenty-five percent. . . . So, that's kind of what happens. You just don't have as much energy left to do as much as you know you really could do if . . . your mind were free." (115)

14.3 Why do sociologists distinguish racism from race-based discrimination and sexism from sex-based discrimination?

STOP
&
REVIEW

The Social Construction of Minority Groups

Louis Wirth stressed that minorities are people who have been "singled out" as different. Naive observers tend to believe that the things that distinguish members of minority and dominant groups are direct reflections of inherent biological or psychological differences.

Take, for example, the concept of race. The term *race* was first applied to humans in 1775 by the German naturalist and physiologist Johann Friedrich Blumenbach. Blumenbach, one of the founders of anthropology, came up with a taxonomy (classification) scheme that divided people into five racial categories: Caucasian, Mongolian, Malay, American, and Ethiopian or African. Although Blumenbach did not make much of racial differences (instead, he stressed the essential unity of humankind), many of the scientists who followed him invested the concept of race with great meaning. In the nineteenth century, in fact, many scientists adhered to *polygenism*—or a belief that different races evolved from different origins, that different races constituted different subspecies of humanity.[3] Here's how this was explained by one such "scholar":

> [The] mass of scriptural and scientific evidence clearly indicates that the pure-blood White is the creature whom God designed should perform the mental labor necessary to subdue the earth; and that the Negro is the creature whom God designed to perform the manual labor. The Negro, in common with the rest of the animals, made his appearance upon the earth prior to the creation of man. With the Negro and the animals of draft, burden and food, it was possible for [white] man to develop all the resources of the earth and not personally till the ground. (Carroll 1900/1991, 101–102)

Race has proved to be a slippery concept. Consider the original five categories proposed by Blumenbach. His placement of groups of people within each category does not mesh with contemporary conceptions of race. Under the category of Caucasian, for example, he placed not only Europeans but Hindus. Under the

---

[3]Polygenistic theories (that is, theories that claim that people of different races evolved from different genetic stock) have been invoked in many cultures to justify discrimination against minorities. In Japan, for example, there are minorities—little known to outsiders—called the *hinin* and the *eta,* or "heavily polluted." Now called the *burakumin,* or "people of the hamlet," these people were long treated as if they were not quite human, and certainly not Japanese. As recently as 1965, a government survey in Japan revealed that 70 percent of the people polled believed that members of the *burakumin* "were of a race and lineage different from the Japanese" (Hane 1982, 40). Yet no empirical evidence can be found to support such a theory. (See also Howell 1996.)

category of Mongolian, on the other hand, he lumped Chinese, Turks, and Eskimos.[4]

Later anthropologists argued for different taxonomies of race. The English anthropologist Ashley Montague showed that these taxonomies varied a great deal, including anywhere from 2 to 2000 different racial groups. Montague himself identified some 40 different races (1960, 1964).

In South Africa, the laws of apartheid ("aparthood") recognized four racial categories: white (those of European descent), coloured (mixed), Asiatic (including those of Indian descent), and African (called *Bantu*). The categories were strict, but they were not entirely based on physical differences. For example, Japanese (who tended to be fairly affluent) could be classified as white.

In the United States, persons of European, African, and North American ancestry are divided into three races: white, black, and Native American. In Mexico, however, the same population would be divided into at least six groups: *Negro* (black), *Indio* (Indian), *Hispano* (white), *mestizo* (Indian and white), *lobo* (Indian and black), and *mulatto* (white and black). The term *mestizo/mestiza* is particularly revealing with respect to the social nature of race. Originally, it meant strictly mixed Indian and white heritage; by the end of the seventeenth century, however, "any person of the lower or intermediate classes who adopted Spanish culture was considered mestizo/mestiza, regardless of his or her [biological] descent" (Appiah and Gates 1997, 455).

Even within the United States, there has been disagreement about who qualifies as what race. In the days when segregation was legal and intermarriage forbidden, it was quite important to know who belonged to which race. But one's race could vary from state to state. Who, for example, was black?

> In Kentucky, anyone having one-fourth or more Negro blood (at least one grandparent)
>
> In Indiana and Maryland, anyone having one-eighth or more Negro blood (at least one great-grandparent)
>
> In Louisiana, anyone having one-sixteenth or more Negro blood (at least one great-great-grandparent)

Still, in other states the law was quite simple. In Arkansas, for example, the law stated, "The words 'persons of negro race' shall

---

[4]Blumenbach's classification was widely accepted among scientists, but conventional observers tended to modify his taxonomy. For example, for the first several decades of the twentieth century, it was illegal for foreigners of Asian descent to buy property. In 1920, a group of Armenians in the United States (whom Blumenbach's scheme had classified as Caucasian) had to go to court to prove they were not of "Mongolian" or Asian descent and thus could legally purchase property.

be held to apply to and include any person who has in his or her veins any negro blood whatever." Likewise, in Georgia, "The term 'white person' shall include only persons of the white or Caucasian race, who have no ascertainable trace of either Negro, African, West Indian, Asiatic Indian, Mongolian, Japanese, or Chinese blood in their veins" (Kennedy 1959, 48–50). These states, then, followed the "one-drop rule"—meaning that a "single drop of 'black blood' makes a person black" (Davis 1991, 51).

What, then, is race? Although the concept of race is not very useful to biologists, it continues to be an important one for sociologists—but only because people's assumptions about race have tremendous consequences for individuals. Race is a socially constructed attribute that is tied to beliefs about differences in the physical makeup of different individuals.

Ethnicity is different. When most people speak of "ethnic differences," they are referring specifically to *cultural* differences. Thus, *ethnicity has to do with shared cultural heritage.* The ties that bind people together into ethnic groups may be varied and frequently include religion, language, dress, music, and food preferences. Sometimes ethnicity has less to do with shared culture than with how people in a social group are perceived. That is, sometimes ethnicity is imposed upon a people. One example involves Italian Americans. Many of the people who emigrated to the United States in the 1880s were surprised to find that they were "Italian." They had thought of themselves as Venetians, Neopolitans, Calabrians, Sicilians, or Corsicans.[5] To them there was no such person as an Italian. But when they came to the United States, their ethnic distinctions were treated as meaningless by members of the dominant group, who lumped all Italians into a single ethnicity. As anthropologist Nancy Lurie put it, "Immigrant communities were not communities when they came; their ethnic identities were, to a surprising extent, constructed in America" (1982, 143). In other words, "The Sicilians, the Neopolitans, and the Calabrians thus became conscious of their common destiny in America" (Schermerhorn 1949, 25). Likewise, it was white Americans who created "Indian" and "African" as ethnicities out of an incredible diversity of cultures.[6]

In conventional language, ethnic labels are not neutral, technical devices. If they were, it would make sense to say that everyone has an ethnicity. But as it is used in society, the concept of ethnicity has connotations of something foreign or exotic.

---

[5]Until these separate states were unified in 1861, Italy did not exist.

[6]The imposition of ethnicity on a minority group by a dominant group is called *ethnogenesis* (Greeley 1971).

Think about it—what is stocked in the supermarket in the aisle marked "ethnic foods"? If those are ethnic foods, what is it that is stocked throughout the rest of the store?

Gender

Gender is a social construction as well. If differences between men and women were biologically determined, then they would be the same across cultures. But they aren't.

In 1935, the American anthropologist Margaret Mead published her famous study *Sex and Temperament in Three Primitive Societies*. This book contained an account of the differences between men and women among the Arapesh, the Mundugumor, and the Tchambuli (pronounced "cham-bully")—small societies in New Guinea.[7] As Mead later explained, she had set out to study the degree to which differences in male and female temperaments (that is, personalities) were a result of socialization rather than physical or biological factors. Mead and her colleagues found that there was what she called a standardized male personality and a standardized female personality in each culture. But the differences across these three cultures were amazing. Here is how Mead summarized the nature of male and female in each society:

> We found the Arapesh—both men and women—displaying a personality that, out of our historically limited preoccupations, we would call maternal in its parental aspects, and feminine in its sexual aspects. We found men, as well as women, trained to be cooperative, unaggressive, responsive to the needs and demands of others. We found no idea that sex was a powerful driving force for men or for women. In marked contrast to these attitudes, we found among the Mundugumor that both men and women developed as ruthless, aggressive, positively sexed individuals, with the maternal cherishing aspects of personality at a minimum. Both men and women approximated to a personality type that in our culture we would find only in an undisciplined and very violent male. Neither the Arapesh nor the Mundugumor profit by a contrast between the sexes; the Arapesh ideal is the mild, responsive man married to the mild, responsive woman; the Mundugumor ideal is the violent aggressive man married to the violent aggressive woman. In the third tribe, the Tchambuli, we found a genuine reversal of the sex-attitudes of our own culture, with the woman the dominant, impersonal, managing partner, the man the less responsible and the emotionally dependent person. (1935/1950, 205)

---

[7]New Guinea is the second largest island in the world (only Greenland is larger). It's located north of Australia.

What to make of these findings? To Mead it was clear: "If those temperamental attitudes which we have traditionally regarded as feminine—such as passivity, responsiveness, and a willingness to cherish children—can so easily be set up as the masculine pattern in one tribe, and in another be outlawed for the majority of women as well as for the majority of men, we no longer have any basis for regarding such aspects of behavior as sex-linked." And, Mead added, "This conclusion becomes even stronger when we consider the actual reversal in Tchambuli of the position of dominance of the two sexes" (1935/1950, 205).

There are, of course, physical differences between men and women, and most societies divide their own population into two groups—male and female—on the basis of these physical characteristics. What sociologists have found most fascinating, however, is what different societies have made of these sex differences. Mead's research in New Guinea brought home the fact that we may have overlooked the real source of most differences between men and women. More specifically, many of the differences between men and women that people conventionally assume are related to biological factors turn out to be products of socialization. Physically, females among the Arapesh, Mundugumor, and Tchambuli were the same, as were the males among the three tribes. Nonetheless, what it meant to be a woman or a man varied tremendously across these groups.

Today sociologists frequently distinguish between *sex differences* (the physical and biological differences between males and females) and *gender differences* (which have to do with social expectations about how males and females ought to act and their respective rights and duties). To put it another way, *sex* is a biological or physical attribute while *gender* is a social/cultural attribute.

Which of the differences that we see between men and women are related to sex and which are related to gender? In other words, which of the differences between men and women have to do with their innate biological selves and which have to do with the kind of socialization they receive? The evidence increasingly shows that gender differences tend to override sex differences—that social expectations, for example, are much more powerful determinants of people's behaviors than their physical attributes.

> Summarizing the differences between women and men is not an easy task, once one leaves the obvious biological domains [that is, differences in reproductive capacities]. . . . The basic repertoires of women and men are quite similar, particularly when it comes to social behaviors. Both women and men know how to be aggressive, how to be helpful, how to smile, and how to be rude. What they

Sex or Gender?

It is often difficult to distinguish sex and gender differences. Read through the following lists. In your judgment, which differences are a result of biology and which are a result of culture?

For Every 100 Girls . . .

For every 100 girl babies born, there are 105 boy babies born.

For every 100 girls aged 5 to 14 who die, 148 boys die.

For every 100 girls enrolled in ninth grade, there are 101 boys enrolled.

For every 100 girls enrolled in tenth grade, there are 94 boys enrolled.

For every 100 high school girls who felt too unsafe to go to school, 104 boys felt the same way.

For every 100 twelfth-grade girls who engaged in a physical fight on school property, 214 boys got into a fight.

For every 100 girls in grades 10 to 12 who drop out of high school, 121 boys drop out of high school.

For every 100 women aged 25 to 29 years who have at least a bachelor's degree, 84 men have at least a bachelor's degree.

For every 100 females aged 20 to 24 who commit suicide, 624 males of the same age kill themselves.

For every 100 women aged 22 to 24 in correctional facilities, there are 1,430 men in correctional facilities.

For every 100 women aged 18 to 24 living in emergency and transitional shelters, there are 86 men living in similar shelters.

SOURCE: Adapted from Tom Mortenson, "'For Every 100 Girls . . .' Postsecondary Education OPPORTUNITY" (Washington, D.C.: The Pell Institute for the Study of Opportunity in Higher Education, 2006). www.postsecondary.org/archives/previous/ForEvery100Girls.pdf

actually do is determined less by differential abilities than by the context in which they are acting. Attitudes and actions of others affect what people do. Societal norms and expectations are also influential. So, too, do people alter their own behavior from one situation to another, depending on their goals and objectives.

Comparisons of women and men cannot be analyzed in a vacuum, independent of their social context. Even in the area of cognitive abilities, the differences between women and men have shifted over time. Now there are fewer differences than there were twenty years ago. . . .

No doubt people will continue to ask how men and women differ. But the answers will never be simple ones. Nor can observed differences between the sexes be used as a simple explanation for the broader gender roles of women and men [for example, the fact that in our society, women are regarded as having more responsibility for nurturing children]. Indeed, the causal direction may be just the reverse: Accepted roles may channel men and women into different patterns of behavior. Whatever the patterns observed, most sex differences will continue to reflect a gendered environment and be subject to further change. (Deaux 1992, 1753)

What To Do with What You've Learned?

Economics was once famously called the "dismal science." In the minds of many students, sociology is regarded as the depressing science. Here's what one of my students wrote on his end-of-term evaluation:

Some of the stuff we talked about is interesting, but by the end of the semester I found the class depressing: All this talk about inequality and discrimination. Maybe leave those parts out for future students. (May 2012)

And, it's not just *my* students who feel this way. Here's how another sociology professor, Sally Raskoff, described her students' reaction to the topic of inequality:

This semester some students reacted with hopelessness. They stated that they don't see that anything can change and that we're doomed to be subject to these pressures since the power always wins. I was not surprised at this reaction, as it is a common one in many sociology classes. Learning about the depth of stratification and exploitation can be demoralizing and depressing. (Raskoff 2011)

I have long observed the tendency of students to become depressed when they study the sources of inequality. I suspect that this sort of depression is especially potent in the United States where citizens pride themselves on living in a meritocracy. Some may disagree with me, but in my judgment, there is nothing inherently depressing about inequality. However, it is certainly depressing to learn that the true nature of inequality differs from what we have all been taught to believe it is.

The belief that equality of opportunity exists in modern society is pervasive and strong. So, when you read these final chapters of *Core Concepts,* it is likely you were dismayed to discover that few modern Western societies are meritocracies. And, it is depressing to think about the facts that prove this: That women tend to earn less money than men who do the same jobs; that people who aren't "white" tend to earn less than people who are white—even when they have the same education and job skills; that just being female or just being black or Hispanic will mean that, over a lifetime, you will lose hundreds of thousands or even millions of dollars for reasons that have nothing to do with your personal talents, dedication.

And, I think learning about such things in a sociology course makes it even more depressing because the most important lesson that you learn in sociology classes is how powerfully society and its institutions, culture, and social structures affect people's live. If the society is imbued with discriminatory beliefs and practices, what can individuals do?

Professor Raskoff goes on to say, "it is imperative to realize that one can't attempt to effectively solve a problem unless one understands the problem." Raskoff's thinking reflects a point made by C. Wright Mills. Recall from chapter 2 that Mills pointed out that people in modern societies feel trapped by circumstances that seem beyond their control. Mills suggested that the way to escape the trap is to use one's "sociological imagination" to distinguish between personal troubles and public issues of social structure (Mills 1959, 5).

Distinguishing between personal troubles and public issues allows us to focus our attention on the true source of our problems. Or, as Mills put it, by using the sociological imagination "the personal uneasiness of individuals is focused upon explicit troubles and the indifference of publics is transformed into involvement with public issues" (Mills 1959, 5). So, while I think that inequality may be inevitable, the bases of inequality need not violate the values of the group. Until people know (from taking courses in sociology?) the real nature of their society's reward structure, however, they are powerless.

14.4 Explain the difference between *sex* and *gender*.

14.5 When a sociologist says that some phenomenon is a *social construction*, what does he or she mean?

14.6 Read each of the research findings reported below. Based on what you learned from this chapter, indicate whether each finding is true or false. (Answers follow Chapter Review.)

    a. Until the 1970s, there were few women musicians who played in major professional orchestras. That situation changed when (in the 1970s and 1980s) orchestras instituted new audition procedures so that those judging the auditions (and doing the hiring) could not see the player auditioning. The evidence suggests that the low numbers of female orchestra members had been a result of gender bias against hiring women.

    b. While women may experience discrimination in the majority of occupations, science tends to be the exception. In a recent study of scientists from a variety of research universities, scientists were shown an application for the job of lab manager from a student—randomly assigned a female or a male name. Then scientists were asked for their judgment about the student applicant's (a) competence, (b) hirability, (c) salary, and (d) potential for mentoring. The results showed that the gender of the student applicant had no significant overall effect.

c. While there was a time when nonwhites were prohibited from even playing on all-white professional teams in some sports, things are different today. In fact, the research shows that African American players earn more than their white counterparts in the National Basketball Association.

d. In the United States, Asian Americans are more likely to die in car accidents than people of any other race/ethnicity.

Chapter Review

1. Below I have listed the major concepts discussed in this chapter. Define each of the terms. (*Hint:* This exercise will be more helpful to you if, in addition to defining each concept, you create an example of it in your own words.)

a dollar is not always a dollar
prejudice
stereotypes
discrimination
Robert Merton, typology of prejudice and discrimination
Gordon Allport, types of discriminatory behaviors
individual discrimination
institutional discrimination
Louis Wirth, minority group, dominant group
"isms," distinguished from other types of discrimination
pyramiding effect of discrimination
race as a social construct
ethnicity
gender as a social construct
sex
Margaret Mead, studies of three New Guinea societies

2. Each of the following jokes is an example of sex-based discrimination, but which are examples of sexism? Explain how you distinguished sexism from sex-based discrimination.

1. Q: What's the difference between a sorority girl and an elephant? A: About 10 pounds.
2. Q: Why did the blonde get fired from the M&M factory? A: Because she threw out all the w's.

3. Q: Why was the blonde happy when she completed the
   puzzle in two hours? A: Because it said on the puzzle
   box "two to four years."
4. Q: What's the difference between men and government
   bonds? A: Bonds mature.
5. Q: What did God say after creating man? A: I can do better.
6. Q: What is gross stupidity? A: 144 men in a room.

3. Just a few decades ago, African American adult males were
   frequently referred to as "boys." Today, adult males of all
   races are generally referred to as "men." However, adult
   women are frequently referred to as "girls." In your judgment, what are some of the implications of this for women?

4. How important is your gender to the way you live your life?
   Imagine that tomorrow morning you woke up and discovered that, overnight, you had changed from female to male
   (or male to female). Describe how the next few days would
   go for you. Will there be any change in what you do or how
   you behave? (Assume that everyone around you acted as if
   your new sex was the one you had always had.) What lessons
   would you learn from this experience?

5. This chapter has used race, ethnicity, and gender as examples
   of how ascribed statuses are bases of inequality. Those examples do not, I think, exhaust the list of ascribed statuses that
   are linked to social inequality. In your informed judgment,
   what other ascribed statuses lead people to be treated differently in society?

Answers and Discussion

14.1 Prejudice is a negative and persistent judgment, based on incorrect
information, about people in a particular group. Discrimination involves
treating someone differently because of membership in some group. The
essential difference between them is that prejudice involves attitudes and
beliefs while discrimination involves behaviors.

14.2 Individual discrimination occurs when a single person discriminates
against another (for example, an owner of a building refuses to rent to
someone because of his or her race, religion, or whatever). Institutional
discrimination is discrimination that is built into the system; the person
who acts out the discrimination (for example, the bank loan officer or the
college admissions officer) may not intend to discriminate (or even know
that he or she is discriminating).

14.3 Any act that discriminates against another based on his or her race
is race-based discrimination. However, not all race-based discrimination
qualifies as racism. Determining which acts are racist and which are not
requires that one look at the social context in which the act occurs.

If a white building owner discriminates against a Japanese renter, that is racism, because whites are the dominant group in U.S. society. On the other hand, if a Japanese building owner discriminates against a white renter in Tokyo, that would be racism, because whites are in the minority in Japan.

There is no difference between the actual behavior (and, to the conventional observers, they both are bad). How "bad" the behaviors are, of course, is not of interest to sociologists. Sociologists distinguish between the two kinds of acts because of the different kinds of effects they have on the people who are discriminated against.

Michael Schwalbe (quoted in the chapter) says that it is important to take into account power differences—that it is perverse to regard all race-based discrimination as the same, because not all people have institutional power to make life difficult for others.

14.4 Sex has to do with physical attributes (such as a person's genitalia). Gender has to do with the meaning that a particular society attaches to those physical attributes. For example, long hair on women and short hair on men are gender attributes (and may vary from society to society).

14.5 To say that something is socially constructed is to say that it is made by people in society. A norm is a social construction (it has no other reality). Similarly, according to sociologists, race is a social construction—the main reality of race is not biological or physical. Race is a social construction, as is gender.

14.6

a. True. The researchers concluded that "blind auditions served to help female musicians in their quest for orchestral positions." (See, Claudia Goldin and Cecilia Rouse. 2012. Orchestrating impartiality: The impact of "blind" auditions on female musicians. *The American Economic Review 90:* 715–741.)

b. False. In fact, just the opposite happened. These university scientists judged the females as less competent and less hirable than the male student; and, when they indicated that they would hire the female applicant, they indicated they would pay her significantly less and do less mentoring. (Corrine A. Moss-Racusin, John F. Dovidio, Victoria L. Brescoll, Mark J. Graham, and Jo Handelsman. 2012. Science faculty's subtle biases favor male students. Proceedings of the National Academy of Sciences, September. www.pnas.org/cgi/doi/10.1073/pnas.1211286109)

c. Mostly false. African American players in the National Basketball Association are, on average, paid more than white players. However, evidence suggests that there is nonetheless a salary premium paid to white players compared with the African American players with comparable productivity (e.g., "shooting, scoring, rebounding, assists, fouls, blocks and turnover statistics."). The salary premium is such that, when controlling for productivity, white players earn "approximately 24.6% more than nonwhite players.") See, Kyle Rehnstrom, business.uni.edu/economics/Themes/rehnstrom.pdf

d. False. As shown in Table 14.4:

Table 14.4 Death Rates and Life Expectancy by Race

	Infant Mortality Rate[1]	Motor Vehicle-Related Deaths[2]	Death by Homicide[3]	% of Children without Health Insurance[4]	Life Expectancy at Birth[5]
American Indian/ Alaska Native	8.28	29.1	7.8	—	75.1
Asian/Pacific Islander	4.55	7.3	2.4	9.1	87.3
Black, non-Hispanic	13.35	14.6	23.1	10.2	78.0
White, non-Hispanic	5.58	15.0	2.7	6.8	78.7
Hispanic	5.41	13.4	7.6	15.1	83.5

[1]Number of deaths among infants less than 1 year of age per 1,000 births, by maternal race and ethnicity, 2006.

[2]Death rate per 100,000 population, 2007.

[3]Per 100,000, 2007.

[4]Percent of families with children without health insurance, 2011. (Data unavailable for American Indian/Alaska Natives.).

[5]2009.

SOURCES: Centers for Disease Control, Health Disparities and Inequalities Report—United States, 2011; National Center for Health Statistics. Health, United States, 2011, With Special Feature on Socioeconomic Status and Health; National Center for Health Statistics. Health, United States, 2010: With Special Feature on Death and Dying. Income, Poverty, and Health Insurance Coverage in the United States, 2011, Current Population Reports, issued September 2012.

AFTERWORD

I nevitably, you will forget at least some of what you have learned in your sociology class. Twenty years from now, you might hear the word *anomie,* for example, and draw a blank because the spot in your mind that anomie occupies will be taken up with other stuff. That's okay.

Still, there are at least two major lessons that I hope you not only remember but also keep supple with use: The first is a tendency to skepticism. In other words, I hope that you always remember what Peter Berger called "the first wisdom of sociology": "things are not what they seem" (1963, 23). This wisdom applies especially in Western societies in which most things are explained in individualistic terms. Sociologists have been persuaded by a great deal of research that people tend to give too much credit (or blame, as the case may be) to individuals. Crediting and blaming individuals makes sense in some circumstances, but individualistic explanations don't work well if the goal is to *understand* why people act as they do. And certainly, having only an individualistic understanding will not work well if we wish to effect change.

This brings me to the second lesson I hope you retain: the importance of having a sociological imagination. You have many tools with which to exercise your sociological imagination; I hope you've been persuaded, for example, that human behavior is shaped by culture and social structure; that the ways in which we carry out our life's arrangements are shaped by social institutions—including the systems of inequality that exist in society; and that if we choose to violate social norms, the ways in which we deviate frequently are influenced by our social environment.

The media are rife with stories of events for which individualistic explanations do not seem to tell the whole stories—the shenanigans of Wall Street brokers, bank managers, and even (in 2012) Olympic athletes. More locally, there are stories about cheating, binge drinking, and date rape. Are you satisfied when these events are explained entirely as the result of individuals'

266

bad choices? I hope not. Certainly, individuals do make bad choices, but frequently there is something going on that transcends individuals and influences their choices.

It is fitting, I think, to end this book as C. W. Mills ended his treatise on the sociological imagination. People, he wrote, "are gripped by personal troubles which they are not able to turn into social issues. They do not understand the interplay of these personal troubles of their milieux with problems of social structure" (1959, 187). Understanding the nature of the interplay of personal troubles with problems of social structure is what having a sociological imagination is all about. And so, Mills exhorts his readers:

> Know that many personal troubles cannot be solved merely as troubles, but must be understood in terms of public issues—and in terms of the problems of history-making. Know that the human meaning of public issues must be revealed by relating them to personal troubles—and to the problems of the individual life. Know that the problems of social science, when adequately formulated, must include both troubles and issues, both biography and history, and the range of their intricate relations. Within that range the life of the individual and the making of societies occur; and within that range the sociological imagination has its chance to make a difference in the quality of human life in our time. (226)

The good news is that, if you are of a mind to save the world or just make it a little better, having a sociological imagination can help you succeed. Anthropologist Margaret Mead is reputed to have said that we should "never doubt that a small group of thoughtful, committed citizens can change the world. Indeed, it's the only thing that ever has." If those citizens exercise their sociological imaginations in the process, it ups their chance of success.

REFERENCES

Ackernecht, Erwin H. 1982. *A Short History of Medicine.* Baltimore: Johns Hopkins University Press.

Acorn, 2000. *Separate and Unequal: Predatory Lending in America.* Accessed at *www.acorn.org/acorn10/predatorylending/plreports/separate.htm.*

Alba, Richard D. 1985. *Italian Americans.* Englewood Cliffs, NJ: Prentice-Hall.

Aleo, Michael, and Pablo Svirsky. 2008. "Foreclosure Fallout: The Banking Industry's Attack on Disparate Impact Race Discrimination Claims Under the Fair Housing Act and the Equal Credit Opportunity Act." *Boston University Public Interest Law Journal,* 18: 1–64.

Allport, Gordon W. 1954. *The Nature of Prejudice.* New York: Doubleday/Anchor Books.

Appiah, Kwame Anthony, and Henry Louis Gates, Jr. 1997. *The Dictionary of Global Culture.* New York: Knopf.

Axtell, Roger E. 1991. *Gestures: The Do's and Taboos of Body Language Around the World.* New York: Wiley.

Ayres, Ian, and Peter Siegelman. 1995. "Race and Gender Discrimination in Bargaining for a New Car." *American Economic Review* 85: 304–321.

Ayres, Ian. 2008. "Discrimination in Consummated Car Purchases." pp. 137–148 in Laura Beth Nielsen and Robert L. Nelson (eds.), *Handbook of Employment Discrimination Research.* New York: Springer.

Badgett, M. V. Lee. 2004. "Prenuptial Jitters: Did Gay Marriage Destroy Heterosexual Marriage in Scandinavia?" *Slate.com.,* May.

Barber, Bernard. 1968. "Social Stratification." Pp. 288–295 in David Sills (ed.), *Encyclopedia of Social Science.* New York: Macmillan.

Becker, Howard S. 1963. *Outsiders: Studies in the Sociology of Deviance.* New York: Free Press.

Been, Vicki, Ingrid Gould Ellen, and Josiah Madar. 2009. "The High Cost of Segregation: Exploring Racial Disparities in High-Cost Lending." *Fordham Urban Law Journal,* 36: 361–393.

Belkin, Aaron, Morten Ender, Nathaniel Frank, Stacie Furia, George R. Lucas, Gary Packard, Tammy S. Schultz, Steven M. Samuels and David R. Segal. 2012. *One Year Out: An Assessment of DADT Repeal's Impact on Military Readiness.* Los Angeles, CA: Palm Center.

Berger, Peter. 1963. *Invitation to Sociology: A Humanistic Perspective*. New York: Anchor Books.

Berger, Peter L., and Thomas Luckmann. 1967. *The Social Construction of Reality: A Treatise in the Sociology of Knowledge*. Garden City, NY: Anchor Books.

Berkow, Robert, ed. 1987. *The Merck Manual of Diagnosis and Therapy*. 15th ed. Rahway, NJ: Merck Sharp & Dohme Research Laboratories.

Berube, Allan. 1990. *Coming Out Under Fire*. New York: The Free Press.

Bierstedt, Robert. 1960. "Sociology and Humane Learning." *American Sociological Review* 25: 3.

Birdwhistell, Ray L. 1970. *Kinesics and Context: Essays on Body Motion Communication*. Philadelphia: University of Pennsylvania Press.

Bishop, Morris. 1968. *Middle Ages*. Boston: Houghton Mifflin.

Black, Henry Campbell. 1979. *Black's Law Dictionary*. St. Paul, MN: West.

Blauner, Robert. 1972. *Racial Oppression in America*. New York: Harper & Row.

Blumenbach, Johann F. 1775. "On the Natural Variety of Mankind." Reprinted in *Anthropological Treatise*. Trans. T. Bendyshe. London: Anthropological Society, 1865.

Bocian, Debbie Gruenstein, Keith S. Ernst, and Wei Li. 2006. *Unfair Lending: The Effect of Race and Ethnicity on the Price of Subprime Lending*. Washington, DC: Center for Responsible Lending.

Bouglé, Célestin. 1908/1971. *Essais sur le Régime des Castes (Essays on the Caste System)*. Trans. D. F. Pocock. Cambridge: Cambridge University Press.

Boxer, Sarah. 1995. "The United States Is the New Bastion of Inequality." *New York Times*, April 23.

Brace, Emma. 1894. *The Life of Charles Loring Brace*. New York: Author.

Brady, Erik, and MaryJo Sylwester. 2004. "High Schools in the Money Are Also Rich in Sports Titles." *USA Today*, June 17, pp. 1, 4–A.

Braun, Denny. 1997. *The Rich Get Richer—The Rise of Income Inequality in the United States and the World*. Chicago: Nelson-Hall.

———. 1995. "Negative Consequences to the Rise of Income Inequality." *Research in Politics and Society* 5: 3–31.

Bremner, John B. 1980. *Words on Words*. New York: Columbia University Press.

Bricker, Jesse, Arthur B. Kennickell, Kevin B. Moore, and John Sabelhaus. "Changes in U.S. Family Finances from 2007 to 2010: Evidence from the Survey of Consumer Finances." *Federal Reserve Bulletin* 98: 2.

Bryson, Bill. 1990. *The Mother Tongue: English and How It Got That Way*. New York: Avon Books.

Bureau of Justice Statistics. 1993. *Highlights from 20 Years of Surveying Crime Victims*. Washington, DC: U.S. Government Printing Office.

———. 1992. *Criminal Victimization in the United States*. Washington, DC: U.S. Government Printing Office.

Campbell, Frederick L., Hubert M. Blalock, Jr., and Reece McGee (eds.). 1985. *Teaching Sociology: The Quest for Excellence*. Chicago: Nelson-Hall.

Carmichael, Stokely, and Charles Hamilton. 1967. *Black Power.* New York: Vintage Books.

Carroll, Chas. 1900/1991. *The Negro a Beast.* Salem, NH: Ayer.

Center for Community Change. 2002. *Risk or Race? Racial Disparities and the Subprime Refinance Market.* Accessed at *www.communitychange.org.*

Chagnon, Napoleon A. 1977. *Yanomamö: The Fierce People.* New York: Holt, Rinehart & Winston.

Chambliss, William. 1973. "The Saints and the Roughnecks." *Society* 11: 24–31.

Chen, Chien-Fei. 1995. "The Impact of American Media and Interpersonal Communication on the Acculturation Process of Taiwanese Immigrants in the United States." Unpublished master's thesis, Washington State University.

Claffey, Jason. 2012. "NH Lawmaker: Kindergarten Leads to More Crime." *ExeterPatch,* June 27. Accessed at *http://exeter.patch.com/articles/nh-lawmaker-kindergarten-leads-to-more-crime.1 August.*

Clark, Kenneth B. 1967. *Dark Ghetto.* New York: Harper Torchbooks.

Cleaver, Eldridge. 1968. Interview. *Playboy,* December, pp. 89–108, 238.

Cloward, Richard, and Lloyd E. Ohlin. 1960. *Delinquency and Opportunity: A Theory of Delinquent Gangs.* New York: Free Press.

———. 1959. "Illegitimate Means, Anomie, and Deviant Behavior." *American Sociological Review* 24: 164–176.

Cooley, Charles H. 1909. *Social Organization.* New York: Scribner.

———. 1902. *Human Nature and the Social Order.* New York: Scribner.

Corbett, Christianne, and Catherine Hill. 2012. *Graduating to a Pay Gap.* Washington, DC: AAUP.

Corcoran, Margaret. 1995. "Rags to Rags: Poverty and Mobility in the United States." *Annual Review of Sociology* 21: 237–267.

Coser, Lewis A. 1971. *Masters of Sociological Thought: Ideas in Historical and Social Context.* New York: Harcourt Brace Jovanovich.

Craig, Albert M., William A. Graham, Donald Kegan, Steven Ozment, and Frank M. Turner. 1986. *The Heritage of World Civilizations.* New York: Macmillan.

Croteau, David, and William Hoynes. 2003. *Media Society: Industries Images and Audiences.* 3rd ed. Thousand Oaks, CA: Pine Forge Press.

Cummings, Scott, and Del Taebel. 1978. "The Economic Socialization of Children: A New Marxist Analysis." *Social Problems* 26: 198–210.

Curtiss, Susan. 1997. *Genie: A Psycholinguistic Study of a Modern-Day "Wild Child."* New York: Academic Press.

Darwin, Charles. 1859/1962. *The Origin of Species by Means of Natural Selection of the Preservation of Favoured Races in the Struggle for Life.* New York: Collier Books.

Davis, Allison. 1948. *Social Class Influences upon Learning.* Cambridge, MA: Harvard University Press.

Davis, James F. 1991. *Who Is Black? One Nation's Definition.* University Park: The Pennsylvania State University Press.

Davis, Kingsley. 1947. "Final Note on a Case of Extreme Isolation." *American Journal of Sociology* 50: 432–437.

———. 1940. "A Case of Extreme Social Isolation of a Child." *American Journal of Sociology* 45: 554–564.

Deaux, Kay. 1992. "Sex Differences." In Edgar F. Borgatta and Marie L. Borgatta (eds.), *Encyclopedia of Sociology.* New York: Macmillan.

Della Fave, Richard. 1980. "The Meek Shall Not Inherit the Earth: Self-Evaluation and the Legitimacy of Stratification." *American Sociological Review* 45: 955–971.

Deutch, Morton P. 1964. "The Disadvantaged Child and the Learning Process." Pp. 172–187 in Frank Reissman, Jerome Cohen, and Arthur Pearl (eds.), *Mental Health of the Poor.* New York: Free Press.

Domhoff, G. William. 2012. "Wealth, Income, and Power". *Who Rules America.* Accessed at *http://whorulesamerica.net/power/wealth.html.*

Douglas, Mary. 1986. *How Institutions Think.* Syracuse, NY: Syracuse University Press.

Downs, A. 1970. *Racism in America and How to Combat It.* Washington, DC: U.S. Commission on Civil Rights.

DuBois, W. E. B. 1968. *The Autobiography: A Soliloquy on Viewing My Life from the Last Decades of Its First Century.* New York: International Publisher Co.

Dumont, Louis. 1970. *Homo Hierarchicus: The Caste System and Its Implications.* Chicago: University of Chicago Press.

Duncan, Greg J., Wei Jun, J. Yeung, Jeanne Brooks-Gunn, and Judith Smith. 1998. "How Much Does Childhood Poverty Affect the Life Chances of Children?" *American Sociological Review* 63 (3): 406–423.

Durkheim, Émile. 1904/1950. *The Rules of the Sociological Method.* Trans. Sarah A. Solovay and John H. Meuller. Glencoe, IL: Free Press.

———. 1897/1951. *Suicide.* Trans. John A. Spaulding and George Simpson. Glencoe, IL: Free Press.

———. 1893/1933. *The Division of Labor in Society.* Trans. George Simpson. New York: Free Press.

Dushkin, Lelah. 1972. "Scheduled Caste Politics." In Michael Mahar (ed.), *The Untouchables in Contemporary India.* Tucson: University of Arizona Press.

Eder, Donna. 1995. *School Talk: Gender and Adolescent Culture.* New Brunswick, NJ: Rutgers University Press.

Emirbayer, Mustafa, and Ann Mische. 1998. "What Is Agency?" *American Journal of Sociology* 103: 962-1023.

Entwisle, Doris R., and Karl L. Alexander. 1993. "Entry into School: The Beginning School Transition and Educational Stratification in the United States." *Annual Review of Sociology* 19: 401–423.

Ettelbrick, Paula A. 2006. "Global Warming to Gay Rights: The Worldwide Trend of Recognizing Same-Sex Marriage Will Likely Continue." *Los Angeles Times,* December 4.

Evans, David, and David Glovin. 2006. "They Flubbed Exams, Get Hired as Executives of Test Companies." *Bloomberg.com,* November 3.

Farb, Peter. 1993. *Word Play: What Happens When People Talk.* New York: Vintage Books.

Feagin, Joe R. 1991. "The Continuing Significance of Race: Anti-Black Discrimination in Public Places." *American Sociological Review* 56: 101–116.

Fine, Gary Alan. 1979. "Small Groups and Culture Creation: The Idioculture of Little League Baseball Teams." *American Sociological Review* 44: 733–745.

Fishbein, Allen J., and Patrick Woodall. 2006. *Women Are Prime Targets for Subprime Lending.* Washington, DC: Consumer Federation of America.

Fussell, Paul. 1983. *Class: A Guide through the American Status System.* New York: Touchstone/Simon & Schuster.

Gamoran, Adam, and Robert D. Mare. 1989. "Secondary School Tracking and Educational Inequality: Compensation, Reinforcement, or Neutrality?" *American Journal of Sociology* 94: 1146–1183.

Gates, David. 1993. "White Male Paranoia." *Newsweek,* March 29, pp. 48–53.

Gerald, Danette, and Kati Haycock. 2006. *Engines of Inequality: Diminishing Equity in the Nation's Premier Public Universities.* Washington, DC: The Education Trust.

Gini, Al. 2000. *My Job, My Self: Work and the Creation of the Modern Individual.* New York: Routledge.

Gleick, James. 1987. *Chaos.* New York: Viking/Penguin.

Goffman, Erving. 1963. *Stigma: Notes on the Management of Spoiled Identity.* Englewood Cliffs, NJ: Prentice-Hall.

———. 1961. *Asylums: Essays on the Social Situation of Mental Patients and Other Inmates.* Garden City, NY: Doubleday/Anchor Books.

Graddy, Kathryn. 1997. "Do Fast-Food Chains Price Discriminate on the Race and Income Characteristics of an Area?" *Journal of Business & Economic Statistics* 15: 391–401.

Greeley, Andrew. 1971. *Why Can't They Be Like Us?* New York: Dutton.

Greenberg, David F. 1988. *The Construction of Homosexuality.* Chicago: University of Chicago Press.

Hallinan, Maureen T. 1988. "Equality of Educational Opportunity." *Annual Review of Sociology* 14: 249–268.

Hallinan, Maureen T., and Richard A. Williams. 1987. "The Stability of Students' Interracial Friendships." *American Sociological Review* 52: 653–664.

Hane, Mikiso. 1982. *Peasants, Rebels and Outcastes: The Underside of Modern Japan.* New York: Pantheon Books.

Holmes, Oliver Wendell. 1891. *Medical Essays, 1842–1882.* Boston: Houghton Mifflin.

Howell, David L. 1996. "Ethnicity and Culture in Contemporary Japan." *Journal of Contemporary History* 31: 171–190.

Hughes, Everett C. 1945. "Dilemmas and Contradictions of Status." *American Journal of Sociology* 50: 353–359.

Hull, Nathaniel R. 2009. "Crossing the Line: Prime, Subprime, and Predatory Lending." *Maine Law Review* 61: 287–319.

Hyde, J. S. 1979. *Understanding Human Sexuality.* New York: McGraw-Hill.

Isaacs, Julia B., Isabel V. Sawhill, and Ron Haskins. 2008. *The Economic Mobility Project of the Brookings Institute.* Washington, DC: Brookings Institution Press.

James, C. L. R. 1967. "Black Power." Pp. 362–374 in Anna Grimshaw (ed.), *The C. L. R. James Reader.* Oxford: Basil Blackwell.

James, William. 1890. *The Principles of Psychology.* Boston: Little, Brown.

Johnson, Allan G. 1997. *The Forest and the Trees: Sociology as Life, Practice and Promise.* Philadelphia: Temple University Press.

Johnson, Charles S. 1941/1967. *Growing Up in the Black Belt.* New York: Schocken Books.

Johnson, Clifford M., Leticia Miranda, Arloc Sherman, and James D. Weill. 1991. *Child Poverty in America.* Washington, DC: Children's Defense Fund.

Kennedy, Stetson. 1959. *Jim Crow Guide to the U.S.A.: The Laws, Customs and Etiquette Governing the Conduct of Nonwhites and Other Minorities as Second Class Citizens.* London: Lawrence & Wishart.

Kennickell, Arthur B. 2009. *Ponds and Streams: Wealth and Income in the U.S., 1989 to 2007.* Finance and Economics Discussion Series, Divisions of Research & Statistics and Monetary Affairs, Federal Reserve Board, Washington, DC.

————. 2006. *Currents and Undercurrents: Changes in the Distribution of Wealth, 1989–2004.* Washington, DC: Federal Reserve Board, Survey of Consumer Finances.

Kerbo, Harold R. 1991. *Social Stratification and Inequality: Class Conflict in Historical and Comparative Perspective.* 2nd ed. New York: McGraw-Hill.

Kluegel, James R., and Eliot R. Smith. 1981. "Beliefs about Stratification." *Annual Review of Sociology* 7: 29–56.

Kottak, Conrad P. 1992. *Assault on Paradise: Social Change in a Brazilian Village.* New York: McGraw-Hill.

Kozol, Jonathan. 1991. *Savage Inequalities: Children in America's Schools.* New York: Crown.

Kroeber, A. L., and Clyde Kluckhohn. 1952. *Culture: A Critical Review of Concepts and Definitions.* Papers of the Peabody Museum of American Archaeology and Ethnology. Vol. 47, no. 1.

Lederer, Richard. 1987. *Anguished English.* New York: Bantam/Doubleday/Dell.

Lemert, Edwin M. 1967. *Human Deviance, Social Problems and Social Control.* Englewood Cliffs, NJ: Prentice-Hall.

Levine, Linda. 2012. *An Analysis of the Distribution of Wealth across Households, 1989–2010.* Washington, DC: Congressional Research Service.

Levine, Robert A., and Donald T. Campbell. 1972. *Ethnocentrism: Theories of Conflict, Ethnic Attitudes, and Group Behavior.* New York: Wiley.

Lewis, Oscar. 1966. "The Culture of Poverty." *Scientific American,* October, pp. 7–25.

Liebow, Elliot. 1967. *Talley's Corner.* Boston: Little, Brown.

Linton, Ralph. 1945. *The Science of Man in the World Crisis.* New York: Columbia University Press.

Liska, Allen E. 1987. *Perspectives on Deviance.* 2nd ed. Englewood Cliffs, NJ: Prentice-Hall.

Lurie, Nancy Destreich. 1982. "The American Indian: Historical Background." Pp. 131–144 in R. Yetmen and C. H. Steele (eds.), *Majority and Minority,* 3rd ed. Boston: Allyn & Bacon.

Mannheim, Karl. 1929/1936. *Ideology and Utopia: An Introduction to the Sociology of Knowledge.* Ed. and trans. Louis Wirth and Edward Shils. New York: Harcourt Brace Jovanovich.

Marx, Karl, and Friedrich Engels. 1848/1964. *Manifesto of the Community Party.* Edited and with an introduction by Francis B. Randall. New York: Pocket Books.

————. 1845–46/1963. *The German Ideology.* New York: International.

Mauer, Marc, and Ryan S. King. 2007. *Uneven Justice: State Rates of Incarceration by Race and Ethnicity.* Washington, DC: The Sentencing Project.

McIntyre, Lisa J. 2005. *Need to Know: Social Science Research Methods.* New York: McGraw-Hill.

McLeod, Jane D., and Michael J. Shanahan. 1993. "Poverty, Parenting and Children's Mental Health." *American Sociological Review* 58: 351–366.

McNeill, William Hardy. 1987. *A History of the Human Community.* 2nd ed. Englewood Cliffs, NJ: Prentice-Hall.

Mead, George H. 1934. *Mind, Self and Society: From the Standpoint of a Social Behaviorist.* Chicago: University of Chicago Press.

Mead, Margaret. 1935/1950. *Sex and Temperament in Three Primitive Societies.* New York: Morrow.

Merton, Robert K. 1976. *Sociological Ambivalence and Other Essays.* New York: Free Press.

———. 1949/1968. "Manifest and Latent Functions." In R. K. Merton, *Social Theory and Social Structure.* New York: Free Press.

———. 1938. "Social Structure and Anomie." *American Sociological Review* 13: 672–682. Reprinted in Merton, *Social Theory and Social Structure.* New York: Free Press, 1949.

Miller, Joanne. 1988. "Jobs and Work." Pp. 327–359 in Neil Smelser (ed.), *Handbook of Sociology.* Newbury Park, CA: Sage.

Mills, C. Wright. 1959. *The Sociological Imagination.* New York: Free Press.

Mishel, Laurence, and Jared Bernstein. 1993. *The State of Working America, 1992–1993.* New York: Sharpe.

Mishel, Lawrence, Josh Bivens, Elise Gould, and Heidi Shierholz. 2012. *The State of Working America, 12th Edition.* New York: Cornell University Press.

Montague, M. F. Ashley. 1964. *The Concept of Race.* New York: Free Press.

———. 1960. *Introduction to Physical Anthropology.* 3rd ed. Springfield, IL: Thomas.

Morrill, John. 1984. "The Stuarts (1603–1688)." Pp. 286–351 in Kenneth O. Morgan (ed.), *The Oxford Illustrated History of Britain.* Oxford: Oxford University Press.

Muller, Edward N. 1985. "Income Inequality, Regime Repressiveness and Political Violence." *American Sociological Review* 50: 47–61.

Murdock, George P. 1945. "The Common Denominator of Culture." In Ralph Linton (ed.), *The Science of Man in the World Crisis.* New York: Columbia University Press.

Murdock, George Peter. 1957. "World Ethnographic Sample." *American Anthropologist* 59: 664–697.

Nelson, M. D., Jr. 1992. "Socioeconomic Status and Childhood Mortality in North Carolina." *American Journal of Public Health* 82: 1131–1133.

Newman, Graeme. 1967. *Comparative Deviance: Perceptions and Law in Six Cultures.* New York: Elsevier.

Newman, Katherine, and Chauncy Lennon. 1995. "The Job Ghetto." *The American Prospect,* Summer.

Oakes, Jeannie. 1994. "More Than Misapplied Technology: A Normative and Political Response to Hallinan on Tracking." *Sociology of Education* 67: 84–89.

———. 1985. *Keeping Track: How Schools Structure Inequality.* New Haven, CT: Yale University Press.

Oliver, Melvin L., and Thomas M. Shapiro. 1997. *Black Wealth, White Wealth.* New York: Routledge.

Parsons, Talcott. 1966. *Societies: Evolutionary and Comparative Perspectives.* Englewood Cliffs, NJ: Prentice-Hall.

Patterson, Orlando. 1982. *Slavery and Social Death.* Cambridge, MA: Harvard University Press.

Pattullo, E. L. 1992. "Straight Talk about Gays." *Commentary,* December.

Payne, Stanley L. 1951. *The Art of Asking Questions.* Princeton, NJ: Princeton University Press.

Perez, Thomas. 2012. *Assistant Attorney General Thomas E. Perez Speaks at the Wells Fargo Press Conference.* Washington, DC: U.S. Department of Justice, July 12. Accessed at *http://justice.gov/crt/opa/pr/speeches/2012/ crt-speech-120712.html.*

Persell, Caroline. 1977. *Education and Inequality: The Roots of Stratification in American Schools.* New York: Free Press.

Pollock, Frederick, and Frederic William Maitland. 1898/1968. *The History of English Law Before the Time of Edward I.* 2 vols. Cambridge: Cambridge University Press.

Quint, Michael. 1991. "Mortgage Race Data Show Gap. Fed Has Apprised Bankers of Disparity in Loan Approvals." *New York Times,* October 14.

Radcliffe-Brown, A. R. 1922/1948. *The Andaman Islanders.* Glencoe, IL: Free Press.

Rank, Mark P. 1989. "Fertility Among Women on Welfare: Incidence and Determinants." *American Sociological Review* 54: 296–304.

Raskoff, Sally. 2011. "Thinking Sociologically about Advertising," December 22. *Everydaysociologyblog.com.* Accessed at *http:// everydaysociologyblog.com/2011/12/thinking-sociologically-about-advertising.html?cid=6a00d83534ac5b69e20168e4f9b349970c.*

Rheingold, Harriet L. 1969. "The Social and Socializing Infant." Pp. 779–790 in D. H. Goslin (ed.), *Handbook of Socialization Theory and Research.* Chicago: Rand McNally.

Robertson, Ian. 1987. *Sociology.* New York: Worth.

Rogers Commission report (1986). Presidential Commission on the Space Shuttle Challenger Accident. 1986. *Report to the President.* Accessed at http://history.nasa.gov/rogersrep /genindex.htm.

Romero, Adam P., Amanda K. Baumle, M.V. Lee Badgett, and Gary J. Gates. 2007. *Census Snapshot December 2007.* Los Angeles, CA: The Williams Institute, UCLA School of Law.

Rose, Peter I., Myron Glazer, and Penina Migdal Glaser. 1979. "In Controlled Environments: Four Cases of Intensive Resocialization." Pp. 323–325 in Peter I. Rose (ed.), *Socialization and the Life Cycle.* New York: St. Martin's Press.

Rosenthal, Robert, and Lenore Jacobson. 1968. *Pygmalion in the Classroom: Teacher Expectations and Pupils' Intellectual Development.* New York: Holt, Rinehart & Winston.

Ryan, William. 1971. *Blaming the Victim.* New York: Vintage Books.

Sadker, Myra, and David Sadker. 1994. *Failing at Fairness. How Our Schools Cheat Girls.* New York: Touchstone.

Sagan, Carl. 1996. *The Demon-Haunted World: Science as a Candle in the Dark.* New York: Random House.

Scase, Richard. 1992. *Class.* Minneapolis: University of Minnesota Press.

Schermerhorn, Richard A. 1949. *These Are Our People.* Boston: Heath.

Schur, Edwin M. 1971. *Labelling Deviant Behavior.* New York: Harper & Row.

Schwalbe, Michael. 1996. *Unlocking the Iron Cage: The Men's Movement, Gender Politics, and American Culture.* New York: Oxford University Press.

Shils, Edward. 1985. "Sociology." In A. Kuper and J. Kuper (eds.), *The Social Science Encyclopedia.* London: Routledge and Kegan Paul.

Shweder, Richard. 1997. "The Surprise of Ethnography." *Ethos* 25: 152–163.

Smith, Huston. 1958. *The Illustrated World's Religion: A Guide to Our Wisdom Traditions.* New York: HarperCollins.

Smith, Tom. 2011. *General Social Survey Codebook.* Chicago, National Opinion Research Center.

Sorokin, Pitirim A. 1928. *Contemporary Sociological Theories.* New York: Harper.

Spalter-Roth, Roberta, Terri Ann Lowenthal, and Mercedes Rubio. 2005. *Race, Ethnicity, and the Health of Americans.* Washington, DC: American Sociological Society.

Speilberg, Nathan, and Bryon D. Anderson. 1987. *Seven Ideas that Shook the Universe.* New York: Wiley.

Spencer, Herbert. 1864. *Social Statics.* New York: Appleton.

———. 1852. "A Theory of Population, Deduced from the General Law of Animal Fertility." *Westminster Review* LVII.

Spitz, René A. 1945. "Hospitalism: An Inquiry into the Genesis of Psychiatric Conditions in Early Childhood." *Psychoanalytic Study of the Child* 1: 53–74.

Sprecher, Susan, and Rachita Chandak. 1992. "Attitudes about Arranged Marriages and Dating among Men and Women of India." *Free Inquiry in Creative Sociology* 20 (1): 59–69.

Sullivan, Andrew. 1995. *Virtually Normal.* New York: Knopf.

Sumner, William G. 1934. *Essays of William Graham Sumner.* 2 vols. Ed. Albert G. Keller and Maurice R. Davie. New Haven, CT: Yale University Press.

———. 1906. *Folkways.* Boston: Ginn.

Sweder, Richard A., 1997. "The Surprise of Ethnography". *Ethos* 25: 152–163.

Szalavitz, Maia. 2012. "Does Kindergarten Lead to Crime? Fact-Checking N.H. Legislator's 'Research.'" Time, July 6. Accessed at *http://healthland.time.com/2012/07/06/does-kindergarten-lead-to-crime-fact-checking-n-h-legislators-research/#ixzz27896dgmq.*

Thernstrom, Abigail. 1992. "Tracking: The Drive for Racially Inclusive Schools." Pp. 131–143 in Harold Orland and June O'Neill (eds.), *Affirmative Action Revisited, The Annals,* September.

Thurow, Lester C. 1996. *The Future of Capitalism: How Today's Economic Forces Shape Tomorrow's World*. New York: Morrow.

Tittle, Charles R., and Robert F. Meier. 1990. "Specifying the SES Delinquency Relationship." *Criminology* 28: 271–279.

Tittle, Charles R., W. J. Villenez, and D. A. Smith. 1978. "The Myth of Social Class and Criminality: An Empirical Assessment of the Empirical Evidence." *American Sociological Review* 43: 643–656.

Tönnies, Ferdinand. 1898/1963. *Gemeinschaft and Gesellschaft*. Trans. and ed. Charles P. Loomis. New York: Harper & Row.

Turner, Victor. 1969. *The Ritual Process: Structure and Anti-Structure*. Chicago: Aldine Publishing Company.

United Nations Human Development Programme. 1994. *Human Development Report*. New York: Oxford University Press.

Vaughan, Diane. 2008. Interview with Diane Vaughan, *Consulting News Line*. Transcript available online at *http://consultingnewsline.com/Info/Vie%20du%20Conseil/Le%20Consultant%20du%20mois/Diane%20Vaughan%20%28English%29.html*.

Visser, Margaret. 1986. *Much Depends on Dinner*. New York: Harper Collins.

Wade, Wyn Craig. 1987. *The Fiery Cross: The Ku Klux Klan in America*. New York: Oxford University Press.

Webb, Eugene J., Donald T. Campbell, Richard D. Schwartz, and Lee Sechrest. 1966. *Unobtrusive Measures: Nonreactive Research in the Social Sciences*. Chicago: Rand McNally.

Weber, Max. *Bureaucracy*. 1920–1958. Pp. 196–266 in H. H. Gerth and C. W. Mills (eds.), *From Max Weber*. New York: Oxford University Press.

———. 1918/1958. "Inconvenient Facts." Pp. 145–147 in H. H. Gerth and C. W. Mills (eds.), *From Max Weber*. New York: Oxford University Press.

———. 1904–1905/1958. *The Protestant Ethic and the Spirit of Capitalism*. New York: Scribner.

Webley, Kayla. 2010. "Brief History of Gays in the Military." *Time*, February 2.

Weissmann, Jordan. 2012. "U.S. Income Inequality: It's Worse Today Than It Was in 1774." *The Atlantic*, , November 3. Accessed at . *http://theatlantic.com/business/archive/2012/09/us-income-inequality-its-worse-today-than-it-was-in-1774/262537/*.

Williams, Lena. 1991. "When Blacks Shop, Bias Often Accompanies Sale." *New York Times*, April 30.

Williams, Robin M., Jr. 1970. *American Society: A Sociological Interpretation*. New York: Knopf.

Wirth, Louis. 1945. "The Problem of Minority Groups." In Ralph Linton (ed.), *The Science of Man in the World Crisis*. New York: Columbia University Press.

Wolff, Edward N. 2006. "Changes in Household Wealth in the 1980s and 1990s in the U.S." In Edward N. Wolff (ed.), *International Perspectives on Household Wealth*. Northampton, MA: Edward Elgar Publishers.

Yinger, J. Milton. 1977. "Presidential Address: Countercultures and Social Change." *American Sociological Review* 42: 833–853.

Yinger, J. Milton. 1960. "Contraculture and Subculture." *American Sociological Review* 25: 625–635.

CREDITS

CHAPTER 2 Allan G. Johnson, excerpt from *The Forest and the Trees: Sociology as Life, Practice and Promise*, (1997): 20–21. Used by permission of Temple University Press. © 1997 Temple University Press. All rights reserved.

CHAPTER 4 Napoleon A. Chagnon, excerpts from *Yanomamö: The Fierce People*. © 1977 Wadsworth, a part of Cengage Learning, Inc. Reproduced by permission, www .cengage.com/permissions.

CHAPTER 6 Interview with Diane Vaughan, http://www.consultingnewsline.com. Copyright © 2008 by ConsultingNewsLine. Used by permission.

CHAPTER 10 René A Spitz, "Hospitalism: An Inquiry into the Genesis of Psychiatric Conditions in Early Childhood," p. 60. *Psychoanalytic Study of the Child*, Vol. 1 (1945): 53–74, Yale University Press.

CHAPTER 11, TABLE 11.1 From Robert K. Merton, *Social Theory and Social Structure*. Copyright 1949, © 1957 by the Free Press; copyright renewed © 1977, 1985 by Robert K. Merton. Adapted with the permission of Free Press of Simon & Schuster, Inc.

Howard S. Becker, excerpts from *Outsiders: Studies in the Sociology of Deviance*. Copyright 1963 by Howard S. Becker. Reprinted with permission of Free Press of Simon and Schuster, Inc.

CHAPTER 12 Frederick Pollock and Frederic William Maitland. 1898/1968. *The History of English Law Before the Time of Edward I*, 2 vols. Reprinted with the permission of Cambridge University Press.

CHAPTER 13 Figure 13-1 Jordan Weissmann. "U.S. income inequality: It's worse today than it was in 1774." *The Atlantic*, November 3, 2012, Chart (3) U.S. Income Distribution: 1774, 1860, 2011; sources Lindert & Williamson, 2012; Census Bureau, via Copyright Clearance Center.

Scott Cummings and Del Taebel, "The Economic Socialization of Children: A New Marxist Analysis." *Social Problems* 26 (1978): 207, http://www.ucpress.edu/journals.

Jonathan Kozol, excerpts from *Savage Inequalities: Children in America's Schools*. Copyright © 1991 by Jonathan Kozol. Used by permission of the author, and by permission of Crown Publishers, a division of Random House, Inc. Any third party use of this material, outside of this publication, is prohibited. Interested parties must apply directly to Random House, Inc. for permission.

Jeannie Oakes, excerpts from *Keeping Track: How Schools Structure Inequality*. Copyright © 1985 by Yale University. Reprinted by permission of Yale University Press.

Erik Brady and MaryJo Sylwester, excerpt from "High Schools in the Money Are Also Rich in Sports Titles." *USA Today*, (June 17, 2004): 1, 4–A.

CHAPTER 14 Figure 14.1 American Association of University Women, *Graduating to a Pay Gap*. Used by permission of the AAUW.

Joe R. Feagin, excerpts from "The Continuing Significance of Race: Anti-Black Discrimination in Public Places." *American Sociological Review* 56 (1991): 101–116. Copyright © 1991. Reprinted with permission from American Sociological Association.

David Gates, excerpt from "White Male Paranoia." *Newsweek*, (March 29, 1993): 48–53.

Sally Raskoff, "Thinking Sociologically About Advertising." Blogpost (December 22, 2011). © W.W. Norton and Company, Inc. Used by permission.

GLOSSARY/INDEX